Mythocracy

Yves Citton is Professor in Literature and Media at the Université Paris 8 Vincennes-Saint-Denis, after having previously taught at the University of Pittsburgh, Pennsylvania (1992–2003), and at the Université Grenoble Alpes (2003–17). He was Executive Director of the Graduate School (EUR) at École Universitaire de Recherche (ArTeC) from 2018 to 2021 and is co-editor of the journal *Multitudes*. He has published a dozen books in French, translated into many languages, including *Mediarchy* (Polity Press, 2019) and *The Ecology of Attention* (Polity Press, 2016). His articles are in open access on his website, yvescitton.net.

Mythocracy

How Stories Shape Our Worlds

Yves Citton

Translated by David Broder

VERSO
London • New York

This work was published with the help of the French
Ministry of Culture – Centre national du livre
Ouvrage publié avec le concours du Ministère français
chargé de la culture – Centre national du livre

This English-language edition first published by Verso 2025

First published as *Mythocratie: Storytelling et imaginaire de gauche*

1 3 5 7 9 10 8 6 4 2

Verso
UK: 6 Meard Street, London W1F 0EG
US: 207 East 32nd Street, New York, NY 10016
versobooks.com

Verso is the imprint of New Left Books

ISBN-13: 978-1-83976-698-5
ISBN-13: 978-1-83976-699-2 (UK EBK)
ISBN-13: 978-1-83976-700-5 (US EBK)

British Library Cataloguing in Publication Data
A catalogue record for this book is available from the British Library

Library of Congress Cataloging-in-Publication Data
A catalog record for this book is available from the Library of Congress

Typeset in Minion by Hewer Text UK Ltd, Edinburgh
Printed and bound by CPI Group (UK) Ltd, Croydon CR0 4YY

With speech of persuasive charms [*thelktêrious muthous*], we will discover devices [*mêchanas heurêsomen*] to release you utterly from your distress.

Aeschylus, *Eumenides*, 81–3

I'm telling people that they've tried everything and now they have to try mythocracy. They've got a democracy, a theocracy – but they should try a mythocracy. The mythocracy is what you never came to be that you *should* be.

Sun Ra

Contents

Introduction

'Scripting' and Soft Power

No one, so far, has determined *what a narrative can do*. Some baulk at the 'myths' people get lulled into believing; others scoff at the 'tales' we are told; still others would like to believe that telling the right 'story' is all it takes to lead donkeys to the polls, sheep to the supermarket, and ants to work. In this book, we won't be offering a string of denunciations or prewritten recipes. Rather, our aim is to explore the power of narrative, and to offer our own account of the mythical nature of power: what we shall call *mythocracy*.

To this end, we are going to bring together three distinct fields of thought. Trying to analyse them separately would be a little over-ambitious. But our hope is that we can gain insight into each of them by looking at common elements that run through all of them. First, we will try to take stock of the *imaginary of power* that has characterised recent developments in the vein of political thought inspired by Baruch Spinoza, Gabriel Tarde, Michel Foucault, and Gilles Deleuze. The aim, here, is to identify and understand the workings of an apparently 'soft power' that operates by insinuation, suggestion, and stimulation, rather than by prohibition, command, or coercion. This is a power that 'conducts conduct' (Foucault) as it circulates in accordance with the desires and beliefs channelled by 'media' communications.

Next, we will try to identify the realities, fantasies, and emancipatory potential that lie behind *the practices of narration and storytelling*. We will draw on a range of disciplines (combining anthropology, sociology, narratology, and semiotics) in a bid to understand in what sense narrative structure is a necessary precondition for human action – and in what sense it is a horizon upon which we rely to give coherence to our various daily acts. This will then allow us to ask why and how the resources of storytelling have been appropriated by reactionary ('right-wing') ideologies, and on what conditions they could be reappropriated by emancipatory ('left-wing') politics.

Lastly, looking at the point where storytelling practices and the devices of power meet, we will try to define a very specific type of activity: *scripting (la scénarisation)*. Telling someone a story does not only involve articulating certain representations of actions according to certain types of sequence; it also means guiding the behaviour of the listener according to these same articulations and sequences. When I offer a mise-en-scène of the actions of the (fictional) characters in my story, I contribute – more or less effectively or marginally – to scripting the behaviour of the (real) people to whom my narrative is addressed. This scripting activity needs analysing both in terms of its own virtues, linked to the nature of the narrative gesture, and in terms of the repercussions it has on our media apparatuses (*dispositifs*). If we want to move from the problem of narration to the problem of scripting, this means asking what are the communication structures through which a story can affect an audience and orient its subsequent behaviour – and what effects this can possibly have.

This book sifts through what are in fact quite common general intuitions about the *power of scripting* (*le pouvoir de scénarisation*). We all know that the distribution of this power corresponds only in some small part to the distribution of political, legal, or economic power. We all know that the decisions that TV news bulletin editors make – whether to include a particular item, a particular question, or a particular interviewee in their daily round-up – play a decisive role in the day-to-day functioning and general direction of our mediatised democracies. We all have the sense that what is said (and what is thought) in our political debates, what is bought in our supermarkets, and what drives us to work, to obey, to accept, to resist or to invent another possible world, depends not only on what we see and hear of the world around us, but also on the various ways in which what reaches us from that world is the object of a mise-en-scène (that is, it is staged and scripted).

What knots tie us together around this power of scripting? What hooks does it use to capture our attention? What are its points of leverage? What kinds of structural inequality are there in the distribution of this power? What obstacles prevent most of us from accessing its multiplier effects? If it were integrated into the way we usually think about power, what new demands for equality would this lead to? How can emancipatory ('left-wing') politics reappropriate this power, without cynicism or false shame? How can we define 'the left' on the basis of a certain mode of enunciation, as well as of a list of demands? These are the questions posed in the six chapters of this book.

As we work through these themes, a literary interlude will delve into the question of the forms of writing that can be seen as part of a 'left-wing' imaginary. Meanwhile, an illustrative interlude will draw on a few episodes from *Jacques the Fatalist and His Master*, Denis Diderot's novel published between 1778 and 1780. The point here is to give concrete examples of the various wellsprings and mechanisms of the power of scripting, and to show us what its real importance is. The characters of Madame de La Pommeraye, Jacques, and the narrator already appear to put the deliciously devious subtleties of scripting into acts and words, with far more grace, lightness, precision, and virtuosity than our theoretical ponderousness could ever hope to achieve.

In other words: the power of scripting described in this book is not, in itself, anything new. It can easily be traced back in time, well beyond the staging of royal power attributed to Louis XIV or the choreography of the Roman emperors' triumphs. Humans have been scripting each other for as long as they have been talking, seducing, fighting, and telling stories. But, while the power of scripting is as old as humanity itself, some things have changed. There are constant evolutions in the conditions in which it is practised, the channels through which it is disseminated, its degree of concentration, and the intensity and precision with which it can hope to influence human behaviour. Our current modes of social regulation are distinguished by the fact that they rely more intensely on the power of scripting than ever before. In a sense, studying these phenomena is today an unprecedentedly urgent task – even if they can be illustrated with the help of a story that is already over two centuries old.

Still, we should be clear from the start that – quite obviously – *not all power has become soft power*. This text could rightly be accused of naivety or idealism if we claimed to be offering *the* theory of power as such. At the start of the new millennium, power also (and still) means bombs destroying homes and lives in the name of national security, soldiers and police firing their guns at crowds, resistance fighters being beaten and imprisoned without trial, and companies being shuttered without any discussion because profit rates are suboptimal. It means prohibitions imposed on women (or the gayest among us) under the guise of all that is holy and sacred; it means the neo-slavery to which undocumented workers are subjected; it means the physical, symbolic, or legal violence directed against alternative and marginal lifestyles. And that is not to mention all the petty bullying, humiliation, stonewalling, and absurdities that are the daily lot doled out by every bureaucratic apparatus. If we wanted to talk about 'power' (in general and in all its forms), we would surely first have to talk about this hard power.

So, our concern here is not at all to deny, relativise, or declare obsolete the massive reality of hard power. Rather, we are trying to point out how it is often relayed by other, apparently 'softer' forms of power. Take the case of the spectacular deployment of 'anti-terrorist' commandos in combat formation against a farm inhabited by a dozen unarmed young people in Tarnac in November 2008 (some of whom were involved with the book *The Coming Insurrection*). One of them was jailed for nearly six months on the basis of an empty case file, and it was later revealed that surveillance had been carried out several months before the assault. This was all done to repress or prevent a 'crime' whose essence seems to be that these people called themselves 'autonomists'. Here we have a combination of both traumatic violence, imposed on a few specific individuals at the end of a machine gun, and a scripting that is aimed at the population as a whole in order to reassure the obedient and frighten the rebellious.

A *story* like that of the 'Tarnac Nine' has an impact far beyond a small village in Corrèze: depending on how it is told, the channels through which it is broadcast, and the audiences' sensibilities, it can serve as a call to order, a revelation, a confirmation of prior suspicions, or cause for indignation. The modes of its scripting open up a space for intervention which, far from cancelling out or supplanting the interplay of political, legal, and economic powers and counter-powers, adds another layer of complexity to these latter. This extra layer is in constant and multiple interaction with this interplay of powers, but nevertheless deserves to be analysed in terms of its own logics. This is what we try to do in the chapters that follow.

The aim, then, is to show that 'telling ourselves stories' is not only unavoidable, but often salutary. 'The society of the spectacle' should be cause not for handwringing, but for efforts in *counter-scripting* (*contre-scénarisation*). The last few decades have been marked by the inability of the political 'left' to tell convincing stories. For reasons that we'll explore, the (securitarian, neoliberal, xenophobic) 'right' has managed to spread an open but relatively coherent set of stories, images, facts, and pieces of information, statistics, slogans, fears, reflexes, and objects of debate that feed off each other within one same 'right-wing imaginary'. This imaginary has had such (soft) power that it has rapidly colonised the discourse of many leaders of parties that officially claim to be 'of the left'. How has this 'right-wing imaginary' been able to shape large swathes of our political life? On what bases could we reinvigorate a 'left-wing imaginary', capable of rivalling its scripting power? These are the questions we have in mind in this book.

The underlying hypothesis is that the current disarray of the (official) 'left' is due to a blockage and a shortfall that can be located exactly at the level of an *imaginary of power* that it has failed to renew. The pathetic disorientation of its leaders and its collective organisations, in France and in many other European countries, contrasts with the vitality of certain 'para-political' movements of resistance and invention. And this disorientation can largely be attributed to the lack of an *imaginary 'glue'* that would allow the left to hold together the sensitivities, feelings, evidence, hopes, fears, slogans, and demands that we instead experience in isolation, without managing to give them the collective force of shared participation.

Many people speak (quite wrongly) of the 'end of ideologies'. They do so for different reasons: either to celebrate it, or else to pine for the good old days when everything was organised around a great binary opposition. But this overlooks the specific character of what urgently needs building today. For we do not again need to look for a coherent, all-embracing system of ideas, firmly rooted in conceptual rigour and able to reassure doubters by claiming to have an answer for everything (an *ideology*). Rather, what we need is a motley assemblage of fragmentary images, dubious metaphors, questionable interpretations, vague intuitions, obscure feelings, mad hopes, out-of-frame narratives, and interrupted myths. These would together take on the consistency of an *imaginary* – not so much because of their logical coherence as because of the interplay of shared resonances which, in cutting across all their varieties, bolster each of them in its singular fragility. This book seeks to make its own modest contribution to helping such an imaginary emerge.

The title of this book is inspired by the African American musician Sun Ra (1914–1993). He invented a *major body of musical work*, of which hundreds of recordings remain (ranging from post-bop compositions to collective experimental improvisations); a *mode of common creative life*, which he maintained for almost half a century within his Arkestra; and a *myth*, in declaring that he hailed from Saturn. In the USA of the second half of the last century, Sun Ra lived, embodied, and illustrated the emancipatory force of myth. When he changed his name, took on an extraterrestrial identity, and looked at earthly society from an interplanetary point of view, all this was part of an effort at counter-scripting the racist, classist, conformist, and anti-intellectualist oppressions that structure(d) American society.

So, the term *mythocracy* does not just refer to a political system in which fairy tales are cynically used to lull infantilised citizens to sleep.[1] It also refers to the capacity of 'myth' – whether a simple 'word' (according to the Greek etymology) or a 'foundational story' (according to modern usage) – to forge new individual and collective futures. To 'try mythocracy', to use the quotation from Sun Ra that provides an epigraph to this book, is, indeed, to confront the *ambivalence* that allows myth (word, story) both to lull us to sleep and to make us dream while we sleep, thereby providing us with a first imaginary access to 'what we never came to be that we should be'.[2]

A final precaution: this book comes from someone who has become a professor of literature. In other words, this author is someone more often confronted with the soft power of librarians than with riot cops swinging their truncheons. He himself wields an institutional power whose perverse effects he does not fully appreciate – and he is someone paid to say and believe that words, forms, narratives, and mises-en-scène count as much as the facts represented or expressed therein. As to whether this ought to grant him some sort of authority, or instead ought to draw the greatest of suspicion towards anything he claims – well, *caveat lector*!

1 This term was first used in French by Christian Mayaud in the 1970s 'to describe the role of propaganda in highly technological democratic societies'. See Christian Mayaud, 'What Is Mythocracy?', sacredcowdung.com, June 2005.

2 See p. v: Sun Ra, quoted by Graham Lock in *Blutopia: Visions of the Future and Revisions of the Past in the Work of Sun Ra, Duke Ellington and Anthony Braxton*, Durham, NC: Duke University Press, 1999, p. 61. The most comprehensive study of Sun Ra is John F. Szwed, *Space Is the Place: The Lives and Times of Sun Ra*, New York: Da Capo Press, 1998.

1

Reformulating Our Imaginary of Power

This book asks a question so straightforward that it may seem downright intimidating: *Who holds 'power' in our rich, liberal, mass media–dominated societies?* Put this way, the question is obviously simplistic: it is clearly misleading to pose the notion of 'power' in the singular, when any specific problem that we may happen to mention is bound to reveal a complex tangle of different forms of power (be they economic, administrative, military, media-communicational, rhetorical, scientific, religious, etc.). Still, such a realisation does not make this question any less pressing: to put off efforts at understanding things by pointing out the inevitable 'complexity of reality' is more likely to generate frustration than to spur our desire to seek further clarification. Much of the contemporary disarray of 'the left' stems from its difficulty in mapping (however roughly) the various relations of force that structure the forms of power today.

We may well still mobilise (with however much difficulty) each time that the electoral circus rolls around again. But even then, we do so in the knowledge that the dice for winning national-level political power are loaded, well ahead of the vote, by the structure of the media field. And we also know that programmes for social transformation are doomed to be eroded, after the votes are cast, under the pressure of transnational economic interdependencies. Even if it is understood that we need far-reaching transformations to bring our societies into line with the demands of justice – and of simple survival – our sensibilities and our behaviour are themselves torn. That is, they are split between moments of *belief* in the possibility of a change in the political order, and long periods of *disillusionment* as we face the falseness of the political circus.

This poses the urgent need for an *imaginary of power* that gives us a better grip (in our beliefs and in our action) on today's social forms. When I speak of an *imaginary* of power (rather than a 'theory') I do so mainly to emphasise the continuum that links the *images* we create of ourselves and the world, the stories we feel swept up in, the understanding and knowledge we develop, and the emotions we feel – without assuming that any one aspect should be prioritised over the others. To speak of an imaginary is also, following Cornelius Castoriadis,[1] to place the capacity for imagination at the heart of the dynamic processes by which human societies are constituted, instituted, and transformed. On this reading, these societies can only orient their development according to the possible futures that their participants have been able to imagine (visualise, envisage, invent, dream). The imaginary of power is not, therefore, a 'theory' that comes along after the fact to provide the analytical explanation of the images circulating around us. Rather, it is a set of schemas that we experience insofar as we use them. It is a set of *imagos*, of 'expansive forms' (patterns, *Gestalt*) that shape our expectations inasmuch as we are able to reconfigure them. They are spectacles that help us see 'reality' only by filtering what we see of it. The aim of this little book is to contribute to the (necessarily participatory, prefigured, and reconfiguring) study of a certain imaginary of power which is emerging in today's world. At the same time, it seeks to offer a brief overview of the question rather than an in-depth scholarly treatment.

1 On this point, see Cornelius Castoriadis, *The Imaginary Institution of Society*, Oxford: Blackwell, 1987, and *Le Monde morcelé. Les Carrefours du labyrinthe III*, Paris: Seuil, 1990.

The dissolution of powers

Over three decades ago, Michel Foucault urged us to stop thinking about 'power' by imagining some King (or President) who wields a force of domination and constraint over his subjects – which would also mean an essentially repressive force, exercised from the top down. Debunking the figure of the King-President is part of a tradition that goes back at least to the *Discourse on Voluntary Servitude* by Étienne de la Boétie, who, already in the mid-sixteenth century, suggested that even the most despotic tyrant has no power other than that which he can draw from the beliefs and actions of his subordinates. For La Boétie, it is only through the eyes, mouths, and hands of his subjects that the Ruler enforces his rule – 'it would be enough' for these subjects to stop obeying his orders, and then the Ruler would be reduced to a weakling, vainly shouting out commands that had long since become ridiculous. An imaginary of theocratic transcendence had long derived power from 'up there' – as in the words of Saint Paul, for whom 'All power comes from God' (through His representatives on different levels, such as the King, the Lord, the Father of the family, etc.). But in opposition to this, a whole modern tradition from Hobbes and Spinoza to Jean Meslier, Léger-Marie Deschamps, the anarchists of the nineteenth century, and the *operaisti* of the 1970s has insisted that the power that appears to be applied from the top down on citizens' heads in fact *emanates from these citizens themselves.*

This is the reversal (from top to bottom) that *demo-cratic* forms of government claim to make a reality. Here, it is the people (or rather *people*, the multitude of bodies and minds that make up the social body) who are supposed to be 'in power', insofar as it is their will (expressed directly or via their elected representatives) that decides the laws meant to govern the future of society as a whole. The disillusionment arising from the real application of this claim is as old as democracy itself: from time immemorial, it has been suspected that the dice in electoral contests were (more or less) loaded, or that structures outside of politics proper heavily conditioned both the selection and the actions of those in power, or that so-called 'intermediary bodies' perverted and became parasites on the channelling of the will of the people into the laws of the State. An entire critical tradition has (rightly) denounced the illusions inherent in democratic forms that (more or less badly) conceal the reality of powers which are in fact monopolised by a tiny oligarchy. But more recently, many thinkers from this critical tradition have come to value anew the formal – or even formalist – dimension of democratic representation. In hyper-reaction to the events of 11 September 2001, various more or less fantastical wars against drugs, crime and terrorism have precipitated a neoconservative upsurge in repressive securitarianism, which had in fact begun much earlier, but which has now reached the point of eroding formal rights won over decades of struggle. Faced with this development, even activists long critical of the inadequacies of 'bourgeois' democracy have felt the need to defend the legal gains achieved in the West during the twentieth century, in terms of individual freedoms and habeas corpus, the presumption of innocence, the protection of privacy, the right to information, and respect for the basic rules of democratic representation.

Faced with the rise of these forces for 'de-democratisation', it has once again become important to assert a certain demand, and therefore a certain *belief*, in the formal machinery of democracy.[2] We could hardly just condemn as naive and misguided those who want to believe that political power in our representative democracies really does emanate from citizens' electoral choices. There have long been demands for a reduction in the discrepancy between the number of votes and the number of human bodies (a gap caused by the exclusion of foreigners, undocumented migrants, and even prisoners and ex-convicts). Many have questioned how much real legitimacy can be derived from representative procedures that are subject to all sorts of distortions. But it is hard not to acknowledge that the perpetuation or transformation of our forms of social life really are based (at least in part) on the *choices* we are

2 For an analysis of the 'de-democratisation' brought about by the resurgence of a repressive neoconservatism which is simply the other face of the dominant neoliberalism, see Wendy Brown, 'American Nightmare: Neoliberalism, Neoconservatism, and De-Democratization', *Political Theory* 34, no. 6 (2006).

solicited to make at election time, on the *preferences* we are led to develop as consumers, and on the whole myriad of small, everyday *decisions* that we often take without the slightest deliberation. We can recognise that economic power and political power do indeed include these individual decisions, preferences, and choices as an important part of their constitutive mechanisms and realise this even without thereby sinking into gullible idealism or falling into the crude traps of liberal or parliamentary ideology.

In this sense, the imaginary of liberal market democracy implies a certain *dissolution* of power: what keeps it on its feet and gives it its form is not some monarchical Leviathan towering over it, but – as in the famous frontispiece that illustrated Hobbes's treatise – a multitude of individuals making myriad choices. Their aggregation alone creates an impression of unity. As in La Boétie, the micro-level, virtually infinite sources of power reside in the daily gestures of subjects' eyes, mouths, and hands.

This trend towards dissolution has become all the more apparent since the 1970s, when we became aware of the plurality of *micro-powers* that shape social reality both below and outside of the prerogatives of political government and market mechanisms. Foucault (along with many others) brought to light the tangle of power relations that structure not only the nation or the town hall, but also the workplace, the classroom, the neighbourhood, and the home. Instead of seeing a global pyramid structure binding the King-President to citizen-subjects via the different layers of Suzerains-Prefects on a gradual scale of domination, we have instead learned to identify the multiple intricate diagonals that may reverse traditional positions of power in each specific instance. For instance, some gay local official may temporarily suffer the domination exercised by a straight constituent of his. This intricate overlapping of micro-powers has led to the recognition of the heterogeneity of the different forms of domination at work within human communities.

Yet this gain in analytical intelligence and ethical sensitivity has come at a cost in practical agency. Faced with such a tangled web, and such tightly interwoven parameters, the ability of the 'political' to hold sway over the 'social' appears to be slipping.[3] What eighteenth-century philosophers called 'mores' (*les moeurs*) – and Pierre Bourdieu reconceptualised as *habitus* – proved to have a substance of their own, which recoiled against (half-hearted) political efforts to reform them. Seeing as this has been combined with a (now-hegemonic) discourse emphasising the primacy of the globalised economy over the still-national political decisions, we can well understand the (partly justified) feelings of *powerlessness* and *disaffection* that have sown disillusionment with the traditional modes of political involvement ('*engagement*').[4]

We all know that governments elected through the channels of representative democracy are neither all-powerful nor impotent: they are certainly often able to initiate legislative changes that can profoundly affect the life of a society, but they are also compelled to constantly replenish their 'power credit'. The last two years of George W. Bush's presidency illustrated the pathetic weakness of the 'most powerful man in the world', when an almost general discredit drained him of almost any sway over the country that elected him. Conversely, the broad support rallied by his successor suggests both the limits and the scale of what can be achieved with the confidence of the people once it has been captured by a certain image and a certain discourse. Short of the US president's formal capacity to unleash a nuclear arsenal capable of annihilating all human life, what exact 'essence of power' was it that the White House was seen to have lost during Bush's second term, which then (momentarily? apparently?) came back again together with Barack Obama? More generally, what makes it possible for an order barked by a Chief to induce obedience from a troop of subordinates, or for a stack of small rectangles of printed paper to command enormous masses of human labour?

3 A recent book by Maurizio Lazzarato succeeds in providing a detailed analysis of this tangle. It gives us a better grasp on what is micro and macro, molecular and molar, in societies remoulded by three decades of neoliberal dominance. See his *Expérimentations politiques*, Paris: Éditions Amsterdam, 2009.

4 On these issues, see Thomas Berns's fine little book *Gouverner sans gouverner. Une archéologie politique de la statistique*, Paris: PUF, 2009.

The economy of attention

To answer such questions, we will look at the microscopic scale, starting from a point that may seem banal and obvious, but is in fact crucial: *no one can obey an order that he has not taken the trouble to listen to*. Without yet knowing what 'power' really consists of, we can already say that its effectiveness is based on the precondition of attention: *that which we do not pay attention to has no power over us*. A flowerpot falling on my head from a sixth-floor balcony may well kill me, and I might tick myself off for carelessly not paying attention to it. Still, even if it undoubtedly exerts lethal violence on my person, it cannot be said to exert power over me. If, from the same balcony, a desperate man points a rifle at me, he will have power over me only insofar as I know that my life relies on the finger touching the trigger. So long as I remain unaware of his presence, or once the bullet he fires actually has reduced my brain to a pulp, he has no 'power' over me, either.

So, let us say that the distribution of power within a collective of individuals correlates to a certain *economy of attention*. The worst loss of power that a president could suffer would not be if every one of his statements and actions were criticised day and night, but, rather, if people stopped paying attention to everything he does, the sounds that pass his lips, and the documents that he signs with his pen. Equally, we can now see that the power of a president can in fact be fuelled by the attacks against him, as long as they help focus attention on his person or on the issues he wants to talk about, and thus divert attention from other, potentially more important problems.

When I speak of an economy of attention, this is not a metaphor but a call to develop a rigorous analysis of this new object of scarcity in our societies of material abundance (however unevenly distributed this abundance may be). What is today genuinely scarce is attention time. As Richard A. Lanham rightly points out, and as Patrick Le Lay explicitly acknowledged when he said that French private TV channel TF1's function was to 'sell available human brain time to Coca-Cola', the new scarcity in our 'information societies' is not information itself, but the time it takes to go through the staggering mass of information, of all kinds and all values, that is offered up to us (hundreds of millions of TV and radio programmes, books, papers and magazines, the millions of websites created each year, etc.).[5] The low cost of internet access, combined with public library collections in most cities in the rich world, means that it is not so much monetary barriers as the limits of the attention economy that stop us discovering this plethora of information.

Unlike most of the resources with which the economy of material goods concerns itself, attention time is affected by a scarcity whose limits are almost impossible to push back. Unless we artificially reduce the sleep we get, which will also cost us in terms of the *quality* of our attention, the amount of waking time available in the course of a human life is eminently limited. This remains the case even if the massive reduction in working hours over the last century surely has helped to free up considerable amounts of attention time. The contrast between this absolute scarcity and the considerable increase in the range of objects and activities on offer to my attention leads to a continual increase in the 'opportunity cost' of each of them – the loss of profit that this activity causes me, in stopping me from doing the myriad other things that also deserve my attention.

As the development of our modes of production allows us to free a growing share of our activities from the sole concern of feeding, clothing, and protecting our bodies, our attention is likely to be drawn in increasingly improbable directions. This could encompass all manner of things: collecting photographs of footballers; mastering the secrets of the art of bonsai; becoming a mine of information about the latest gadgets that can be fitted to such and such a make of car; memorising the dates of the last European tour on which Eric Dolphy accompanied Charles Mingus; and so on. The question of how and for what purposes we should use the time thus freed up makes ever more important the question of the best distribution of our attention time. It is true: many of us

5 For some good insights into this economy of attention, especially in its profound relationship to rhetoric, aesthetics, and scholarship, see Richard A. Lanham's *The Economics of Attention. Style and Substance in the Age of Information*, Chicago: University of Chicago Press, 2006.

see ourselves as chronically short of 'free time'. On a global scale, many people's days are still taken up by the search for the most basic necessities of life (water, food, shelter). Still, the ancient gesture of the 'wise men' who spurned material wealth – today followed by welfare recipients who readily claim to have 'chosen' a frugal existence – shows how our attention time is often distributed according to priorities that depend on us (even if they seem to be imposed on us by others).[6] Of course, when we add up these 'preferences' across the whole population, we see that their apparently 'individual' character rings hollow. Even if we are not violently forced to do it, we are at least strongly pressured to listen to a particular singer, see this or that film, take up some sport, or work overtime at our place of work – and we do all these things *en masse*.

In fact, in our consumer societies and our representative democracies, capturing people's attention time is the key issue at the heart of all economic and political life. These phenomena are part of a cyclical relationship that makes it difficult to even tell apart the chicken and the egg, that is, to separate the *attention* from the *desire*. Whether we are dealing with a question that affects our immediate well-being (getting some inkling of my boss's mood before I ask him for a pay rise) or something apparently trivial (remembering whether guitarist Marc Ducret really did appear on a recording by saxophonist Tim Berne), my attention follows my desire, which is largely the result of my attention. The direction in which our desire-attention points both reveals and helps to reorientate the way in which we plug in to the power structures that govern us. Between the chicken and the egg, the decisive thing is the moment when our attention-desire is captured. You do not need to take much of a step back from our everyday existence to see that we spend most of our time putting ourselves in a position to capture our fellow human beings' attention. It is not just that ad men, political advisers, PR managers, DJs, or teachers are professionally on the lookout for what will attract their audiences' attention. Each of us is constantly trying, through most of our daily gestures, to direct and shape the attention of the people around us

6 On this point, see the film by Pierre Carles, Christophe Coello, and Stéphane Goxe, *Attention danger travail* (2003).

(to get noticed by them, to make a good impression on them, or to distract them from our mistakes).

We can only choose or prefer things whose existence we have previously recognised (and which we think we can develop a specific idea of). As a consequence, from the individual point of view, the economy of attention has a function logically prior to the economy which governs the sphere of market exchange – as well as that which determines the distribution of political power in a democratic system. The goods or services which I engage in some monetary transaction over can only become the focus of my 'preferences' insofar as they have previously captured my attention and my desire. And the candidates or parties for whom I cast my ballot will only get my vote insofar as they have said, done, or shown something that I find noteworthy and desirable.

The economy of affects

Trying to understand the mechanisms behind the constitution of the powers that govern us today thus implies situating oneself in a field of problematisation that falls under what Maurizio Lazzarato has proposed to call a '*noo-politics*' (a politics of the intellect, of the action that one mind can exert on another by mobilising its attention and making its mark on its memory). Or it can be said to belong to what Pascal Sévérac terms a 'theory of the occupation of the mind', in the sense of competition for the conquest of those very special terrains of activity that are human brains.[7] However, this expression's rather military connotation perhaps demands that we specify what exactly the occupation of a mind could possibly consist of. Of course, the first step may be to occupy the land, to prevent an enemy from seizing it and turning it into one of his strongholds. From this unfolds the whole negative imaginary that Pascal sketched out under the heading of *divertissement* ('diversion' in the sense

7 On these points, see Maurizio Lazzarato, *Les Révolutions du capitalisme*, Paris: Les Empêcheurs de penser en rond, Seuil, 2004, pp. 83–6; and Pascal Sévérac, *Le Devenir actif chez Spinoza*, Paris: Champion, 2005, pp. 203–301.

of 'entertainment') or that Marx denounced in the register of the 'opium of the people'. Ever since the Romans' bread and circuses, it has been possible to understand the occupation of the mind as a way of diverting attention away from problems that would deserve to be the object of intellectual effort, but which the interests of a dominant social group (or some curse of human nature) turn us away from. It does not matter what is occupying the mind: all that really matters is what this occupation *excludes from the mind.*

Such strategies are surely still part and parcel of political combat. But the aim of all advertising activity is (also) to make certain particular images (such and such a brand name, such and such a desire, such and such a hope, such and such a fear) penetrate their way into the mind. What occupies the mind is no longer simply a repellent, the content of which is itself neither here nor there. Rather, it is occupied by a certain impression, with which a particular affective orientation is always necessarily associated (desire, joy, sadness, love, hatred, fear, hope). Even in the case of entertainment, as argued by Pascal, or the oft-denounced dumbing down of the masses in today's 'Tele-cracy', the diversion always involves *the mobilisation of a certain desire* (generally supposed to be located at the 'basest' level of our most 'primal' instincts).[8]

In other words, the economy of attention can never be separated from an economy of affects.[9] Drawing on Spinozist philosophy, an *affect* can be defined as an emotion felt internally by the mind, which conditions the individual's thoughts, will, and future behaviour on the basis of a fragmented perception of the reality that surrounds and constitutes us. For Spinoza, the field of affects was initially divided into three main

8 See Bernard Stiegler, *La Télécratie contre la démocratie: Lettre ouverte aux représentants politiques*, Paris: Flammarion, 2006, and *Économie de l'immatériel et psychopouvoir*, Paris: Mille et une nuits, 2008.

9 On the notion of the economy of affects, see Maurizio Lazzarato, 'Gabriel Tarde ou l'économie politique des affects', *Chimères*, no. 39 (2000); and Yves Citton, 'Esquisse d'une économie politique des affects', in Yves Citton and Frédéric Lordon, eds, *Spinoza et les sciences sociales. De la puissance de la multitude à l'économie des affects*, Paris: Éditions Amsterdam, 2008, pp. 47–123. See also Brian Massumi, *Parables for the Virtual: Movement, Affect, Sensation*, Durham, NC: Duke University Press, 2002.

branches, which distinguished desire, joy, and sadness, before branching out into a complex combinatorial structure producing love and hate, jealousy and pity, pride and humiliation, and so on. Where the classical moralists spoke of 'passions', the term 'affect' not only makes it possible to account for the 'affective' dimension of our personal experience (in contrast with the 'cognitive' dimension) but, above all, encourages recognition that my inner feelings should be understood in terms of the impressions that affect me from the outside. Even if we may think that they emanate from the innermost core of our personality, emotions should thus be understood as, above all, relational, intersubjective or, better still, transindividual phenomena. This is the term Gilbert Simondon uses to denote the common fabric from which subsequent individuations are formed.[10]

To speak of an 'economy of affects' thus means, on the one hand, that my various inner emotions constitute a system with its own dynamics and equilibria. But this also implies, on the other hand, that my affective regime is directly articulated, in a *transindividual* way, around the affective regimes of those around me whom I recognise as akin to me. Here we have no intention of devaluing the virtues of scientific knowledge and communicational rationality – we know that Spinozist philosophy makes causal intellection its highest Good. But an approach to social realities that takes note of the laws of the economy of affects will place the phenomena of suggestion, magnetism, emotional contagion, and waves of imitation at the heart of its analysis of communication processes.[11]

It is easy to see how the economy of attention and the economy of affects depend on each other. What I pay attention to (or not) depends on my affects (fears, desires, jealousies), which are in turn conditioned by what I pay attention to. Watching the news on TF1 (a private station,

10 See Gilbert Simondon, *Individuation in Light of Notions of Form and Information*, Minneapolis: University of Minnesota Press, 2020.

11 On Spinoza's notion of affect, see Pierre Macherey, *Introduction à l'Éthique de Spinoza. III La vie affective*, Paris: PUF, 1995; and Chantal Jaquet, *L'Unité du corps et de l'esprit. Affects, actions, passions chez Spinoza*, Paris: PUF, 2004. For a theory of communication that integrates the economy of affects, see Daniel Bougnoux, *Introduction aux sciences de la communication*, Paris: La Découverte, Repères, 2001.

but the same may be said of its lookalike on the 'public' broadcaster) is part of the mutual reinforcements and feedback loops that bring about a certain type of affective economy. When we are exposed every night to news stories about sexual predators or drug traffickers (who are generally not 'from here') – rather than seeing images of police brutality or hearing critical reflections on crime statistics – this will not, of course, automatically drive viewers to vote for politicians who make tough-on-crime law-and-order rhetoric their bread and butter. However, this steady diet of anxiety-provoking images, alternating with scenes of policemen taking criminals to prison, cannot fail to impress the population that is subjected to all this. It is hardly surprising if the aggregate of this same population's individual affective economies 'meets' with a discourse that captures their attention with talking points that play on the same fears and the same need for protection nurtured on their TV screens each night.

'Facilitation' and publics

Simplistic as it may be, this example shows why the notion of 'facilitation' – of forging paths, paving ways (*frayage*) – is essential for grasping the intimate link between a certain economy of affects and a certain distribution of attention time and memory traces. The effects of circular reinforcement and feedback loops mentioned above rely on the fact that one flow passing through forges a path which facilitates and attracts the passage of subsequent others. Through molecular friction (*frayage* comes from the Latin *fricare*, 'rubbing'), this forges paths which are both conditioned by previously developed paths and themselves condition future ones (the term *frayage* is modelled on the German *Bahnung*, in which we recognise the word *Bahn*, 'way, path'). An affect embodies the passage, carved out by previous passages, which channels the attention whose thrust constitutes the frictional force always seeking easier progress, while simultaneously smoothing the path it takes, paving the way for further passages. We can see that the vocabulary of economics is never far beneath this imaginary of psychic path-forging: the attention that I (temporarily) 'pay' (*prêter*, 'lend') to an event today traces the lasting imprint of a path that may more easily 'earn' my attention tomorrow.

Once we have situated the individual economies of attention and affects within the trans-individual phenomena that structure them collectively, we may then define an *affect* – from the viewpoint of a noo-political theory of the occupation of the mind – as an agent of facilitation in the psycho-social distribution of attention time and memory traces. It is an agent of facilitation in that, in response to some stimulus, it 'eases' the mind in the direction of some reaction of joy or sadness, hatred or love, and thus 'traces' a path towards which subsequent reactions will more easily tend to be oriented. This two-sided process – clearing a new path and sending subsequent behaviour along this same track, articulating the labour of attention to that of memory – always acts simultaneously both within my *psyche* and within the *social* body. According to a logic of communication, what is individuating itself through this forging of paths within me is always a society (a 'culture'). And, conversely, a society is nothing other than the communicative movement of the trans-individual facilitations through which individuals inter-trace their affects on each other's minds.

This inter-tracing of our affects can take place in the most varied contexts and institutions. A couple in love, a large family, a sports team, an infantry regiment, a classroom, an editorial board, a congregation of parishioners, a jazz concert: each of these interaction structures induces a certain collective arrangement of attention, memory, and affectivity. Among all these structures, of which we have all developed a (generally very detailed) practical knowledge, there is one that is worth analysing a little more closely, insofar as it plays a central role in the distribution of power that characterises our current mediarchic societies – that which constitutes what we call a 'public'. It is intuitively obvious, indeed a commonplace sentiment – but also something of a delusion – to say that what feeds (economic, political, media) power is the favour accorded to it by 'the public': public opinion, the public sphere, the same stuff which is sounded out in opinion polls and periodically recorded at election time. Well before and well after Jürgen Habermas proposed his famous analysis of the 'public sphere', the sociologist Gabriel Tarde (1843–1904) (recently revisited by the contemporary philosopher Maurizio Lazzarato) conceptualised the notion of the 'public', in a manner which offers many precious insights.

Gabriel Tarde suggests that we should draw a distinction between the principle of a public and that of a crowd. Whereas the notion of a crowd refers to a group of individuals gathered together in the same place whose affective interferences and contagions relies on the fact that they can see and hear each other in real time, a public refers to a collection of apparently autonomous and independent individuals who neither see nor hear each other, but who, notwithstanding this spatial separation, tend to think and act in the same way. They do so because – in a circular logic – they 'cross paths' in media (understood in the broadest sense) that inform their sensibilities and ideologies, according to a logic that is more a function of the laws of the market than of direct political control.[12] The various 'members' of a public have the remarkable characteristic that they are completely unknown to each other, are scattered across space and separated by thousands of miles of distance, and yet feel and move in the same way at the same time. For instance, this is what happens once every four years when half the world's population simultaneously jumps up from their seat when a footballer manages to get his leather ball inside a large net-lined rectangle during the World Cup final.

It follows from this definition that, while all human societies have experienced crowd phenomena, most past societies only had 'publics' in rather embryonic forms compared with the last two centuries. In fact, there is no public worthy of the name unless there are 'media' capable of disseminating information and representations relatively extensively and quickly. In Europe, that only began in the second half of the eighteenth century with the acceleration of postal routes and the first rise of the periodical press. It has since accelerated with the wider circulation of print media in the nineteenth century, and then with the arrival of radio,

12 On this point, see Gabriel Tarde, *L'Opinion et la foule*, Paris: PUF, 1989 (1901); and Maurizio Lazzarato, *Puissances de l'invention. La Psychologie économique de Gabriel Tarde contre l'économie politique*, Paris: Les Empêcheurs de penser en rond, 2004.

television, and the internet in the course of the twentieth. Seen in the broad sweep of human history, the mass publics we have today are completely new communications phenomena, whose long-term development patterns are doubtless still poorly understood.

A world of increasing plasticity

Indeed, the various centuries-long developments discussed in this chapter join together in the new power of the public. These major developments in the collective life of our affluent societies can be summed up in the following eight points.

A formal democratisation of political institutions. Since the end of the eighteenth century, our Western societies have (gradually) equipped themselves with formally democratic mechanisms of government, through which political power is attributed on the basis of the aggregate 'choices' of the electorate.

The expansive commodification of goods, services, and access rights. Ever-more aspects of our existence are governed by the competition among consumers, producers, and investors, based on a price set within a now-global market, on the basis of individuals' needs and 'preferences'.

Technological 'levitation' above the constraints of subsistence. Under the pressure of workers' demands in the first half of the twentieth century (reducing working hours, establishment of welfare-state institutions), European societies have come to provide large sections of their populations with a standard of living that allows them to devote a significant proportion of their time and available income to so-called 'pampering' (hobbies, tourism, culture, entertainment),[13] detached

13 On these notions of 'levitation' and 'pampering', see Peter Sloterdijk, *Foams: Spheres III*, Los Angeles: Semiotext(e), 2016.

from the constraints of survival. This has given their development a certain plasticity, which is, of course, far from absolute – as we are reminded by the sharp environmental constraints that are today bearing down on us. But it does increase, indeed in an absolutely unprecedented way, the possible range of forms of life that we can imagine and invest in.

The centrality of demand-driven production in consumerist economic dynamics. In direct proportion to this 'levitation', the logic of our classical economic conceptions has gone haywire. Rather than the bulk of our productive activities being guided by the *satisfaction of the inherent needs of material life* (food, shelter, protection), it is now instead the *artificial production of socially induced desires* (through advertising, art, the interplay of mimetic behaviour, and attempts to distinguish ourselves) that commands the overall dynamics that mark our economic cycles.[14]

The massification of higher education. From the doubling of literacy rates in the eighteenth century to the middle classes' broadened access to further and higher education in the 1950s to the 1990s – and now through the 'magic' of Wikipedia – ever-wider sections of our Western populations have become able to shape their desires and beliefs based on a shared written culture. This latter acts both as a shared platform and as a site for the infinite diffraction of the individual.

The turn from an industrial capitalism towards a cognitive capitalism. Faced with new possibilities for production, as well as the emancipatory demands raised in the late 1960s by these strata who had been newly empowered by the welfare state and mass higher education, capitalism was driven to start adapting its structures. Even if

14 John K. Galbraith had already sketched out the broad outlines of this reversal in his book *The Affluent Society*, London: Houghton Mifflin, 1958. Dominique Quessada drew the philosophical and anthropological consequences in *L'Esclavemaître. L'Achèvement de la philosophie dans le discours publicitaire*, Paris: Verticales, 2002 (see in particular pp. 363–88).

innovation has always played a central role in the capitalist dynamic, the strata generating the greatest profits are now located in the massification of a diffuse capacity for invention, within the webs of a collective intellect. This latter increasingly appears to constitute a common good, fed not so much by homogenisation as by individuals' bid to distinguish themselves.[15]

The doubling-up of disciplinary societies with societies of control. The ways in which individuals are expected to collaborate in the adaptive reproduction of our forms of life has become increasingly complex and intensive. This has led disciplinary societies, in which individuals had to be programmed to repeat certain behaviours known in advance, increasingly to be permeated by mechanisms of control, in which individuals need to be given a wide margin of self-determination, so that they can themselves inventively adjust their behaviour to the novel requirements of the (interactive) tasks they have to perform.[16] This is no longer simply a matter of moulding predetermined reactions (as the army, boarding school, or spelling class did), but of building the capacity for the self-regulation of relationships that have become too complex to be programmed in advance.

The intensification and globalisation of media networks. Media have built networks for communicating information, images, and sound that now reach most of the world's populations nigh-on instantaneously. These media technologies now make it possible to generate mobilisation, interference, and resonance effects without equivalent in any previous era of human history.

---

15 On the great transformation that this hypothesis of a 'cognitive capitalism' suggests, see Yann Moulier Boutang, *Cognitive Capitalism*, Cambridge: Polity, 2012; and Carlo Vercellone, ed., *Sommes-nous sortis du capitalisme industriel*, Paris: La Dispute, 2002, as well as nos. 2, 10, and 32 of the journal *Multitudes*.

16 On this point, see Gilles Deleuze, 'Post-scriptum sur les sociétés de contrôle', in *Pourparlers*, Paris: Minuit, 1990; Bruno Karsenti, 'La Politique du dehors. Une lecture des cours de Foucault au Collège de France (1977–1979)', *Multitudes* no. 22 (2005), pp. 37–49; and Maurizio Lazzarato, 'Biopolitique/Bioéconomie', *Multitudes* no. 22 (2005), pp. 51–62.

In fact, these eight long-term developments combine to make my *(trans)individual choices* (as a voter, consumer/producer, reader/listener/viewer) the obligatory passage point – a site of forging paths, of identical reiteration, or of possible bifurcations – for the forces that determine the development of our forms of collective life. We began this chapter by naively asking who really holds 'power' in today's rich, Western, liberal, mass media–dominated societies. The overview that has taken us from the dissolution of a monarchical imagery of power to the economies of the micro-level (attention spans, memory traces, and affective regimes) leads to the intuition that we now need to imagine power in terms of the facilitation mechanisms that operate within this form of diffuse sovereignty, specific to our era, that 'publics' constitute. Having thus reworked our imaginary of power, the next stage will try to reconstruct, on this basis, a model of how power works. It will have a specific task: to model the way that the diffuse logic of micro-level choices constitutes the apparatus of conditioning, control, or emancipation.

2

Modelling the Circulation of Power

We could sum up our findings in the previous chapter by saying that, in the imaginary that Gabriel Tarde, Michel Foucault, Gilles Deleuze, Félix Guattari, and Maurizio Lazzarato invite us to sketch out, power is not *something that anyone holds*, but *something whose circulation itself constitutes us*. It is, indeed, something whose circulation must reconstitute us in each moment, by the very act of its passage. Power thus appears as a current that constantly needs to be replenished – like a magnetising influx that can be observed both through the channels that serve as its conductors and through the magnetic wave fields that orient the sensitivities and behaviours of the publics it informs.

The development of such an imaginary is by no means a novelty peculiar to our supposedly 'postmodern' age. It has, rather, developed through myriad smaller developments over the last two centuries, in close parallel with the socio-technological conditions listed at the end of the previous chapter. Gabriel Tarde suggested that we conceive of social life on the magnetic model of 'a somnambulist [who would] imitate his medium to the point of becoming a medium himself and magnetising a third person, who, in turn, would imitate him, and so on, indefinitely'.[1] But even a

1 Gabriel Tarde, *The Laws of Imitation*, New York: Henry Holt, 1903, p. 84.

century before that, Jean-Jacques Rousseau, in his paranoid *Dialogues*, had already described the epidemiocratic spread of ideologies among publics. Similarly, André Chénier had already compared to 'a sort of electric chain' the way in which Jacobin networks and periodicals managed to ensure that in 'the same moment, in every corner of the Empire, [activists were] agitating together, crying out the same things, churning out the same movements, which [they] certainly had no great difficulty in predicting in advance'.[2] From the discovery of electrical phenomena and 'Mesmerism' in the Enlightenment era, to the spread of large daily newspapers and the telegraph in Tarde's time, to the wireless and internet-based networks that form the backdrop to Maurizio Lazzarato's thinking, we can see the gradual emergence of an imaginary that represents modern societies as *a collective mental universe* informed by the circulation of magnetic currents and resonance waves.

How can we move beyond this surface-level imaginary and try to imagine the structuring logics that govern these movements of circulation and resonance? That is what this second chapter sets out to do. It does so by constructing an abstract model, cobbled together from six elements drawn from sources that may appear rather different from each other, but which are all linked to successive reinventions of Spinozist thought. I do not claim here to offer an exhaustive overview, or for that matter to be particularly original. In the pages that follow, I will assemble quotations borrowed from a few select authors, which seem to me to

2 André Chénier, *Œuvres complètes*, ed. Gérard Walter, Paris: Gallimard, Pléiade, 1950, p. 275. On Rousseau's epidemiocratic visions in the *Dialogues*, see my articles 'Liberté et fatalisme dans les *Dialogues* de Rousseau: Hyper-lucidité politique de la folie littéraire', *Méthode!*, no. 5, Vallongues (2003), pp. 115–24, and 'Fabrique de l'opinion et folie de la dissidence: Le "Complot" dans *Rousseau juge de Jean-Jaques*', in *Rousseau juge de Jean-Jacques. Études sur les Dialogues*, Ottawa: University of Ottawa Press, 1998, pp. 101–14 (republished by Champion, 2003). On the imaginary of resonance and magnetic suggestion in the eighteenth century, see Chapters 8 and 14 of my book *L'Envers de la liberté. L'Invention d'un imaginaire spinoziste dans la France des Lumières*, Paris: Éditions Amsterdam, 2006; and, with regard to André Chénier, 'Imitation inventrice et harpe éolienne chez André Chénier: Une théorisation de la productivité par l'Ailleurs', in François Genton, ed., *Ferments d'Ailleurs*, Grenoble: ELLUG, 2009.

provide a set of small modules whose patchwork arrangement may bring some clarity on our question. As the various elements fall into place, I hope that this modelling operation will shed some light on power relations that we all have some practical intuition of, but whose general articulation we cannot spontaneously map in our heads, and whose decisive moments are not always so readily identifiable.

Flows of desires and beliefs

If power is not something we can hold but something whose circulation itself forms us, then we must surely begin by defining what this 'something' is that runs *between* and *within* each of us. Maurizio Lazzarato's reading of Gabriel Tarde's work, which simultaneously reconstructs his thinking and brings it into our own present, answers this question by providing us with the first element of our model. What constitutes the 'substance' of power (which, as we shall see, is not very substantial) are the flows of *desires* and *beliefs*.

'Desires and beliefs are forces in the sense that they circulate like flows or currents between brains. These latter function as relays in a network of cerebral or psychic forces, in passing currents (imitation), or bifurcating them (invention).'[3] The forces circulating in and between brains that push, pass, cause friction, and forge paths, therefore belong to two closely associated types. These are *desires*, a term under which we here include everything that the previous chapter attributed to affects (emotions, passions, feelings); and *beliefs*, which include all the forms of adherence to some knowledge, information, or doctrine. Desires are therefore affective, while beliefs are cognitive.

Although we indiscriminately place all forms of both rational knowledge and fanatical faith on one same register of 'belief', this in no way denies the difference in nature between 'scientific' knowledge (the HIV

3 Maurizio Lazzarato, *Puissances de l'invention. La Psychologie économique de Gabriel Tarde contre l'économie politique*, Paris: Les Empêcheurs de penser en rond, 2001, p. 27.

virus is the cause of AIDS) and 'superstitious' illusions (some animal sacrifice will lead to a rainfall pattern that should result in a better harvest this year). It is simply to recognise that this mechanism of adherence characterises both the mental state of someone who believes in the danger of the HIV virus, and that of someone who believes that spilling the blood of an animal will win over the deities who are in charge of the rain. Belief may be more or less absolute, more or less critical, and, in either case, its intensity may vary over time. But we will be measuring one same *force of adherence* in either case.

Similarly, by placing all forms of affects on one same register of 'desire', we are not denying that there is a difference of degree (of content, of compatibilities, of properties, etc.) between the hunger that assails the undernourished and my consumerist fancy to buy a new pair of shoes. It just means recognising that there is one force of impulse that pushes us to want to do certain things (an appetite, hope, ambition, or hatred) or that holds us back from doing others (fear, humility, respect, etc.).

Using one fixed syntagm to refer to the *flows-of-desires-and-beliefs* implies both that I desire certain objects because I believe in the reality of certain representations, and that I develop certain beliefs because I experience certain desires. These two modes of implication are but two sides of processes that are in fact intimately linked. The same kind of feedback loops that feed attention and affect are here found linking desires and beliefs: it is because I believe that the streets are full of criminals on the lookout for their next victim that I feel fear when my eyes lock onto a suspicious gaze; it is because I fear being attacked that I will perhaps interpret someone looking at me as a threat. Likewise, I need to worry about the weather because I am hoping for a good harvest, and that is also why I will develop (as best I can) the understanding necessary to anticipate it. It is because I have come to identify certain correlations between the colour of the sky in the evening and the weather the next day that I want to rush to harvest my wheat rather than leave it standing for another twenty-four hours. And it is because I have noted other correlations between Monsanto's commercial practices and their consequences for society and the environment that I will join an activists' action against a field of genetically modified maize rather than a field of wheat.

Maurizio Lazzarato adds a valuable clarification on the origin of these flows of desires and beliefs: 'It is not that brains are the origin of these flows; rather, they are contained within them. The ontology of the "Web" is to be found in these currents, in these networks of cerebral forces, in these powers of differentiation and imitation.'[4] The flows of desires and beliefs are not so much circulating *between* people as *through* individuals. The 'sources' of these fluids are not so much located in a particular brain as in the trans-individual nature of our affects and beliefs: an emotion is not generated *by* me, but *in* me by *what connects me to others*. The forces of impulse or adherence are thus best conceived not as individual properties but rather as relational realities, which emanate from the differential relationships between what is interior and exterior to me.

The individual is not the place from which these flows originate, but the site through which their paths evolve. As the first quotation emphasised, my status within the general circulation of flows of desires and beliefs implies that I can either let a certain current pass through me, or stop it, or else make it bifurcate in another direction. This behaviour can be termed *imitation* in the first case, *counter-imitation* in the second case, or *invention* in the third case. In other words, in the imaginary proposed here, individuals are nothing but moments of path-clearing. They are neither a substance definable in and of itself, nor a source of original impulses, nor pure elements of structure. They exist only as sites of marking, tracing, and forging (either aligned or bifurcating) paths, traversed by currents that constitute individuals only insofar as they flow through them.

In other words, 'in Tarde's theory, circulation has priority over production. But the circulation of commodities, manufacturing processes, economic needs, and representations is subordinate to and dependent upon the molecular, pre-individual circulation of flows of desires and beliefs'.[5] We may simply add – to return to our main point – that the constitution of the various forms of power also depends on this molecular and pre-individual circulation of flows of desires and

4 Lazzarato, *Puissances de l'invention*, p. 27.

5 Ibid., p. 28.

beliefs. To 'reduce' individuals to the forging of paths that takes place in and through them in no way condemns them to impotence or passivity. The flows of desires and beliefs to which I contribute neutralise the simplistic opposition between activity and passivity: insofar as I am driven by these flows, I can certainly be considered passive. Yet, insofar as the path of these flows does not pre-exist the selection of which I am the locus, I can be attributed some share of activity (and thus of power).

In between Gabriel Tarde and Maurizio Lazzarato, Gilles Deleuze and Félix Guattari popularised the imaginary of flows with their 1972 work *Anti-Oedipus.* Returning in 1980 to the 'tiny little something' that this book brought, Gilles Deleuze situated it precisely in the process of forging an unpredetermined path:

> We spend our time being traversed by flows. The process is the course that a flow takes, it's the simple image of a stream digging its bed . . . it's a movement of travel insofar as the path has no pre-existence, in other words, insofar as it traces its own path. In another way, we called these 'lines of flight' [*lignes de fuite*].[6]

The percolation of *potestas* into *potentia*

I borrow the second element of the model from a distinction highlighted by Antonio Negri in his reading of Spinoza. It contrasts two different notions of power, as either *potestas* (*pouvoir*) or *potentia* (*puissance*). The most intuitive way of presenting this distinction is, without doubt, to go back beyond Spinoza, to Étienne de La Boétie's aforementioned *Discourse on Voluntary Servitude* (1548), and read two passages in which he clearly poses the question at the heart of his argument:

> I should like merely to understand how it happens that so many men, so many villages, so many cities, so many nations, sometimes suffer

6 Gilles Deleuze, *Cours du 27 mai 1980*, available as 'Anti-Œdipe et autres réflexions' at webdeleuze.com.

> under a single tyrant who has no other power than the power they give him; who is able to harm them only to the extent to which they have the willingness to bear with him . . . He who thus domineers over you has only two eyes, only two hands, only one body, no more than is possessed by the least man among the infinite numbers dwelling in your cities; he has indeed nothing more than the power that you confer upon him to destroy you. Where has he acquired enough eyes to spy upon you, if you do not provide them yourselves? How can he have so many arms to beat you with, if he does not borrow them from you? The feet that trample down your cities, where does he get them if they are not your own? How does he have any power over you except through you?[7]

Potentia is what the multitude of subjects provide the tyrant as they place their vital energy, the competences of their bodies and minds (their eyes, their hands, their feet, their gazes, their vigilance, their actions), in his service. *Potestas* is what the ruler can turn back on the members of the multitude, as he re-applies to them the forces he draws from their service – which he can do to harm them, as in the case of a tyrant, or to help them better organise themselves, as we can expect from a better form of government.

We can also present this distinction in another way by defining *potestas* as the capacity for collective action which human institutions mobilise insofar as they succeed in capturing the *potentia* of (parts of) the multitude. The multiple and multidirectional powers of human bodies and minds become *potestas* only when they are brought together, inflected, aligned, and channelled through collective institutions. This is emblematically illustrated by Abraham Bosse's famous frontispiece for Hobbes's *Leviathan* (1652), in which the Sovereign is made up of the multitude of bodies of citizens, who thus duplicate their existence, each being both a subject (subject to the laws, in the city represented at the bottom of the image) and a part of the Sovereign (in the body of the

7 Étienne de La Boétie, *The Politics of Obedience: The Discourse on Voluntary Servitude*, Auburn, AL: Mises Institute, 1975, pp. 46–8.

Leviathan that towers over them, threatens them, and orders them around from up there):

Figure 1. Frontispiece for Thomas Hobbes's *Leviathan* (1652), engraving by Abraham Bosse.

Still, such a reading should not be taken to suggest that each individual is originally endowed with their own *potentia*, which would be only in a separate and second moment placed in service of the common institutions (either spontaneously or under constraint). This is the libertarian's illusion. Rather, it is mostly from the *common potentia of the multitude* that each individual derives their *individual potentia*. This is well illustrated by the fact that the individual can develop their capacity for reflection and personal rationality only by using a necessarily shared language. The *potentia* harnessed by institutions, who place it in service of our rulers, should not then be imagined in the form of a collection of small parcels of energy and capacities which are simply added together into an 'aggregate'. Rather, we should think of this more in the form of a radiating influence or a *trans-individual* fluid that individuals not only bathe in, but in which they are constantly (re)constituting themselves.

Another quotation – directly inspired by La Boétie although written two centuries later by the priest (and clandestine atheist) Jean Meslier – makes clear the liquid nature of the imaginary that is necessary to give a proper sense of the notion of *potentia*:

> For your tyrants, however powerful and formidable they might be, would have no power over you without yourselves. All their grandeur, all their wealth, all their force and power come only from you . . . it is only from you and from your industry and your harsh labors that come the abundance of all the goods and wealth of the land. It is this abundant sap, which they draw from your hands, that maintains them, that fattens them and that renders them as strong, as powerful, as proud and as haughty as they are.[8]

According to Meslier, this 'abundant sap' that tyrants extract from their subjects' labours can be readily imagined in the form of streams of wealth drawn from the workers' sweat in order to shower luxury on the palaces of the princes. Still, the end of the sentence shifts from what 'maintains and fattens them' to what makes them 'proud and haughty' – in other words to flows that satisfy mind rather than body. Indeed, this capturing of the *potentia* of the multitude has to do with flows of affect (pride, glory, courage). This 'sap' anticipates another fluid notion that theorists of new technologies have introduced in recent years: *wetware*. Whereas hardware refers to the solidness of computers as material machines, and software to the flexibility of the programs that can be coded and operated on them, wetware draws on a liquid analogy to refer

8 Jean Meslier, *Œuvres complètes*, Paris: Anthropos, 1970 (1733), vol. 3, pp. 146 and 152. Translation by Mitchell Abidor from marxists.org.

to the work of a specific 'wet' part of the body, the brain.[9] Without a brain to command the fingers moving across a keyboard, or to integrate the data displayed on the screen into a thought-process, the computer and the software will be nothing more than inert and useless objects. What makes a fleet of computers and a range of programs productive are the interactive flows of knowledge, questions, suppositions, desires, suspicions, intuitions, imaginations, and interpretations – in other words, desires and beliefs – that are exchanged between and through human brains by means of hardware and software.[10] All of humanity's intellectual, cognitive, and emotional *potentia* is thus realised only at the level of wetware. The liquid analogy is a good one: for humanity's productivity depends on its capacity to spread, to leak, to infiltrate beneath the rigid barriers of the past in order to communicate ideas, feelings, and disciplines that had previously been separate.

The energy and the physical capacities of the body, the intellectual competences and sensibilities of the mind, are all part of a *potential* that only becomes productive of life through a dialectic of capturing (channelling) and release (leakage). This is the dialectic through which Antonio Negri theorises the distinction between *potentia* and *potestas*, which he places at the heart of his interpretation of Spinoza's thought. It has been shown that Spinoza did not distinguish between the two terms in any absolutely systematic way.[11] But it is clear that the frequent use of these words in contrasted ways does point to a profound and structural contrast. This is the case, for example, in the *Tractatus Politicus* (*TP*), where we read that 'it is clear that the right of the supreme authorities (*summarum potestatum*) is nothing else than simple natural right, limited, indeed, by the power (*potentia*), not of every individual, but of the multitude, which is guided, as it were, by one mind' (*TP*, III, p. 2). As he draws this scandalous

9 On the three-sided division between hardware, software, and wetware, see, for example, Richard R. Nelson and Paul M. Romer, 'The Economics of Software and the Importance of Human Capital', *CyRev*, no. 8 (Winter 2004).

10 On this point, see my *Avenir des humanités. Économie de la connaissance ou culture de l'interprétation*, Paris: La Découverte, 2010.

11 See the entry 'Puissance' in Charles Ramond, *Dictionnaire Spinoza*, Paris: Ellipses, 2007, pp. 149–50.

equation between right (*jus*) and power (*potentia*), which is the foundation of his political ontology, Spinoza seems to be inviting us to see *potentia multitudinis* as capacities that emanate from the bodies and minds of the myriad individuals that make up the social body, and which need the conduit (*ducitur*) of a gathering and unifying capture (*una veluti mente*) to assert their own right as a power (*potestas*). Antonio Negri highlights this when he characterises *potestas* as 'the subordination of the multiplicity, of the mind, of freedom, and of *potentia*' or when he asserts that *potestas* 'can mean only one thing: *potentia* toward constitution'.[12] Political life consists of capturing, reorientating, and channelling the *potentia* of the multitude through the institutions of *potestas*. Doubtless this is the formulation in which we find the most general definition of 'class struggle'.

Still, in the first chapter of the *Political Treatise*, Spinoza takes the trouble to make clear that, unlike other theorists who deluded themselves into believing 'that the multitude or men distracted by politics can ever be induced to live according to the bare dictate of reason', he starts from the principle that 'men are of necessity liable to affects' and that these latter should be considered not as 'vices of human nature, but as properties, just as pertinent to it, as are heat, cold, storm, thunder, and the like to the nature of the atmosphere' (*TP*, I, pp. 4–5, translation edited). So, the *potentia* of the multitude cannot be channelled – put into conduits (*induci*) – based on a postulation of the rationality of human behaviour, but only based on the economy of affects (even if this also includes the possibility of sometimes directing minds towards 'active affects', based on a rational intellection of reality).

In cobbling together my model from various sources, I will here take the liberty of assuming that the circulation of the 'sap' we mentioned earlier – the *potentia* of multitude – follows the paths traced by the circulation of the flows of desires and beliefs which I described in the previous section. If *potestas* is constituted through the capture of *potentia*, this capture is only possible, only has profitable effects, insofar as it involves the capture of the flows of desires and beliefs that circulate within the multitude.

12 Antonio Negri, *The Savage Anomaly*, Minneapolis: University of Minnesota, 1991, pp. 190–2.

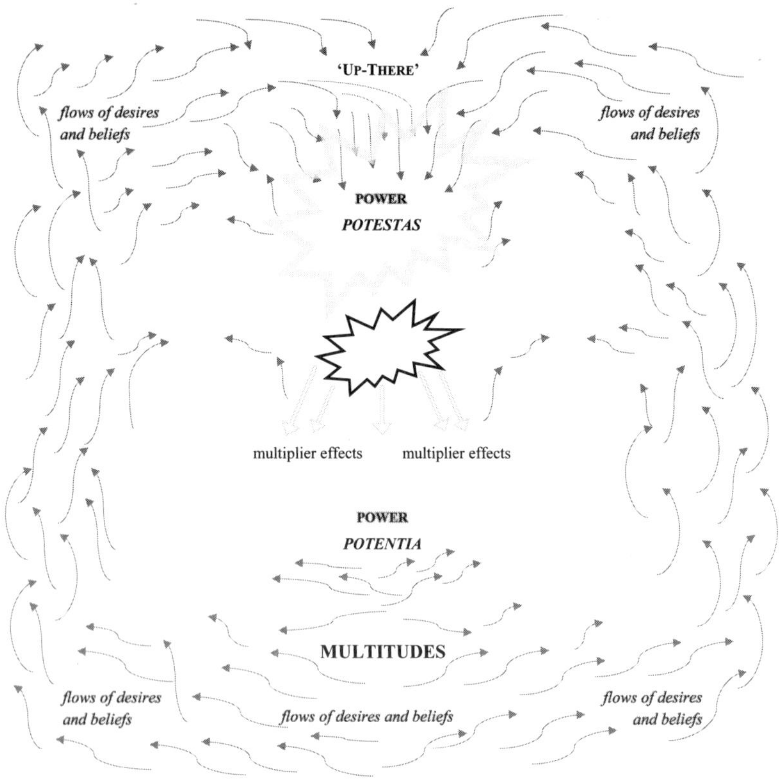

Figure 2. The flow of beliefs and desires, *potestas* and *potentia*.

The first element of my diagram provided us with the raw material (though there is not much material about it) of what circulates between us and within us to constitute our power: the flows of desires and beliefs. This second element gives us the general form of this circulation: that of a percolation of the *potentia* of the multitude into institutional *potestas*. I say percolation – an image today associated with a coffee machine. So, to use that analogy, the *potentia* of the multitude is channelled in such a way that it rises up from itself, surges above and then falls back down on individuals, now in the form of institutional *potestas*. It should be pointed out that, while this movement from *potentia* to *potestas* is always a trans-individual dynamic, it can be observed in collective expressions (the power of the State, the power of money, the power of religion) as well as in its individual ones, according to the now well-known process of 'empowerment'. For what can be more 'empowering' than the (always interactive) capacity that a person or a social group gains to collect, direct, and channel its own *potentia* – giving it the kind of overhanging, composed, solid character so typical of an institutionalised *potestas*?

Institutions as mediations with multipler effects

Following in the footsteps of Alexandre Matheron,[13] the author who has most clearly described this 'percolation' is the philosopher-economist Frédéric Lordon. He has devoted much of his recent work to using Spinozist concepts and frameworks to rethink phenomena like the origins of money or the way that institutions operate. Through his work, he has come to develop an 'energetic structuralism' that grasps the form of the structures governing the social world as concentrations of 'dead energy with which the living energies of present actors will combine'.[14] In the terms I set out in the previous two sections, this 'dead energy' can be seen as the firmly consolidated effects of earlier facilitation, of the already forged paths. That is, the desires and beliefs that have previously been engaged along certain stable courses have carved out *pathways* or *channels* that seem naturally to lead further desires and beliefs into these already solidly established structures.

This explicitly leads to a highly stimulating definition of the notion of power:

> The highest concentration of dead energy is to be found in the structure's Archimedian points. These are its sites of power. Indeed,

13 See Alexandre Matheron, *Individu et communauté chez Spinoza*, Paris: Minuit, 1988 (1969).

14 Frédéric Lordon, 'Conatus et institutions. Pour un structuralisme énergétique', in *L'Année de la régulation*, vol. 7, Paris: Presses de Sciences-Po, 2003, p. 128. See also, by the same author, 'L'Empire des institutions', *Revue de la regulation* 7 (Spring 2010).

> the topological-energetic intuition could lead to another way of defining power, which is characterised phenomenologically by the disproportion between its efforts and its effects: A barely whispered word triggering a war, bringing millions of people out into the streets, or overthrowing governments – that is what power means . . . Reconsidered in these energetic-structuralist terms, power may thus be redefined as the occupation of the Archimedian points of the structure, and the enjoyment [*jouissance*] of the immense collective resources that are there made available for living energies' activities. This, then, is an *intensive* conception of power. Power is an intensity; it is a quantity. A physicist would say: it is the moment of leverage. Fundamentally, power is a multiplier effect: it is the ability to access large quantities of dead energy, in order to multiply one's own living energy.[15]

This approach allows us to map out the aforementioned percolation of *potentia* into *potestas* – even if this cartography simplifies things in the extreme. Institutions (whether political, military, religious, economic, educational, linguistic, literary, etc.) appear as structures for capturing, arranging, composing, aligning, and channelling the flows of desires and beliefs that circulate within society. These structures materialise in a physical and spatial form, for example, when they arrange a few dozen students in a classroom to pay attention to a teacher, when they compose a regiment's movements according to a colonel's battle plan, or when they synchronise the parishoners' genuflections to the rhythm of the priest's words.

Lordon also shows – and in a much more suggestive way, in light of the imaginary we are drawing on here – that phenomena such as money and finance result not only from visible and localised institutions (a central bank, a stock exchange), but, above all, from a complex interplay of beliefs that permanently and diffusely circulate among individuals. The banknote in my hand has value for me only because I believe that others believe that everyone believes that it has the value in question. If

15 Lordon, 'Conatus et institutions', p. 128.

this circulation is interrupted by some sort of accident (I am shown that the banknote is a fake, my bank declares itself insolvent) – then, suddenly, everything that had made the paper in question valuable evaporates. As soon as the belief in the value of a paper note is broken, it is no longer valid, then that money no longer circulates. All I will have in my hand is a piece of paper: as etymology suggests, the value of a *currency* is only worth the trust that allows it to run on and on (*correre*).[16]

Institutions appear as *mediating bodies*, which structure social life insofar as they manage to collect and distribute flows of desires and beliefs through relatively stable structures. In the last analysis, it seems that their entire reality is reducible to the pure effects of trans-individual beliefs, and thus to a 'self-affectation of the multitude' itself. It is my belief that – conforming to and confirmed by others' beliefs – gives substance to the value of a currency which, when crisis erupts, will turn out to be based on nothing more solid than trust. It is, therefore, the multitude that gives the banknote its effective reality (its *Wirklichkeit*, its capacity to produce effects), insofar as it auto-affects itself into believing in this value.

Lordon (following in the footsteps of his colleague André Orléan) is right, however, to insist that this self-affection, while surely part of circular logics, is never direct, but always requires the constitution of a mediation in between. My belief in the value of a particular banknote becomes effective through the intermediary of others' belief: for money to function and 'stand on its own feet', for the genuflecting worshippers to be synchronised, for the movement of soldiers to conform to a battle plan, the desires and beliefs of the multitude must be joined in a mediation, which is the institution of power itself. 'Power [*potestas*] is thus born with *mediation*, and the self-affection of the multitude takes on a mediated character in the moment when the power [*potentia*] of the multitude transits through an intermediary in which its concentration is

16 On this point, see Frédéric Lordon and André Orléan, 'Genèse de l'État et genèse de la monnaie', in Yves Citton and Frédéric Lordon, eds, *Spinoza et les sciences sociales: De la puissance de la multitude à l'économie des affect*, Paris: Éditions Amsterdam, 2008, pp. 127–70.

realised, before it is again discharged onto those who are in fact its producers – and who have now become its subjects.'[17]

This insight into the real nature of institutions allows us to add a further element to the model. For the element that captures the flows of desires and beliefs which direct the multitude's *potentia* – raising this *potentia* above itself before discharging it onto the multitude once more via some mediation – is institutional structures. These structures consist of a web of channels and already forged paths, which have various multiplier effects. These multiplier effects can be observed in a number of ways: there is a multiplication of force when the institution (for instance, an industrial or military one) enables individuals to coordinate their physical movements. There is a multiplication of value when the (financial) institution has become the focus of such trust that it can lend sums that it does not currently have. There is a multiplication of visibility and access when the (media) institution allows the same discourse to be disseminated to millions of households. Institutions can thus be imagined as channelling structures built around nodal points (the headquarters, the bank, the news programme) defined in relation to the nature and scope of their multiplier effect.

Power as a meta-conduct conditioning 'free' conducts

Michel Foucault's thinking on these issues in the 1970s was directed at imagining power as a structuring of behaviours. For Foucault, 'to govern . . . is to structure the possible field of action of others' and 'guiding the possibility of conduct and putting in order the possible outcome'.[18] Despite a still-common perception – and Foucault's own dogged efforts to dispel this confusion – it would be a mistake to identify power with

17 Frédéric Lordon, 'Derrière l'idéologie de la légitimité, la puissance de la multitude. Le *Traité politique* comme théorie générale des institutions sociales', in Chantal Jaquet, Pascal Séverac, and Ariel Suhamy, eds, *La Multitude libre. Nouvelles lectures du* Traité Politique *de Spinoza*, Paris: Éditions Amsterdam, 2008, p. 116.

18 Michel Foucault, 'The Subject and Power', *Critical Inquiry* 8, no. 4 (Summer 1982), pp. 777–95; quote on p. 789.

repression or constraint. Power should be seen less as something that *prevents us from doing* what we want, than as something that *incites us to (want to) do* what we want. While power is often limited by the threat of constraint and violent reactions, this threat is only its outer limit, not its inherent nature. Power is 'a total structure of actions brought to bear upon possible actions; it incites, it induces, it seduces, it makes easier or more difficult; in the extreme it constrains or forbids absolutely; it is nevertheless always a way of acting upon an acting subject or acting subjects by virtue of their acting or being capable of action'.[19]

By pointing out that the very essence of power is to *induce* – with an etymology (*inducere*) that relates to 'conduct', both in its guidance and in its plumbing connotations – Foucault adds an important nuance to the model. To 'guide the possibility of conduct' is to structure flows of desires and beliefs by channelling them along solidified, previously paved paths, but always within a certain margin of deviation and adherence which is left up to the acting subject. Unlike 'constraining' – which is experienced by the constrained individual as a necessity forced upon them from the outside – 'inducing' implies a certain degree of internalisation of an option that is chosen from among multiple possible behaviours. Hence, for Foucault,

> When one defines the exercise of power as a mode of action upon the actions of others, when one characterizes these actions by the government of men by other men – in the broadest sense of the term – one includes an important element: freedom. Power is exercised only over free subjects, and only insofar as they are free. By this we mean individual or collective subjects who are faced with a field of possibilities in which several ways of behaving, several reactions and diverse comportments, may be realized.[20]

The freedom in question here need not be based on an ontological assumption of 'free will'. It can be grounded in the empirical fact that we

19 Ibid.
20 Ibid, p. 790.

cannot predict with certainty which of several possible behaviours the subject will ultimately choose to adopt. Power thus appears as a characteristic of all those types of conduct that manage to condition free conduct (which is 'free' in the specific sense that it is a priori unpredictable). Here, we should understand 'conditioning' not in terms of an ineluctable determinist sequence, but rather as a combination of external conditions which will induce an individual to make certain choices in a given situation. The social reformer Robert Owen (heir to a whole tradition of Enlightenment thought) took up the most rigid determinist positions and thus set himself the goal of 'governing circumstances' (in the sense of 'combining' and 'regulating' them) in order to 'remove the causes' of society's ills.[21] This idea of 'conditioning' is built on the understanding that individuals' apparently free choices are always the result of the 'conditions' in which they have to be made. From this it follows that the human power to act resides less in the moment of the choice which triggers the action, than in the configuration of the parameters that will determine future choices (my own, and those of others). The notion of *gouvernement*, which is so important in the late Foucault's thought, thus appears to stem from a discrepancy between two levels of action. Here, power is located at the (higher) level, which exercises a meta-conduct on the conduct of an agent, who conceives of himself as free to choose between several behaviours at the (lower) level at which he situates his action.

But let us keep this lesson for our model: within the flows of desires and beliefs that direct the expression of the multitude's *potentia*, and that are captured and channelled by various institutional mediations, *power manifests itself as the capacity to meta-conduct*. Which is to say, the capacity to influence, to suggest, to induce certain behaviours, by conditioning the voluntary choices that subjects over which the power (*potestas*) in question holds sway are led to make.

21 Robert Owen, *A Discourse on a New System of Society*, New York: Humanities Press, 1970 (1825), pp. 26–7.

Social life as an entanglement of strategies

As we saw, Michel Foucault defines the exercise of power as 'a mode of action upon the actions of others'. But, in so doing, he makes clear that the actions in question must always be analysed in terms of relations that belong to the domain of *strategy* (understood in its various possible meanings).

> If it is true that at the heart of power relations and as a permanent condition of their existence there is an insubordination and a certain essential obstinacy on the part of the principles of freedom, then there is no relationship of power without the means of escape or possible flight. Every power relationship implies, at least in potentia, a strategy of struggle, in which the two forces are not superimposed, do not lose their specific nature, or do not finally become confused.[22]

Power struggles and strategic relationships are not the same thing, insofar as power is situated on this side of the open violence that characterises warlike confrontation, in which one side conquers and defeats the other, who is actually killed or (temporarily) suppressed as a 'free subject'. But power struggles and strategic relations are inextricably bound together. For the guiding of conduct is always experienced in the context of gestures of *affirmation* and *resistance*, through which 'we try to get a grip on the other' or, on the contrary, to escape his hold.

Laurent Bove's analysis of the Spinozist *conatus* offers, I think, the most enlightening description of the strategic nature of power relations: 'a singular *potentia* of affirmation and resistance, the Spinozist *conatus* is a strategic practice of decision on problems and their resolution'.[23] In ontological terms, the 'strategy' in question here is, indeed, a certain form of 'war', in that it is a struggle in which – in accordance with the definition of the *conatus* as the tendency to persevere in one's being

22 Foucault, 'The Subject and Power', p. 794.

23 Laurent Bove, *La Stratégie du conatus: Affirmation et résistance chez Spinoza*, Paris: Vrin, 1996, p. 14.

– each individual strives to ensure their survival and therefore to avoid death: 'The affirmation of existence is called strategy, first of all from the perspective of this dynamic of the active resistance of the *conatus* to being totally crushed by more powerful external forces.'[24] Less than the idea of 'war' per se – which makes us think of human enemies and a fight to the death – 'strategy' evokes the parallel idea of both an effort to survive and an effort against the forces that threaten to crush us. The essence of the *conatus* thus lies in a movement with two distinct faces: the *affirmation* of a form of life that is trying to force its way into being, and the *resistance* against those dynamics which tend to stifle the development of this form of life. So, for Bove, when we think about what a strategised activity confronts, its model should be found not in the image of combat but in that of a problem. Whereas a combat situation presupposes the existence of some enemy, the problem does not exist ready-made as an external reality; rather, it must be formulated by the effort of affirmation-resistance itself:

> The concept of strategy thus first of all refers to a body's capacity to pose and resolve the problems posed by its own actualisation in a situation of risk and impotence that immediately denotes it as a victim . . . The problem is not a 'given fact' encountered in experience. It is a product of the force of affirmation of any being (an individual or society) in its complex dynamic articulation with reality.[25]

If there are, necessarily, forms of 'insubordination', 'restive freedom', and 'resistances', this is because each being poses itself different problems, which befit its own modes of existence. No transcendent Providence has taken the trouble to harmonise each and every *conatus* in a way that ensures that they will all fit together. As Rousseau famously points out in his *Discourse on the Origin of Inequality*, the mode of interaction observed in our societies 'necessarily bring men to hate one another to the extent

24 Ibid.
25 Ibid., pp. 15, 308.

that their interests are at cross-purposes with one another.'[26] Given these overlapping and rival interests, each course of conduct is likely to be met with *counter-conducts*. Yet, more crucially, each individual conduct may itself appear as a counter-conduct to the strategies that pre-exist it. The fabric of social relations thus appears as *a tangle of strategies*. This is not only the way that society patterns its collective being, but also the way that each individual carves their own mode of individuation: 'In reality, there are only individuation strategies. The Real is strategies.'[27]

Given these considerations, we should make strategising a constituent element – disseminated at the level of each *conatus* involved – of our modelling of power relations. The tensions between the different expressions of affirmation and resistance – which are always (more or less well) strategised – govern the relations of opposition and composition which arrange the individual *conatuses* within the collective *conatuses* into which societies organise themselves. The flows of desires and beliefs do not circulate through channels that are naturally aligned with each other, as if they could ensure a perfect fluidity. Rather, they are at every level agitated by turbulence which results from contradictory currents and conflicting interests, as they make their way along paths which are constantly being opened up but are not predetermined. The capturing of *potentia*, on which all *potestas* feeds, should be seen in the context of conflicting strategies that simultaneously constitute both the affirmation of certain forms of life and the resistance which these forms of life put up against all that threatens to extinguish them.

Verticality in immanence

We are working with a model of power relations which sees reality as a tangle of conducts and counter-conducts, corresponding to conflicting flows of desires and beliefs. To add a further element to this model, it is

26 Jean-Jacques Rousseau, *Discourse on the Origin of Inequality*, note 9, trans. D. A. Cress, in *Basic Political Writings*, Indianapolis: Hackett Publishing, 1987, p. 90.

27 Bove, *La Stratégie du conatus*, p. 173.

worth thinking further about strategy – again, without getting caught up in the reductive imaginary of warfare. We have said that power should not be identified with the level of overwhelming violence, and that the enemy is *never given* (since an enemy has to be constructed at the end of some prior process of problematisation). The notion of the 'battlefield' in any case risks being misleading for the way we imagine power relations. Contrary to what the frontal opposition between conduct and counter-conduct may suggest, this entanglement of strategies should not be imagined in terms of some flat space, a battlefield, on which each rival *conatus* deploys its opposed forces. Rather, it should be grasped within a vertical superposition of multiple levels of embeddedness.

It is, of course, right and important to see the model proposed here as part of a way of thinking about *immanence* – a way of thinking that denies any transcendent source of the ways of organising human lives. By imagining power in terms of currents and circulation mechanisms, this model implies that nothing comes from Elsewhere, and that anything can and must be found within one same plane of immanence. The beauty and the virtue of thought that draws on the notions of the 'multiple' and the 'multitude' is that it takes us beyond established hierarchies (which are often imagined to be natural and impossible to go beyond) and delves into their micro-level (even if trans-individual) component forces. Such thought has the great merit of taking us to the level of the infinitely diverse powers-to-act, desires and beliefs that are scattered throughout the multitude.

However, this radical egalitarianism, as well as the cult of spontaneity that sometimes goes with it, carries a major risk. For it would be mistaken to confuse the plane of immanence with a flattening of reality. It is all well and good to challenge falsely naturalised hierarchies, assert the constituent role of the multitude's spontaneous desires, and make equality (of intelligences) the central postulate of all democratic politics. Indeed, it is absolutely necessary. But, in so doing, we should not reduce social life to a flattened horizontality. Rather, we need to take seriously the vertical relationships through which the multitude gives itself structure.

This verticality is at the heart of Frédéric Lordon's thinking on the mediated self-affection that allows the *potentia* of the multitude to *rise* above itself, through the percolation mentioned previously. The difference of levels of which we have spoken – between conducts and the meta-conducts that condition them – is, on a microscopic level, part of this same verticality: not everything is at the same level *within* immanence. Since the eighteenth century, biology has often been a discipline at the forefront of thought on immanence. It has identified how life emerges through *a multiplicity of levels of organisation*; while it is always possible to question and problematise the thresholds supposed to separate these levels, they reflect *a vertical superposition* that can be mapped in terms of levels of emerging 'complexity'. This superposition of levels of entanglement and complexity also needs to be integrated into our model of the circulation and composition of power.

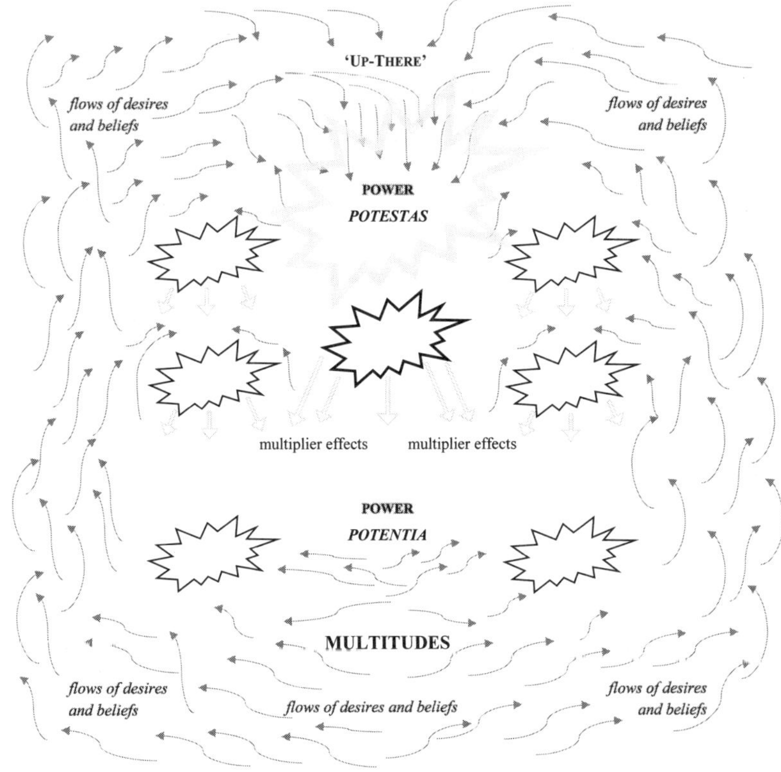

Figure 3. Entanglements and verticality.

I can think of no more evocative – and provocative – way of imagining this vertical relationship than Jacques the Fatalist's refrain in Diderot's novel, a *ritornello* he constantly repeats as a quote from his Captain: 'Everything good or bad that happens to us here below is written up there [*écrit là-haut*].'[28] This line has often disoriented critics (which was surely what Diderot intended). Immanentist thinkers saw it as a mere joke – the work of a Spinozist Diderot who took pleasure in portraying the most indefensible (and anti-modern) form of determinism, simply for the sake of fun and mischief. The flustered defenders of free will saw it as a repentant realisation on the part of a fatalist who (finally!) starts to reckon with the limits and the absurdities of fatalism. Both were wrong. Clearly, it would be absurd to imagine that Diderot could have believed for a second in the existence of a Book of Laws in which our fate has always been written by some transcendent Authority. One way out of this problem would be to point out that Diderot was already thinking in terms of a Laplacian imaginary, which asserts that, if only we knew the laws of nature and the exact position of each point of matter, we could calculate and predict the future evolution of the entire system that constitutes the universe. Still, the fact that everything that happens to us may – according to the principles of this mechanistic determinism – be 'written' into such a system of equations is hardly sufficient to establish a distinction between a *here below* and an *up there*. Quite the contrary: immanentist readings of *Jacques the Fatalist* imagined that they were showing their own 'modernity' (their materialism, their anti-providentialism) by reducing the world to a pure *here below*, and in denying that what our naive ancestors located *up there* was in any way real.

Lordon quite rightly points out that power (*potestas*) is the product of 'the *capturing* of *potentia multitudinis* by whoever "wields" it, and the fact that those over whom it is wielded are unable to recognise themselves as its true origin.'[29] In this sense, historically immanentist thought

28 Denis Diderot, *Jacques le fataliste et son maître*, ed. Pierre Chartier, Paris: Livre de Poche, 2000 (1780), p. 43.

29 Lordon, 'Derrière l'idéologie de la légitimité', p. 116.

certainly did play an emancipatory role, insofar as it debunked the idols supposedly belonging to a transcendent 'up there'. Yet the multitude's inability to recognise the *vertical* topology of embedded power structures is no less damaging than its inability to recognise how much its own power is percolating through the actions of the powers that are striding over them. Jacques's jibe, which Diderot mischievously dumps on the shoulders of immanentist thinking, ought to be understood in terms of its ability to provoke a reaction. Diderot's intention is to 'lead' us to think about what exactly is this '*up there*' where our everyday destiny is supposedly written. It certainly means recognising that it is not each individual who spontaneously writes it for themselves, down here, based on their personal free will. When an individual casts their vote into the ballot box, or puts their bottle of Coke in their trolley, they should be aware of just how far their behaviour down here has been *written up there* (*écrit là-haut*). It is written through all the power structures, all the paths that have been broken open and which have consolidated in the past, which have contributed to *meta-conducting their conduct* in this particular moment. Even if that 'up there' is the pure product of the trans-individual percolation of the multitude's own power (*potentia*), it is indeed this vertical relationship that they must try to understand and to map. That is, unless they want to avoid (somewhat) the fate of becoming a mere puppet, like another figure in Diderot's novel, Jacques's Master (a kindly idiot). If the expression 'thinking about power' means anything, it consists precisely in thinking about *the superposed layers of the entangled embedding of (strategic) meta-conducts that induce our (strategic) conducts.*

We can see what makes Diderot's novel so provocative. Jacques is perfectly right to say that 'all the good and the evil which befalls us here below was written up there'. After all, he is a character in a novel: so, everything that happens to him in his fictional world really has been written 'up there', that is, by the (quite real) hand of Diderot himself. The provocation lies in the fact that this novel, whose narrator spends his time interrupting the story of Jacques's love affairs to call out to his reader, both openly asserts and blurs the difference of levels between the fictional world and the real one. The reader is made well aware that they are reading a novel: the arrangement of Jacques's flows of desires and beliefs, respectively frustrated and shaken by the narrator's constant interruptions, is staged in a way that aims to fully display the author's own meta-conductive activity, exercised over his reader. The reactions of both the (real) reader and the (fictional) character are therefore also written 'up there', on the great scroll written by Diderot's hand.

Neither our common experience as readers nor critical interpretations of the novel generally take the provocation or the blurring of levels much further. We know that, by keeping our eyes on the text, we are immersing ourselves in a fictional narrative: all we have to do to get out of (and free ourselves from the grip of) the narrative meta-conduction is to look away from the page. It is quite obvious that someone is directing (part of) my behaviour when I am reading a book that they have written; it is equally obvious that my real-life story (as soon as I close the book) has *not* been written up there. The game that Diderot plays (with us) in *Jacques the Fatalist* belongs to the series of the disconcerting hypothesis that Descartes has us imagine with the possible illusion generated by his *malin génie*, of the hallucination which Jean Potocki plunges us into at the start of *The Manuscript Found in Saragossa*, of the one which the creators of *The Matrix* immerse us in, or of the one that leaves us so uncomfortable when we watch Michael Haneke's *Funny Games U.S.* Beyond their various differences of narrative genre and stylistic tone, each of these works question 'the reality of reality'. But they all do it within the limits of their fictional world.

The singularity of the way in which *Jacques the Fatalist* stages the tangled web of meta-conducts comes from the fact that he directly questions our position as a reader in our actual life: *who is telling my (real-life) story?* At first glance, of course, the answer is easy: *nobody is*. There is no great scroll, no providential pen, no evil genius, no all-encompassing conspiracy (no Evil Empire, no totalitarian state, no conspiracy of big business, no collusion of multinationals, no Bollywood-style intrigue) dictating my daily actions. As we have seen, there is nothing but a tragicomically chaotic tangle of conflicting (and generally 'half-baked') attempts to capture our flows of desires and beliefs.

But things change when we translate this question – who is telling my story? – into Foucauldian language. Then, we see it as the question raised by *any* analysis of power relations: *Who is meta-conducting my conduct?* In other words, *who plays a role in inducing my choices, nudging me towards my desires and influencing my beliefs?* Admittedly, these questions fit quite poorly with the imaginary of the writer who determines the actions and the fate of his characters as they please, or that of the puppeteer who pulls their wooden creations' strings at will – an image that Jacques also brings up in order to describe how he directs his Master's behaviour.[30]

However, we can get a better image of these questions when we think of the sheer variety of musical practices. Translated into this field, the overly simplistic character of the way we commonly imagine power (and freedom) would be like imagining only a binary alternative between, on the one hand, a hyper-rigid classicist approach which recognises nothing as music other than a (marionette) instrumentalist's execution of a score written up there by some all-powerful composer, and, on the other, the free improvisation developed on the extreme edge of jazz, in which concert performers make a principle of not pre-empting things by agreeing in advance on any theme, rhythm, key, structure or pre-established hierarchy among themselves. Yet we all know that most music played today is the product of complex combinations, which can be located at countless points on the spectrum of possibilities bounded between these two extreme cases (each of which is, in itself, an extremely meagre offering). Classical musicians (fortunately) can and must add much of their own hinterland from 'down here' to the (necessarily incomplete) prescriptions provided in the score written by the composer from up there; even the freest improvisers can usually be expected to imbue their instantaneous compositions with references to pre-existing themes or structures. Musical practices more broadly may be characterised in terms of the *conduction* outlined by Lawrence 'Butch' Morris. This term

30 Diderot, *Jacques le fataliste*, p. 352; English edition, *Jacques the Fatalist and His Master*, trans. David Coward, Oxford: Oxford University Press, 1999, p. 235. Some translations will be amended to stay closer to the French original.

refers to the real-time arrangement work a conductor performs to trigger, coordinate, superimpose, interrupt, synchronise, dephase, blend, and modulate the performances of a group of improvisers. These latter still retain a great deal of control over the thematic, rhythmic, and timbral material which they draw from their instruments, some variable part of which may have been prescribed in advance, while the rest is left up to the inspiration of the moment.[31]

Gabriel Tarde spoke of 'cascades of successive and interlinked magnetisations', to make us imagine the life of a society on the model of a multitude of sleepwalkers who push the imitation of their medium so far as to become mediums themselves. But the most fitting image of the meta-conduct of conducts is doubtless that of a criss-crossing of conducting strategies, through which each conductor-instrumentalist seeks to arrange the performances of those around them, so that they will together play the music that most suits them. If we do not want to flatten out power relations and end up with a merely illusory egalitarianism, then these sets of conductor-improvisers need to be situated within the *institutional* embedded levels which define the entire economy of the performing arts: musicians can only make a living from their performances insofar as other types of improvisers manage to meta-conduct the behaviours of spectators ready to shell out a few quid to come and hear the concert. But, to reach the crowds, these promoters also need the strategic relationships they have forged with the press services who improvise the content of their television news programmes or advertising inserts on the spur of the moment . . . At each level of this series of improvisation-conductions, each agent tries to capture the flow of desires and beliefs of the other agents, to get them to sing their own little tune or tell their own little story.

Who tells my story? Who is meta-conducting my conduct? Clearly, if these questions are misleading, this is not really a problem of the

31 On the notion of conduction, see 'Lawrence D. "Butch" Morris, Conduction', conduction.us. For a broader discussion of these issues, see Alexandre Pierrepont, *Le Champ jazzistique*, Marseille: Parenthèses, 2001; and Yves Citton, 'L'Utopie jazz entre liberté et gratuité', *Multitudes*, no. 16 (2004), pp. 131–44; and 'Le Percept noise comme registre du sensible', *Multitudes*, no. 28 (2007), pp. 137–46.

difference between the two planes of 'reality' and 'fiction'. Indeed, we would be mistaken to consider these levels truly autonomous of each other: in a world of improvisers, social reality is itself largely a product of the fictions we make of it.[32] Rather, these questions are mainly deceptive insofar as they conjugate the verb in the *singular*. For our reality as a whole (and my individual story within it) result from the entangled embedding of *multiple* fictionalising modulations.

We therefore need to do a little violence to English syntax and rewrite the question: 'Who are the *we-they*, who are telling our stories?' Based on what (hierarchical) superposition of 'up there'? By meta-conducting what conducts? In the interest of which strategies? These are the questions that our next chapters will try to answer, by looking more specifically at the way in which a particular type of meta-conduct – scripting – can modulate our desires, beliefs, and behaviours.

32 For a rewarding exploration of the *mises en abyme* of multiple levels of fiction created in the world of sci-fi, see Ariel Kyrou, *Paranofictions. Traité de savoir-vivre pour une époque de science-fiction*, Paris: Climats, 2007.

3

Scripting as an Activity

Once upon a time, managers, advertisers, and politicians almost simultaneously discovered a wonderful mantra. It had long been lying dormant in the dusty binders of old literary theorists – but it was also ripe to bring fame, wealth, and power to anyone who could whisper it persuasively enough into the ears of their victims. This all happened around the year 1995, in a large and, well, somewhat dull-witted Empire beyond the Western seas. These adventurers were well aware of the power of the hidden treasure they had unearthed – but, sadly, they were also entirely unscrupulous. They made shameless use of this mantra over the decade that followed. Nothing could resist them: their panacea, which they baptised 'storytelling', bewitched hearts and minds and converted countless souls. Through their 'incredible' 'hijack[ing of] the imaginary', they became vastly wealthy and awfully powerful. They racked up successes all the more abrasively because they had no qualms about openly extolling the virtues of their invention at conferences, seminars, and publications. This was also why they did not just win the devotion of the masses, but also kept getting fat pay cheques: 'In the hands of the forces that [sought] to control people's minds, storytelling machines ma[d]e it possible to regulate media, economic, financial, political and military transformations, in direct contact with the individuals who [were] the objects of these processes.'

The great Empire, which had now been irredeemably stultified, was already beginning to extend the tentacles of this mantra towards the noble kingdoms of the East and (what horror!) even preparing to make incursions into Gaul – that proud land of druid-citizens and diehard intellectuals. But then, an intrepid Christian knight blew into his ivory horn, just as two traitors were about to abuse this alien mantra to (even more horror!) 'delegitimise politics'. He called for a crusade – and it rallied the brave more than could ever have been hoped for. Baptised with the very name of the enemy, the breathtaking story of *Storytelling* drew on all the mantra's power to capture the general attention, break all sales records, allow its author to live happily ever after and expect many children . . .

Despite all the perhaps questionable pastiches that one can build on top of it, Christian Salmon's book *Storytelling* surely has struck a chord in the era we are living in. Its success no doubt reflects the endemic nature of the 'new narrative order' that it so devotedly exposes: in its denunciation of the narrative machines that capture beliefs, it was itself able to capture beliefs. For what *Storytelling* documents is, first and foremost, the inflation of discourses that present narrative as an apparatus for capturing and shaping our minds by telling us stories: 'Beneath the immense accumulation of narratives produced by modern societies, a "new narrative order" (NNO) is emerging that presides over the formatting of desires and the propagation of emotions – through their narrative formatting, their indexing and archiving, their dissemination and standardisation, and their instrumentation through all the levels of control.'[1]

1 Christian Salmon, *Storytelling. La Machine à fabriquer les histoires et à formater les esprits*, Paris: La Découverte, 2007, p. 199. The quotes above are taken from pp. 210–11. The author himself plays with the narrative dimension of his own argument by concluding his remarks with phrases which are doubtless best heard with a wry smile (and which perhaps partly excuse my hamming up of this book's claims, most of whose views I otherwise share). Hence Salmon writes, 'The empire has confiscated narrative. This book tells the incredible story of how it has hijacked the imaginary': Christian Salmon, *Storytelling: Bewitching the Modern Mind*, London: Verso, 2017, p. 20.

Ubiquitous (right-wing) narratives

Surely, there can be little doubt that our 'modern societies' are, indeed, drowning us in an 'immense accumulation of narratives' – this is what is worth noting. From films to TV series, celebrity gossip, various current events, 'tell-all' reality shows, historical milestones, politicians' careers, presidential weddings, obituaries, anecdotes, 'slices of life', pulp fiction, and the great mania for autobiography: each day the media serve up countless narratives that we are encouraged to consume, more or less willingly. On a happier note, we are all familiar with the craze for tale-tellers' festivals, which draw huge crowds to hear a *conteur* take their audience into the worlds of the *Odyssey*, medieval fables, or African tales. In an era that is said to be addicted to special effects, the captivating power of a simple voice, with its scansion, its energy, and its story remains attractive and powerful, still able to create a community around the same flight of the imagination.[2]

What *Storytelling* denounces is not so much the fact that narratives are so ubiquitous, or the attraction they have. It is rather about the hegemony building, imperialist inroads that narrative forms have made outside their 'natural' fields of practice, as they conquer other areas of activity such as managerial motivational speak, advertising hype, and politicians' rhetoric. It is certainly symptomatic that, as Deirdre McCloskey already pointed out in the 1980s, economists often prefer to say in their lectures or articles that they have a 'story' (rather than a 'theory' or a 'hypothesis') to explain such things as the causal links between the minimum wage and the unemployment rate.[3] It is indeed a serious problem that, instead of giving us a picture of the main events in the world, each night the evening news gives us a barrage of inane stories – at best annoying, at worst frustrating and infuriating – which provide a breeding ground for all today's Le Pen–isms and all the fascisms of tomorrow.

2 Bruno de La Salle, Michel Jolivet, Henri Touati, and Francis Cransac, *Pourquoi faut-il raconter des histoires*, Paris: Autrement, 2005; and Bruno de la Salle, *Plaidoyer pour les arts de la parole*, Vendôme: Centre de Littérature Orale, 2004.

3 Deirdre McCloskey, 'Storytelling in Economics', in Christopher Nash and Martin Warner, eds, *Narrative in Culture*, New York: Routledge, 1990, pp. 5–22.

But beyond these transgressions into reserved domains – surely a significant expression of the new narrative order we are living in – it is perhaps worth asking how exactly 'narrative formatting' contributes to the 'formatting of desires and the propagation of emotions'. For all its qualities, Salmon's book is mainly based on the premise that the mere act of telling a story is a kind of original sin: 'We are being told stories . . .' In other words, we are being taken for a ride, and we are going to get screwed. From the works of Louis Althusser to Clément Rosset or Frédéric Lordon, we are told, time and again, that being a good materialist means agreeing to *stop telling ourselves stories.*[4] With good reason, a whole vein of sociology raises the banner of 'objective analysis' and 'demystifying things'. More generally, all the human and social sciences strive – again, quite rightly – to see *beyond* and *through* all the stories that we tell ourselves.

Of course, our concern here is not to cross swords with the intellectual and methodological requirements which are at the heart of all research in the social sciences. But we do want to note the deep allergy to stories which is seemingly felt by many voices who claim to be 'left-wing' – whatever sense may still be attached to this label, whose meaning has been unnervingly hollowed out. Too quick and too superficial a reading of Jean-François Lyotard's (remarkably profound) arguments on the postmodern condition seems to have induced 'the left' to move from a (healthy) disbelief in 'grand narratives' to develop a (suicidal) allergy towards any form of story at all. For, while 'the left' nobly applied itself to this cause – to stop telling itself stories – much of its base was instead won over to the simplistic but highly effective stories told by the grand masters of neoliberal, neoconservative, and neofascist narratives.

If stories are indeed omnipresent in the political discourse of our time, it has to be said that the vast majority of them are 'right-wing' ones. The Reagan administration's great assault on the welfare state was spearheaded by the outrageous story of the 'Welfare Queen': *Once upon a*

4 Clément Rosset, *En ce temps-là. Notes sur Louis Althusser*, Paris: Minuit, 1992, p. 22 (quoted in Frédéric Lordon, *L'Intérêt souverain. Essai d'anthropologique spinoziste*, Paris: La Découverte, 2006, p. 45).

time, a welfare recipient was photographed at the wheel of a Cadillac, even as the valiant workers could barely even pay their bus fares. Fortunately, a defender of the little people, alerted to this scandal by a watchful citizen, put a stop to such abuses, and raised a hue and cry about a social security system which encouraged laziness and parasitism – in short, one which favoured a 'welfare society' (*une société d'assistés*) instead of stimulating a 'society that goes to work' (*une société qui travaille*). Some supposedly 'left-wing' French Socialist leaders (Lionel Jospin, Claude Allègre) would adopt this story, too, with a couple of decades' delay.

Twenty-five years later, the Welfare Queen found a perfect French translation in President Sarkozy's 'Widow of the Île de Ré': *Once upon a time*, there was a poor widow living modestly in her little house on an enchanted island, on a pension close to the minimum wage. City dwellers in search of fresh air and tourist-resort developers discovered her corner of paradise – and built all over it. Property prices soared, giving her cottage the face value of a château and making the poor widow a virtual millionaire. The cruel Ogre of the Solidarity Tax on Wealth (ISF) fell cowardly upon her, demanding that she pay more tax than her income, forcing her to sell the piece of land where she had spent her life, and from which she was now exiled by the cursed socialist ideology. Fortunately, a Prince Charming took pity on this widow struck by such a wicked fate, and freed France from the cruelties of the ISF fairy (even if 95 per cent of the revenue did come from taxing 'real' millionaires).

In France again, the noble cause of privatisation has succeeded in 'shaping people's minds' through the tale of the Telephone Fairy: *Once upon a time*, there was a state-owned telecommunications monopoly, which made it ever so expensive to ring your uncle in the States or your Sicilian godfather. Fortunately, a few free-market cats were able to capture the attention of the ('left-wing'?) prince and wax lyrical about the wonders of competition. And now, with one wave of the neoliberal magic wand, prices have tumbled! How can we resist the proof of such a marvel, which we see every month on our bills, cut by half, three-quarters, even 90 per cent in the space of just a few years? If only an Electricity Fairy came along to do the same!

Would it really have been so beneath 'the left' – already so complicit in such neoliberal narratives – to push more actively the little story of Technological Changes, which explains this magical fall in the price of telephone calls much better than the fable of Competition does? What about if we consider that the said competition has done nothing to stop mobile networks from shamelessly stuffing their pockets? Should we find fault with those who told the tragic story of the Undocumented Migrant Grandfather who was arrested like a dangerous thug in front of his granddaughter when he was picking her up from school, even though his only crime was his wish to come and work in France (where, incidentally, he was much needed)? Could not 'left-wing' stories be just as effective, but also much more empowering and emancipatory, than the tales spread by the right? Is there some incurable curse, some original sin, involved in telling (ourselves) stories? Before we can hope to answer such questions, it may be a good idea to get a better definition of these 'narrative forms', which stand accused of 'formatting desires' and 'propagating emotions'.

The nature and power(s) of narratives

Our era surely has no great love for the structuralist adventure. Still, one good idea might be to start again with the definition of stories given by the narrative semiotics of the 1970s. We could say that a *narrative* is a discourse that tells a story, and that a *story* can be basically defined as a *transformation from one condition to another* which affects the relationship between a certain *subject* and a certain *object* (which is not necessarily material).[5] If I said that my cousin in Calcutta is a talented painter who earns a living from the import-export business, and I described in detail one of his still lifes, the house where he lives, his current political

5 On these issues, see Joseph Courtès, *Introduction à la sémiotique narrative et discursive*, Paris: Hachette-Université, 1976; and Groupe d'Entrevernes, *Analyse sémiotique des textes*, Lyon: Presses universitaires de Lyon, 1979; as well as Gérard Genette, 'Discours du récit' in *Figures III*, Paris: Seuil, 1972, pp. 67–280.

views, his general philosophy of life – I could fill pages and pages with all this and still not have a narrative. But, if I said in just a single sentence, that my brother-in-law went to the airport to catch a plane to the USA but was denied boarding because his passport did not meet the new biometric requirements – well, that is enough for a narrative. For here, there is indeed a subject in some initial condition (Apu wants to go to the USA), a transformation (he heads off to the airport), and an eventual condition (he does not get the desired object, which in this case was a trip to the USA).

This barebones example is enough to illustrate the first characteristics by which narrative is defined. These are well set out in the overview which the sociologist Francesca Polletta gives at the start of her study on the power of storytelling for activists as a tool of mobilisation.[6]

1. Insofar as it represents a *transformation* between at least two conditions, a narrative must describe a story that unfolds over time, with a beginning, a middle, and an end.

2. Every story has at least one *main character* (the protagonist) and presents the narrative world from a certain *point of view*, or at any rate specific points of view.

3. The plot involves both a certain *unity* (according to a closure effect), and a certain *causal consistency* (which may be different from that of our actual world). Hence, the insertion of a series of transformations from one condition to another into the frame of a story involves drawing upon causal explanations to account for the story's unfolding. These explanations may be more or less suggested or caught out by the narrative itself.

4. A narrative implies not only a transformation from one condition to another, but the (at least implicit or potential) association of certain values with the said conditions. In Apu's case, we understand that, to his mind, entering the USA would have been a Good Thing and that he considers the frustration of his travel plans a Bad Thing. But it only takes a little adding to the story and these values change to the point of being flipped on their head: the plane he was supposed to fly on could have

6 Francesca Polletta, *It Was Like a Fever: Storytelling in Protest and Politics*, Chicago: University of Chicago Press, 2006, pp. 8–28.

crashed into the sea (and what appeared to be a Bad Thing ultimately would have turned out to be Good for him). Apart from what it does to capture our attention, a story is therefore *a machine for capturing our desires and beliefs*: as Apu's story becomes more complex, I am successively 'led' to first desire and then to fear the same thing (his trip to the USA). From this point of view, a narrative represents a (more or less complex) transformation from one condition to another, in which the interpreter invests their desires and beliefs in terms of the supposed desires and beliefs of the story's subject, according to evaluation operations that unfold on several levels and which are capable of successive reversals.

5. To be well received (in our world), a narrative must both respect *certain canonical norms* that define its place within social discourses and institutions, and – at least for us modern adults – it must simultaneously provide an element of *surprise*, meaning that it cannot be entirely predictable just on the basis of these canonical norms. In her study of the effectiveness of storytelling in political mobilisation, Francesca Polletta stresses how important it is for activist movements to grasp the subtleties of the different functions that a society (or social group) recognises narratives as having (or forbids them from having): What makes a narrative powerful has often less to do with its particular nature than with the situation in which it is used. At the same time, the need to capture audiences' attention, and hold on to it, means that it is not enough to simply copy pre-existing narrative frameworks, forms, and contents. Similarly, a narrative must – as we have seen – fit into patterns of causal explanation that allow it to be recognised as having a certain logical consistency, and at the same time allow the recipient a certain margin of interpretative freedom. Later on, we will see in greater depth how it is from this kind of tension that narrative activity derives both its capacity to bring people together (in a potentially conformist way) and its power of social transformation (which is potentially emancipatory).

6. Finally, many theorists of storytelling look to Paul Ricœur for an essential property of narrative experience: the ability to *distil the hypercomplexity of reality into a schematic, unifying imaginary model.*

> With narrative, the semantic innovation lies in the inventing of another work of synthesis – a plot. By means of the plot, goals, causes, and chance are brought together within the temporal unity of a whole and complete action . . . The plot of a narrative . . . 'grasps together' and integrates into one whole and complete story multiple and scattered events, thereby schematizing the intelligible signification attached to the narrative taken as a whole.[7]

It is this 'synthesis' of different elements and this capacity for 'schematisation' that make immersion in a narrative a quite particular (indeed, an especially powerful) form of *understanding*. This is an 'operation that unifies into one whole and complete action the miscellany constituted by the circumstances, ends and means, initiatives and interactions, the reversals of fortune, and all the unintended consequences issuing from human action'.[8] We have said that narrative is a machine for capturing affects and modulating the formulation of values. But it also offers an *integrating structure* that helps us to constitute the heterogeneous multiple of our perceptions into a coherent plane, on which our power to act can begin to find its bearings.

Of course, this kind of narrative structure is not confined to the stories we consume in books, films, plays, or TV series. It also organises our perception of the transformations from one condition to another that we directly experience in our own lives: *it is by narrating the events of my life that I make sense of them*. That is, I give meaning to these events by setting them in an interconnected sequence of (possible or actual) facts, in which I believe I can identify relationships of causality, incompatibility, convergence, and divergence. We could also say that I orient myself in the field of present action by situating the possible future consequences of my present choices within narrative sequences.

It is also worth mentioning the studies that David Snow and his colleagues have made into social movements' forms of mobilisation.

---

7 Paul Ricœur, *Time and Narrative*, vol. 1, Chicago: University of Chicago Press, 1991, pp. ix–x.

8 Ibid.

They have developed a whole field of research which poses similar problems – problems of producing meaning by inscribing scattered elements within some cohesive horizon – but they do so using the notion of *frames* rather than narratives.[9] However, it is quite easy to show that narratives operate as frames, and that frames are also (implicitly) based on narrative structures. Whether we are talking about diagnostic framing, prognostic framing, or motivational framing, in all cases what is mobilising the actors involved is the articulation of the analysis (framing) of a certain state of affairs with the possible transformation of this initial state into a more desirable final one.

Establishing narrative sequences between the facts and states of affairs that make up my own life is necessary both for the constitution of an identity fed by my own past events (and this is what psychoanalysis invites us to piece together as a 'history of the subject') and my capacity to project myself, by means of the imagination, to multiple other possible worlds, which I will have to make choices between with a view to the future (and this is what theorists of utopia set at the root of all historical change).[10] Insofar as we construct them as internal narratives, the stories we tell ourselves do indeed work as *machines for orienting our own flows of desires and beliefs.*

Reconfigurations and re-concatenations

However, this power to capture desires and beliefs also has a certain ability to reorient them. Paul Ricœur's theory of mimesis distinguishes three moments in the representational dynamics to which narratives contribute. A first moment of *pre-comprehension* simply involves finding and

9 For a good critical overview of theories of 'frames', see Kimberly Fisher, 'Locating Frames in the Discursive Universe', in *Sociological Research Online* 2, no. 3 (1997).

10 On these points, see Lubomir Dolezel, *Heterocosmica. Fiction and Possible Worlds*, Baltimore: Johns Hopkins University Press, 1998; Jean-Marie Schaeffer, *Pourquoi la fiction*, Paris: Seuil, 1999; Thomas Pavel, *L'Univers de la fiction*, Paris: Seuil, 1988; Raymond Ruyer, *L'Utopie et les utopies*, Brionne: Monfort, 1988 (1950).

recognising elements in the story with which we are already familiar. On the basis of this familiarity, a second moment invites us to *immerse ourselves* in the (often fictional) world in which the story takes place. A third moment enables us, based on this immersion in a world that is not our own, to get to grips with novel experiences and thus to induce a *reconfiguration* of our habitual ways of linking together facts and deeds. 'What is at stake, therefore, is the concrete process by which the textual configuration mediates between the prefiguration of the practical field and its refiguration through the reception of the work.'[11]

For Paul Ricœur, narrative activity is most centrally a mechanism of reconfiguring the sequences of action. A striking connection can be drawn between the mechanism Ricœur describes and proposition 10 of the Part V of Spinoza's *Ethics*. This passage is pivotal to the entire path of emancipation and empowerment proposed by Spinoza's book, in that it indicates what exact power a human being has to strive for the 'freedom' promised by the title of this same Part V: 'So long as we are not assailed by emotions contrary to our nature, we have the power [*potestas*] of arranging and associating [*concatenare*] the modifications of our body according to the order of the intellect' (*Ethics*, V, 10).

This ability to *re-concatenate* our affections involves redistributing our attention time and 're-routing' the established affective paths that orient our behaviour.[12] The chiasmus between the affections of the body and the order that suits the intellect may seem both insightful and rather problematic. But we can understand these 'affections of the body' as likely to refer to both the *sensory images* that occupy our minds, and so, too, the more or less voluntary *gestures* that characterise our bodily ways of being (our 'sensory-motor schemas'). The human being's power (and the pivot of our emancipation) is thus located in our ability to arrange in different sequences 1) the images, thoughts, affects, desires, and beliefs that we associate in our minds, 2) the

11 Ricœur, *Time and Narrative*, p. 53.

12 On this notion, see Yves Citton, ' "ConcateNations": Globalisation in a Spinozist Context', in Diane Morgan and Gary Banham, eds, *Cosmopolitics and the Emergence of a Future*, London: Palgrave Macmillan, 2007, pp. 91–117.

phrases that come out of our mouths, and 3) the movements that emanate from our bodies.

The long scholium that Spinoza appends to this proposition gives examples of all these kinds of rearranged sequences. These might include adopting a certain conduct in our practical life, as we make our outward behaviour conform to certain rules; attaching certain images to the repeated imagination of these rules; or concentrating our attention on what is good in each thing, in order to fend off the affects of sadness and hatred that might risk assailing us at any moment, etc. Ultimately, this allows for a re-arrangement of our thoughts, desires, and beliefs in different sequences. And all this leads, in the last sentence of the scholium, to the conclusion (which contradicts many common clichés about Spinozism) that observing these rules is 'not difficult' and that whosoever does so 'will verily, in a short space of time, be able, for the most part, to direct his actions according to the commandments of reason' (*Ethics*, V, 10, scholium).

It is easy to see how this Spinozist re-concatenation closely matches the reconfiguration of our usual ways of linking facts and actions, as described above by Ricœur. But this quotation from the *Ethics* also adds two new elements to what has been said so far; and these are crucial if we want to gain a better understanding of the relationship between narrative activity and the distribution of power within society in general.

First, we should note that Spinoza used the word *potestas* (and not *potentia*) to refer to this activity of re-concatenation. In line with the distinction discussed in the previous chapter, we may usefully see this as an indication that this capacity to re-concatenate does not emanate from a pregiven and spontaneous *potentia* that lies within each individual, but rather from an *instituted power* (*potestas*) – which must always be constructed both collectively and individually. On the one hand, the ability to rearrange our body's affections results from the *institution of a certain way of life governed by certain guiding rules*: I put myself in a position to conduct my own conduct by enacting, on my own, principles through which to channel my desires, my beliefs, and my future behaviour (principles necessarily inspired by the common resources of books, existing examples, and the stories of the wise men of days gone by).

The ability to tell stories capable of reconfiguring the usual sequence of facts and actions also requires the *active construction of a particular skill.* Indeed, we have no innate faculty of knowing how to assemble the elements of a narrative that 'makes sense' (i.e., that is articulated through tenable chains of events and connected in a relevant way with our perceptions of reality). Rather, this faculty is a potential that needs to be actively cultivated, by both personal effort and collective institutions. Hence the power that humans may acquire to conduct their conducts (by setting themselves rules for life) and the power to produce reconfiguring stories come together in the institution of a common storytelling. This is, indeed, what Christian Salmon suggests when he concludes his book by saying that 'to struggle for their emancipation . . . people need to reconquer their means of self-expression and narration'.[13]

Let us now move to a second lesson of proposition V, 10, which directly concerns storytelling. It offers an insight that may be useful to us when we make a first attempt to sort 'good' stories from 'bad'. The rules of life which Spinoza proposes we establish should, he says, allow us 'to gain a knowledge of the virtues and their causes, and to fill [our] spirit with the joy which arises from the true knowledge of them' (*Ethics*, V, 10, scholium). We could thus set narrative activities the *ultimate* (though not immediate) goal of arranging mental activity 'according to the order of the intellect' (*secundum ordinem ad intellectum*, i.e., literally 'in an order conducive to intellection'). There is nothing inherently wrong with 'telling ourselves stories': it all depends on *what the stories are doing*. The tales of the Welfare Queen, the Widow of the Île de Ré, or the Telephone Fairy are not toxic simply because they are stories. Rather, they are harmful because they induce the human mind to resent individuals who are already disadvantaged, to reject tax measures that rein in income inequalities, or to delude ourselves about the real value of certain forms of economic regulation. Insofar as affects of joy (or at least, ones without harmful side effects), help the mind to move towards rational understanding of causal relations, and insofar as compassion helps us to align our behaviour with humane principles, stories can be much more

13 Salmon, *Storytelling: La Machine*, p. 212.

exciting and useful than stern moral lessons. The inherent power of stories lies in their capacity to reconfigure chains of actions. It is thus perfectly possible to imagine a narrative aesthetic that values the most passionate, the most exciting, the most 'immoral', even the most irrational of stories. The important point is that they should produce conflicts and shift boundaries in a way liable to guide us towards re-concatenating facts and actions in a new order more conducive to causal intellection.

The dangers of 'tertiary retentions' and the virtues of props

As we said at the beginning of this book, paraphrasing Spinoza, despite all the old books on narrativity and all the recent ones on storytelling, no one, so far, has determined what a narrative can do.[14] When we study what narratives can do (within the definition of power sketched out in the preceding chapters), we need to ask *at what scale* and *by what means* are established the narrative sequences that condition our ability to orientate ourselves in a world of actions. In a rough ascending scale, we could start with the private labour that each of us does to give meaning and unity to the events of our own lives, without necessarily needing to tell anyone about them. The experience of psychoanalysis or of friendship suggests, however, that the stage of putting things into words in front of another subject plays a major role in this effort. As it takes on some external manifestation, the narrative is not only summoned to take on the form of language – as it does as well for the speaker themselves – but it also gains the propensity to impress those who hear it.

Humans have, of course, developed many technical means for recording narratives over the centuries. These range from the memory of storytellers and the written record of their inventions, to phonographic recording, film, and the digital camera. This allows us to elevate these

14 In the great scholium to *Ethics*, III, 2, Spinoza writes that 'no one, so far, has determined what a body can do', drawing on the example of sleepwalkers.

narratives to the status of what Bernard Stiegler (drawing on Husserl) calls 'tertiary retentions'. In this schema, *primary* retentions are made up of what I grasp on to at any given moment in my current perceptions (where I inevitably carry out an initial filtering process, which makes me pay attention to certain characteristics of material reality, while ignoring others); *secondary* retentions are those that my memory enables me to retrieve after the event, thanks to a recording faculty internal to my consciousness; *tertiary* retentions, for their part, correspond to the recording of perceptions (and narratives) by material techniques independent of my person, and which can be circulated around the world in identical form, regardless of the vagaries of my consciousness or my own person.[15]

Once narrative sequences have 'emerged' from private consciousnesses to acquire an independent material existence that can be disseminated to a virtually unlimited audience (in the form of tertiary retentions), their effects can be evaluated on a radically new scale. While primary and secondary retentions are in principle imbued with a certain idiosyncrasy, tertiary retentions are today endowed with a technical reproducibility that guarantees their unlimited and identical multiplication. After all, while the perception of a cup of tea or the memory of the taste of a madeleine will vary minutely according to the singular individual consciousness, the film shown in a South Korean multiplex will be (almost) exactly the same as the one shown in Northern Virginia (even if the sound volume chosen by the cinema, the quality of the loudspeakers, and the acoustics of the room will surely reintroduce some margins of individual variation in each screening).

But Bernard Stiegler also expresses great concern about the mechanical reproducibility of tertiary retentions. This is because he thinks that it involves the risk of a *formatting* of human experiences, with the effect of homogenising them. Just now, I spoke as if everything starts at the

15 See Bernard Stiegler, *Technics and Time 3: Cinematic Time and the Question of Malaise*, Stanford, CA: Stanford University Press, 2010. Stiegler makes rich and suggestive use of the imaginary of flux and facilitation to explore both the virtues and dangers of the reproduction of narrative through machines and mass media.

individual level: as if, in the beginning, there are the stories I tell myself in my head to make sense of the events that happen in my life. This was, of course, a misleading simplification: for when I narrativise the events of my life to give them meaning, I do so by drawing (at least some) inspiration from the stories I have seen and heard told around me. In other words: my ability to string together the scattered data of my perceptions into narratives that give meaning to my life is profoundly informed by the narratives which the tertiary retentions around me make available to me (be they fairy tales, bedtime reading, children's programmes, TV series, films, etc.). Hence the danger denounced by Bernard Stiegler: in a world where almost everyone was subjected to the same television regime – from infant hours watching *Teletubbies* to more geriatric cruise-liner entertainment – there is a danger that the same causes (standardised programmes) will produce the same effects (standardised subjectivities, with a desperate and sometimes pathological need to distinguish themselves).[16]

Recent neurobiological discoveries open up new avenues of thought that are remarkably consistent with the construction of identity in proprioception (the internal perception I have of my actions) and in the external images through which I recognise the gestures of other people. Researchers observing brain activity have identified 'mirror neurons' whose activation suggests that my own motor patterns (such as when I reach out to grasp an object) and those I perceive in someone else's motor action (when I watch someone else grasp an object) pass through the same neural pathways. Whether I am doing it myself or watching someone else do it, the same pathways in the brain are activated, opened up, and reinforced. In the book summarising the results of their research (which is often based on the projection of video images), Giacomo Rizzolatti and Corrado Sinigaglia stress the importance of the same two properties that we have just identified as being at the heart of the power of narratives: 1) linking together a multiplicity of small, scattered movements within one unified and directed act, and 2) constructing in

16 On this point, see Bernard Stiegler, 'Faire la révolution: Interview with Ariel Kyrou', in *Constituer l'Europe*, Paris: Galilée, 2005, pp. 93–129.

parallel my understanding of the sequences made by others and my understanding of the ones I arrange myself.

> In the human observer, the sight of actions performed by others immediately triggers the motor areas responsible for organising and performing the same actions. Moreover, in both monkeys and humans, this involvement makes it possible to decipher the meaning of the 'motor events' that are being observed, in other words to understand them in terms of action . . . Finally, as in monkeys, this understanding in humans concerns not just particular acts, but entire chains of acts.[17]

Here, we get right to the heart – or better, right to the brain – of the political, ethical, and anthropological power of the narratives that circulate among us in the form of tertiary retentions (films, ads, clips we see online). Insofar as my sequences of actions are constructed in mirror image around the sequences of actions observed in the moving image, we can effectively believe ourselves to be immersed in the imitative universe of late-nineteenth-century somnambulists magnetising one another in cascades. But does that really mean that we are condemned to ape ourselves in mirror-images, faced with the few dominant tertiary retentions imposed upon us and reproduced endlessly and identically by multitudes of perfectly standardised screens?

In today's media landscape, we should not underestimate the factors which push towards the homogenisation of most images. But we can also look to other conceptions of tertiary retentions, whose effects may be harder to predict. In *Les Imaginaires médiatiques*, Éric Macé is perfectly right to analyse our media cultures as driven by 'an unstable conformism', a 'temporary and reversible conformism' conditioned by the 'greater or lesser ideological and institutional stabilisation of compromises that result from symbolic and political conflicts among actors in society'. On the programmers' side of things, this conformism 'translates into a

17 Giacomo Rizzolatti and Corrado Sinigaglia, *Les Neurones miroirs*, Paris: Odile Jacob, 2008, p. 138.

constant search for ways to keep up with new trends and concerns as they may be perceived, theorised and negotiated by the various actors in the television production line'. A homogeneous pressure to 'do something new' thus drives everyone to constantly look for ways to (temporarily) break away from homogeneity. Following on from the work of Arjun Appadurai, Éric Macé also stresses the importance of the 'dynamics of appropriation of mediacultures by individuals'.[18] The same television programme, broadcast to all four corners of the planet, may produce radically different effects – it depends on the expectations, interests, sensibilities, and struggles of social groups, who will always reinterpret such a programme through the lens of their own specific context.[19]

The American philosopher Kendall L. Walton has proposed a theory of artistic representation that helps us account for the – always *re-interpretative* – creative activity that is at work in such appropriations. In so doing, he offers a stimulating reframing of our power to act *through* and *on* the narratives that circulate among us. For Walton, tertiary retentions should not be conceived on the model of (memorial) perception, but on that of a game of make-believe, which should further be set within the framework of wanting-to-believe. Stories, like artistic objects in general, no longer appear as disquieting 'capturing machines', but as what he more cheerfully calls 'prompters' or 'props' (literally the kind used on stage, but also all those material aids that help the imagination to fictionalise possible worlds).

When I venture into the forest with my little cousins, I suggest to them that the cut tree trunks and fallen branches are the silhouettes of bears. Our walk in the woods becomes the in-progress story of a journey into grizzly country. These props (both the trunks and bears) are evidently produced and conditioned by our (playful and hallucinatory) projection of a swapped identity, which stems from our own make-believe. But our game-story also includes countless perfectly

18 Arjun Appadurai, *Modernity at Large: Cultural Dimensions of Globalization*, Minneapolis: University of Minnesota Press, 1996.

19 Éric Macé, *Les Imaginaires médiatiques. Une sociologie postcritique des médias*, Paris: Éditions Amsterdam, 2006, pp. 84 and 102.

unexpected twists and turns, as the product of the form, the groupings, the perspectival illusions, and the relative distances of the props which we come across during our walk through the forest. These props (as models of the intellectual dynamics conveyed by an artwork) are both the products of our game and also have a certain autonomy, even if this autonomy is set in motion by our play itself. Instead of being subjected to tertiary retention as a passive impression and alienating magnetisation, the spectator actively uses props to playfully project themselves into the fictional worlds of make-believe, of which they are simultaneously the co-creator and surprised explorer. They do so with an attitude of intellectual DIY (*bricolage*) which was once foregrounded by Claude Levi-Strauss's analysis of 'wild thinking' (*pensée sauvage*), and is remobilised today in Cultural Studies when observing reappropriations of media products.

Kendall Walton's approach accounts for the fact that most of the time, when we allow ourselves to be immersed in some narrative, we remain clearly aware that we are indeed being told a story (and that this is not a real experience that we ourselves are living in real time). In contrast to the world of dreams, which often entails a direct attachment with no sense of distance, the world of narration prompted by tertiary retentions continues to be perceived as make-believe. Of course, even this does not stop what we consciously experience as play from actually affecting us unconsciously far more than we are aware. Doubtless, a slightly more advanced theory of the power of stories would have to go beyond questions of scale and the modes of narrative rearrangement and take into account the great differences in the intensity with which stories are received. From the almost total empathy I may feel when I am being told about an accident that has befallen a loved one to some TV series that I more or less distractedly follow as I tidy my stuff and prepare dinner, the narrative's power to sway people depends enormously on the spectators' own level of attention and impressionability.

Make-believe activity – which Kendall Walton defines as the use of prompters that set the imagination to work and of props that clear the pathways from which it starts – has a certain 'magic' to it:

> Props insulate fictional worlds from what people do and think, conferring on them a kind of objective integrity worthy of the real world and making their exploration an adventure of discovery and surprise. Yet worlds of make-believe are much more malleable than reality is. We can arrange their contents as we like by manipulating props . . . Games of make-believe, however, are easily shared; we play them together.[20]

In this power 'to arrange content' by manipulating props, we recognise both Ricœur's reconfiguration and Spinoza's re-concatenation. Within the theories of 'possible worlds', the element Walton adds is a reflection on the mediating role of props, which enable an articulation between our perceptive experience of actual reality and the projective work of our powers of imagination. These props may consist of sounds, still images, moving images, bronze statues, blocks of perceptions, or sequences of words. They are both real objects, endowed with a material existence available to our senses, and the vectors of an imaginative rearrangment of the data of our experience. To go back to the vocabulary set out in the previous chapter, we could say that the ability to rearrange props – a capacity which is always (unequally) shared between the producer of the narrative and its receiver – puts the subject in a position to play with what channels our flows of desires and beliefs, as if these channels were the pieces of a game of building blocks (open to an infinite activity of reordering, reconnecting, recombining). The rules of this game conduct our conducts according to certain facilitated paths which constitute the specific form of each game of make-believe. But, at the same time, the interaction between the subject and the props, as well as the different subjects playing this game together, enable the participants to rearrange what drives their behaviour and to redirect the paths that direct their flows of desires and beliefs.

These all-too-brief considerations about 'what a narrative can do' should be enough for us to understand that recent thinking on narrative activity is deeply ambivalent. Does the sheer ubiquity of narratives

20 Kendall L. Walton, *Mimesis as Make-Believe: On the Foundations of the Representational Arts*, Cambridge, MA: Harvard University Press, 1990, pp. 67–8.

entrap us in a homogenising New Narrative Order, subjecting us to forms of control which are all the more pernicious because they guide our behaviour right from the depths of our affective pathways – and which never openly expose themselves, such that they could be grasped by rational intellection? Or does the omnipresence of narratives instead surround us with stimuli that magically enable us to become rebuilders of our own world, re-concatenators of our own chains, through the imagination's power to reconfigure things? Faced with such an inevitably reductive alternative, we must, of course, preserve the interrogating force which is inherent in the ambivalence itself. We should then ask, faced with each narrative, what makes for its strength, its dangers, and its virtues.

From storytelling to scripting

When I talk about 'scripting' (*scénarisation*), I want to help explain the multiple and deeply ambivalent ways in which narratives *act on* those who listen to them, watch them, or read them. To write a *scenario* is to arrange a web of actions, scenes, and episodes that structure certain characters' progress through life. These characters are, in the main, fictitious and played by actors. But the idea of a scenario might also be used, in real life, to refer to some projected future situation that we attempt to anticipate. Given the current state of affairs and the trends that direct their likely development, we imagine a certain number of conflicting possible scenarios, and we try to prepare to act appropriately in response to the specific constraints each of them entails.

This section attempts to analyse this scripting activity. To this end, we could well make use of theories inspired by the notion of the *frame*, as originally outlined by Erving Goffman. He makes a somewhat chaotic distinction (although one clarified by his followers) between primary frames (equivalent to sensorimotor schemas), which allow us to orient ourselves practically in our everyday actions, and then the various *transformations* which draw on these frames in order to divert and direct the aim or effects of these actions. Goffman uses the term 'keying' to refer to the various forms of 'staging' that represent these actions at a secondary level (make-believe, sporting competitions, ceremonies, etc.). Within these different scripting operations, he isolates the particular cases of 'fabrications', defined by the fact that such secondary stagings take place without the knowledge of certain participants (manipulations, dissimulations, espionage, etc.).[21]

From this it follows that, beyond the scripting of fictional characters played by actors, there is also scripting in my own behaviour as a real individual (with or without my awareness that I am indeed participating in a script) in the context of the collective actions that may play out in future reality. In this second case, I treat real people (myself and those involved in the actions in question) as fictional characters, with a certain consistency of their own as well as the plasticity inherent in the world of props. When the time comes to take action, success will depend on how faithfully each of the real people conforms to the behaviour imagined by the script: I will try to stick as closely as possible to my scripted character, while at the same time hoping to see the other agents carry out as closely as possible the sequence of actions they are expected to fulfil.

Scripting is based on what narratology calls a *metalepsis*. This refers to the breaking of some difference of narrative level which was theoretically meant to ensure that two embedded universes remained sealed off from one another.[22] When the narrator of *Jacques the Fatalist* invites the reader to descend into the fictional world in order to check whether it is real, or when a character/actor in *Funny Games U.S.* turns to the camera to ask what the viewer is feeling, or when the same character, internal to the fictional world created by director Michael Haneke, grabs a remote control and rewinds the DVD of the film he is starring in, in order to go back in time and take an earlier off-ramp into a different sequence of events – each of these narratives jumps over a supposedly uncrossable

21 Erving Goffman, *Frame Analysis: An Essay on the Organization of Experience*, Boston: Northeastern University Press, 1974.

22 On this notion, see Gérard Genette, *Métalepse. De la figure à la fiction*, Paris: Seuil, 2004.

narrative level, thereby opening up the space of a 'paratopic' non-place.[23] This is the hallmark of metalepsis.

But at what level of reality should we situate the script that I use to anticipate and conduct the conducts that would best respond to the future real situation as it unfolds? By scripting various paths for how things could play out, starting from the real, current situation, I project *into the imaginary* fictional behaviours that solely emanate from my power to establish narrative sequences between actions. Yet this work of the imagination is also doing something else: for, by doing so, I am already carving out the reality of these future developments in the reality of my brain and of the props I thereby produce (battle plans, road maps, messages sent to others, warnings, forward projections). The activity of scripting is metaleptic precisely in that it articulates a (fictional) scenario, imagined for the future, with the actual facilitation of the (real) happening of this fiction.

Yet here we are not only concerned with such practical scenarios, which are geared towards the immediate development of some particular situation. For the stories we tell ourselves – even if they explicitly concern the past, distant lands, or worlds that are explicitly unreal – can always be seen as part of (more or less self-conscious) *thrusts (poussées)* that inscribe the readers-spectators in scenarios within which they become both heroes and (more or less malleable) puppets. These thrusts, which mould the imaginary through the breaking of paths into future reality, are the result of two reciprocal movements that branch off from each other in a kind of loop.

On the one hand, as we have already seen, insofar as a narrative succeeds in capturing the attention of an audience, the latter is led to engage its own flows of desires and beliefs in the narrative machine which is being offered to it. Reading a novel, listening to a story, or watching a film involves projecting one's causal explanations, affects, and (ethical, or

23 For Dominique Maingueneau, *paratopia* is the space created by a creative discursive gesture insofar as it is situated at the frontiers joining the possible world of fiction and the actual world of reality. See Dominique Maingueneau, *Le Discours littéraire. Paratopie et scène d'énonciation*, Paris: Armand Colin, 2004.

political) values into the sequence of events depicted by the story. It is, of course, quite possible that the knowledge that this is a make-believe situation will lead me to moderate my reactions – holding me back from the fullest attachment to whatever is being shown to me. And yet we all know that props (even ones that are artificial, conventional, and quite obviously props) manage to make us laugh, cry, shudder, gasp, think, hope, doubt, and even make our hearts beat faster (in the physical reality of our affective economy). And all these are reactions to what happens to characters whom we are well aware do not actually exist.

On the other hand, no one ever tells a story without the act of telling it having some purpose: to entertain, to inform, to make people laugh, to worry them, to reassure them – and, beyond these immediate goals, such concerns as drawing attention to oneself, charming people, being loved, or making money. However unlikely the story's actual content, the act of telling it is always a *real* act, directed towards certain objectives that motivate and condition it. This effort may, of course, go all wrong: the person to whom I am telling my story may not pay any attention to me, or get bored and lose me along the way, or react to my story in a completely unexpected way. But every story that 'gets across' is intended to move people to do something (to make them laugh, cry, fear, say something, buy a product, get riled up, become involved, vote). In this sense, a story always functions like a prompter: a stimulator of action, a trigger, a driver. So, the sequence of (fictional) actions represented by the story is meant to produce a certain sequence of actions in the reality to come.

Here I will use the term *scripting* (*scénarisation*) to refer to the inscription of a narrative effort within the transformations it is oriented towards inducing in reality: this takes place through the metaleptic force that transmutes the behaviour of imagined characters into the behaviour of real people, as the narrative experience clears a path for their future actual conduct. The title of this book refers to *the scripting power of myths* (*le pouvoir scénarisateur des mythes*). By 'myth' I mean not only the foundational 'grand narratives' that are generally described as 'mythical' but also the 'little stories' that we tell ourselves on a day-to-day basis in order to deal with the powers that be or to accommodate to them, and even the simple (not formally narrative) 'words' that we use in our many scripting activities. Admittedly, to justify calling these latter 'myths' we need a little etymological detour: the Greek root (*muthoï*, μύθοι) first refers to speech in general, before designating more specifically certain narrative words with a fabulist vocation.

Myths as 'enchanting words'

The most insightful formulation of 'myth' as words involved in scripting activity is offered by Apollo in Aeschylus's *Eumenides* (450 BCE). The play opens with the image of Orestes, who has just killed his mother Clytemnestra, being hunted down by the Furies who want to avenge his act in the name of a brutal concept of justice identified with *lex talionis* (an eye for an eye, a tooth for a tooth, murder for murder). Apollo advises Orestes to take refuge in Athens, where the goddess Athena sets up the court of Areopagus to judge his case. This tragedy can, therefore, be read as a staging, before the gathered people, of the foundation of Athenian democracy. Indeed, the goddess declares that the case is too complex to be decided by any one man or god: she will defer judgement to a collective decision, by vote of a jury selected from among the best citizens. She will ensure that the indictment procedure allows for adversarial debate based on the presentation of evidence, critical cross-examination, and rational argument.

But this institutionalisation of public reason – as illustrated by the debates between the Furies, who lead the indictment against Orestes, his defender Apollo, and Athena in the role of even-handed judge – above all reveals the rhetorical power of sophistry, unfounded prejudice, and underlying power relations. By doing so, it shows the mystifications of storytelling. From the outset, Aeschylus depicts democratic institutions as overdetermined by the criss-crossed paths of storytelling strategies, in which the role of rhetorical virtuosity far outstrips that of logical rationality.[24]

24 For this reading of the tragedy, see Yves Citton, 'Does Democracy Ensure the Triumph of Right over Might as Aeschylus Maintains in *The Eumenides*?', in *History in Dispute*, vol. 19, *Classical Antiquity and Classical Studies*, Columbia: University of South Carolina Press, 2005, pp. 56–64.

Apollo gives us the finest expression of the potentially liberating force of 'myths' when he urges Orestes to go to Athens to seek a judgement that will absolve him of his crimes: 'and there, with judges of thy cause and speech of persuasive charms [*thelktêrious muthous*], we shall discover means [*mêchanas heurêsomen*] to release thee utterly from thy distress.'[25] With these words, Apollo sets out the script for Orestes's future behaviour: if you become the protagonist of the story I am proposing, which will take you to Athens and bring you face to face with the human jury chosen by Athena, you will escape the vengeance of the Furies. This story itself sets out a scripting activity: we need to 'discover means' (*heurêsomen*: same root as the famous *eureka* or *heuristic*) to tell the story of the murder that will persuade the judges to declare you innocent. This is your story, and we have to turn it into a real machine of persuasion, conceiving it in the mode of machination, according to the different connotations of *mêchanê*: machine of war, stage machinery, clever device, ingenious invention, expedient, ruse, artifice. We will have such means once we have devised words (*muthous*) of a very special kind, for which we have to resort to a rather rare epithet: *thelktêrious*.

Thelktêrion is the magic charm, the *enchantment* that soothes troubles and enthrals even the gods. The word comes from the verb *thelgô*, which means 'to charm by magical enchantments', to 'fascinate', to 'seduce'. Whether narrative or otherwise, the *muthoi* that make mythocracy powerful are enchanting words whose inextricably aesthetic and magical charm seduces and fascinates us, momentarily taking us outside what we consider the limits of 'reality', but thereby also enabling us to act on that reality much more incisively.

Even when they incite rebellion against the injustices of men and gods, these *muthoi* have a fundamentally soothing quality. The machines of war they can be used to mount are always a stage machinery, which operates through deception and ruses rather than through open violence. Their aesthetic charms carry the balm of gentleness: if they win the

25 'Κἀκεῖ δικαστὰς τῶνδε καὶ θελκτηρίους / μύθους ἔχοντες μηχανὰς εὑρήσομεν, / ὥστ' ἐς τὸ πᾶν σε τῶνδ' ἀπαλλάξαι πόνων' (Aeschylus, *The Eumenides*, v. 81–3, here using Herbert Weir Smyth's English translation, Loeb Classical Library, 1926).

battle, they do so not through explicit coercion but through soft power: their capacity to persuade us, even through artifice, sophistry, wordplay, and verbal sleight of hand.

The *thelktêrious muthous* that Apollo and Orestes have to devise will also be soothing in the sense that their aim and effect is to curb the vengeful violence of the Furies, by enabling them to escape the dismal cycle of revenge (an eye for an eye, a tooth for a tooth), which might otherwise go on indefinitely. There is more. Following the machinations to free Orestes from his distress (*apallaxai tôn ponôn*), the magical and soothing quality of the enchanting words allows for the liberation of the community at large, for it is now freed from the Furies' *lex talionis*. Behind the specific fate of Agamemnon's son, what Aeschylus is staging before his Athenian audience is the collective development of Greek democracy. The dramatised myth of the Furies appeased by the scripting machine devised by Apollo makes *thelktêrious muthous* both the first origin of the democratic institutions and the source of their constant renewal, since it is through the enchanting words of his tragic poems that Aeschylus helps to script his city's future.

Illustrative Interlude

Scripting from Up There

Once upon a time, there was a proud woman. Having been unhappily married to her first husband, she had become a widow, and thus free. She swore that she would never get caught up in such a situation ever again. But a handsome and honest Marquis tried to win her back to faith in love. She resisted, made him swear loyalty to her, allowed herself to be persuaded by his solemn oaths, made him happy, and shared a lasting contentment with him. But after a few years, as the Marquis's visits became less frequent and more lukewarm in tone, she sensed that she was no longer the object of his affections. She decided to provoke him to confess his true feelings by pretending to confess the cooling of her own affections – presenting this, with false shame, as a moral failing of hers, which betrayed their most sacred oaths of fidelity. Surprised but relieved to see his own estrangement mirrored by the woman whose wrath he so feared, the Marquis opened his heart to her: 'I am confounded by your candour and honesty which fill me with shame. Ah! how infinitely superior you are to me at this moment! How tall you stand in my eyes and how small I feel! You were the first to speak and yet it was I who was guilty first. My dear, your sincerity is contagious. I would be a monster if it were not, and I will confess that the history of your heart is also the history of mine, to the letter. Everything you have ruminated upon I have ruminated upon myself.'[1]

Thus begins the richest example of scripting provided by all French literature: Madame de La Pommeraye's revenge against the Marquis des Arcis, as related in Diderot's *Jacques the Fatalist and His Master* (1778–80). I shall use this work to briefly illustrate the mechanisms, issues, virtues, and limits of scripting.

From this first manipulation of the Marquis through the projection of a false mirror image, we see that the 'story' (of the heart) serves as a trap and a ploy, designed to extract from the listener a behaviour which he had until then shied from. Her whole revenge will also consist of a vast 'story' which she will not simply tell, but plot and script in the most masterly of fashions: a machination to punish her inconstant lover. While continuing to pass herself off as his friend and confidante, she recruits a poor girl, Mademoiselle d'Aisnon, whom poverty had condemned to prostitution. Madame de La Pommeraye restores her to health, beauty, fortune, and reputation and arranges for a few 'chance' encounters to dazzle the Marquis with her charms, to the point of making him fall madly in love with her. By choreographing Mademoiselle d'Aisnon's every move, dictating her every letter in the notes of false prudishness, and meticulously arranging every element of the décor in her apartment, Madame de La Pommeraye perfectly calibrates what needs to be shown and what needs to be hidden in order to inflame the Marquis's desire. This goes on until he can bear it no longer and is reduced to proposing to the girl. Yet, once their union is consummated, the proud manipulator takes off her mask, makes the unworthy origins of the Marquis's new wife public knowledge, and savours the pleasures of 'a revenge such as would serve to put the fear of God into any man who might thereafter feel tempted to seduce and betray an honest woman.'[2]

1 Denis Diderot, *Jacques the Fatalist and His Master*, trans. David Coward, Oxford: Oxford University Press, 1999, pp. 94–5. For a more detailed analysis of this novel, see my article '*Jacques le fataliste*: Une ontologie de l'écriture pluraliste', in 'Diderot Philosophe', ed. Colas Duflo, special issue, *Archives de la philosophie* (April 2008), pp. 77–93.

2 Ibid., p. 104.

Listening to this story being told to him, Jacques's master has his fears right from the start: 'I'm very much afraid that the marriage of the Marquis des Arcis with a tart is written up there.'[3] The great merit of Diderot's novel is that it allows us to see clearly the different layers of this 'up there' where our 'fate' is written on a daily basis. Madame de La Pommeraye provides a marvellous example of *strategic meta-conduction*. The Marquis des Arcis pursues his own strategy for winning the unknown beauty's heart in the most skilful and 'freest' of ways. He does everything we do every day to achieve the goals we set ourselves: he strives to understand, to please, to influence, to convince – in other words, to use Foucault's definition of power, 'he incites, he induces, he facilitates, he makes more likely' the success of his seduction of Mademoiselle d'Aisnon. To this end, he meticulously scripts his appearance, his dress, his gestures, and his words, all of which he takes pains to calculate in minute detail, the better to 'bait' a young woman whom he knows to be in dire straits.

And yet, although he uses his power as freely as possible, it is perfectly accurate to say that 'his marriage to a tart is written up there'. His entire seduction scenario was in fact *meta*-scripted in and by Madame de La Pommeraye's vengeful machinations. Each of his strategies, each of his gestures, each of his choices, each of his own lies had been written 'up there': in the great spectacle machine devised by the proud widow. The phrase which the Marquis uses to announce his decision to marry makes clear the ambivalence of his own behaviour: 'I have returned with my mind determined [*déterminé*] to embark upon the greatest folly a man of my birth, age, and character could possibly commit. But I shall be better off marrying her than suffering like this.'[4] His mind is 'determined' by whom, and by what? By himself, no doubt, since the proposal is a voluntary decision, not only fully intentional but the result of serious deliberation. But this choice is itself *(over)determined* by the machinations of his former lover, by Mademoiselle d'Aisnon's own charms, by the beliefs and desires produced in him by a whole series (itself largely scripted) of external images and circumstances.

3 Ibid., p. 142.

4 Ibid., p. 127.

Madame de La Pommeraye perfectly illustrates what Jacques says elsewhere to his Master (after having arranged for him to fall, by undoing the straps of his horse's saddle): 'It was written up there and guaranteed by my foresight' that this would, or would not, happen. Prudence – the highest virtue of Spinozism – is nothing but an effort to rise to a higher level of meta-writing and meta-scripting of future behaviours: humans elevate their limited capacities to approach divine Pro-vidence thanks to their fore-sight, which allows them not only to see, but to meta-script their and other people's behaviours.[5]

But what does such meta-scripting actually involve? Here, too, Madame de La Pommeraye is a paradigmatic example. After deciding on her objective (to marry her fickle lover to a tart), the meta-conductor imagines a possible scenario for achieving that goal. This is the *writing* phase, properly speaking. The equivalence Jacques draws between 'up there' and 'foresight' implies that this first phase of writing involves a particular form of freedom: it is true that Madame de La Pommeraye could have written any of an infinite number of possible stories (a lost girl other than Mademoiselle d'Aisnon could have done the job, another house could have been rented for her, other elements of décor could have adorned the walls, etc.); and yet, each of these possible stories would also have had to tightly conform to the particular conditions which characterise the unique complexion of the Marquis's desires and beliefs. Madame de La Pommeraye's scripting of this scenario thus reflects both the freedom of her imagination and her accurate work of observation. Insofar as observation can be refined to an infinite degree, and insofar as our human foresight is condemned to have its constant limits and hesitations, this labour of writing cannot be confined to some initial stage which then simply needs to be 'realised'. Rather, this writing must continue on and on throughout the

5 Ibid., p. 235. We get a marvellous definition of prudence from two quotes at the beginning and end of the novel: 'My Captain believed that prudence is an assumption we make which says that experience justifies regarding present circumstances as the cause of certain future effects which we can only hope or fear will happen' (p. 10); and '[Jacques] tried to prevent bad things happening and acted prudently, while at the same time despising prudence' (p. 150).

realisation of the project. This is what we see in the scripting of *feuilleton* novels or soap operas which are written one day at a time, according to the twists and turns of the news, the illnesses or pregnancies of the actresses, uncertainty over future funds, etc. Scripting, surely, is a matter of projection, foresight, and anticipation – a matter of *programming*: writing the future ahead of time – and yet, it always includes an element of improvisation, trial and error, and constant rearrangements and readjustments. This process goes on as a story unfolds whose parameters are largely beyond our control, since we are striving to meta-conduct free subjects' conducts.

As well as scripting the Marquis's marriage to a tart, Madame de La Pommeraye acts as a director (*metteuse en scène*), who stages the events in question. She not only prescribes, in the form of a list of injunctions, the manners that Mademoiselle d'Aisnon should adopt, she not only dictates the letters she should write to her bashful suitor, but she also tells her what tone to answer him in, when to hide her face, sigh, or blush – while doing the same with the Marquis himself (whose confidante and adviser she also poses as). Through the double role she assigns herself in her revenge scenario, she also has to be an actor: she has to be able to weep on command, to affect the feelings that are in fact the feelings of another, and to force herself to appear indifferent at the exact moment when she is seething inside. We can see that the work of scripting, when pushed to its logical limit, transforms every act into a *gesture*: since soft power consists in making others act of their own free will, we must neither resort to open violence nor stick immediately to who we are, but modulate appearances so as to produce the hints and prompts that will lead the other person to do what we want them to want to do.

The practice of scripting thus immerses us in a world that is wholly concerned with the artificiality and plasticity of *spectacle*. Madame de La Pommeraye shapes reality in such a way that it becomes impossible to distinguish between what is 'fake' and what is 'authentic'. Her virtuoso skill allows her to 'frankly' tell the Marquis truths that he hears perfectly well, but is incapable of understanding: 'Marquis, you really must take care, for you are building up trouble for yourself'; 'I am a vindictive woman.'[6] To a good meta-scripter, speaking truth to power is a moment of the false. Once she has succeeded in capturing the Marquis's flow of beliefs and desires, the manipulator moulds not only an 'artificial' world of spectacle, but the very reality of the affects that move the protagonists: the Marquis falls in love with Mademoiselle d'Aisnon who, for her part, despite her own double-dealing, also comes to share his feelings.

Madame de La Pommeraye's masterful scripting succeeds in this transmutation of the artificial into the authentic. Yet this same transformation is also at the root of its eventual reversal. Thanks to her genius as a scriptwriter, her plan has unfolded exactly as she had foreseen: the Marquis has blindly fallen into her trap; his marriage to a tart, written in the 'up there' part of her script, has come about with seemingly inescapable inevitability; and the proud woman's revenge ends in an unalloyed triumph. As we have already seen, the Marquis genuinely acknowledges her superior status of quasi-divine meta-conductor of conducts from 'up there': 'Ah! how infinitely superior you are to me at this moment!'

Except that the consequences of the perfect realisation of this perfect scenario end up completely escaping her grasp – and producing directly opposite effects to the ones which she had hoped for. The initial reaction is shock, surprise, scorn. But the monstrous marriage which has been confected 'up there' by the vengeful script ends up as a match made in Heaven. For 'the Marquis des Arcis was one of the best husbands that ever lived and had one of the best wives who ever breathed'; 'this Pommeraye woman, far from having her revenge, has done me a great service,' he concludes.[7] But what about this attempted revenge's supposed value in setting an example and deterring male infidelity, in the interests of preserving honest women in the future? Here, too, the perfectly successful scripting leads to an abortive outcome: 'Since then, women have not been any less vilely seduced and betrayed,' admits the landlady who tells Jacques the whole story.[8]

6 Ibid., p. 128.
7 Ibid., p. 132.
8 Ibid., p. 104.

If the result of the scripting, counter-scripting, and meta-scripting inevitably turns out to be uncertain, this is – of course – because, for a Spinozist like Diderot, the entanglement of behaviours is, ultimately, the result of a necessity that bears a striking resemblance to chaos (in the absence of any divine Providence arranging the universe in advance with a view to some transcendent end decided 'up there'). The central point of this fatalistic novel, however, is perhaps not so much a metaphysical principle as an ethical and sociopolitical one. Individual conducts and counter-conducts – even those which, as in Madame de La Pommeraye's script, involve several actors coordinated in a single staging of reality – are set not only within the ontological chaos of a nature without finality, but, above all, within a human framework of collective institutions. For Diderot has found that there is something above the (immanent) 'up there' of individual foresight: he discreetly but surely points out, at a still higher level, the 'up there' of *social foresights*.

At the start of the novel, Jacques and his Master debate the Captain's statement that 'everything good or bad that happens to us here below is written up there'. The Master worries that, if we subscribe to this principle, 'no crime we commit can ever be followed by remorse'; for Jacques, the question is whether there is 'some way of rubbing out what's written up there'. The narrator then breaks them off to poke fun at these 'two theologians [who] were arguing and not agreeing, as sometimes happens with Theology', and to take us back to the far more concrete and important realities of their journey. We learn, for example, that they 'were traversing a part of the country that was never very safe and was even less so at that time as a result of maladministration and poverty, which had resulted in a huge increase in the criminal population [*malfaiteurs*]'.[9] The chaotic and conflicting criss-crossing of individual and group strategies should thus be seen in terms of *two kinds of structural 'up there'* immanently determining what happens among us, 'here below'. There are the *material* living conditions that themselves 'condition' our actions ('poverty'). But there are also the *institutions*, laws, and behavioural norms that structure our social interactions ('maladministration').

9 Ibid., p. 8.

Just as Madame de La Pommeraye meta-scripts the seduction of Mademoiselle d'Aisnon by the Marquis des Arcis, the rules decreed by the 'administration', whether good or bad, meta-script the antagonistic strategies developed by travellers and brigands who cross each other's paths on the highways and byways of unsafe parts of the country. It is written *up there* – in the penny-pinching laws that cut back social benefits – that poverty will multiply the number of criminals. The victims and culprits we see every day on the television news are all, like each and every one of us, meta-scripted by the frameworks for action put in place by parliaments, administrations, and the norms of the day. Maladministration is the culprit to blame for the multiplication of *malfaiteurs*.

You may be tempted, reader, to rebel against the above statements. Well, 'feel free to speak your mind, for as you observe, we are in the mood for frank and open exchanges', as Madame de La Pommeraye puts it in her initial confession to the Marquis des Arcis.[10] I hear you grumbling: unlike Jacques's Master, who behaves like an automaton, we are *not* puppets whose strings are pulled by talented manipulators or Big Brothers in parliaments! Far from conforming to the deterministic imaginary, human affairs are not as simple as all that: you can cut welfare budgets without automatically seeing an increase in the number of *malfaiteurs*. Not every poor person in a poor land is a criminal, or a Pulcinella! No one, so far, has determined what an image or a story can do: who knows if the daily carnival of morbid news stories does not cause us secret joys, apart from concerns over security and calls for law and order?

Here, too, Diderot is at pains to bypass the great theological themes of freedom and determinism. He wants us to pay attention not only to the shady (in all senses) forests through which we travel, but also to the practical, concrete interaction which we have with him when we are reading his novel. *Above* (in terms of narrative levels) *and beyond* the spectacle confected by Madame de La Pommeraye's machinations, or the fictional forest where Jacques goes for a walk, but at the heart of all storytelling

10 Ibid., p. 96.

activity, the dialogues between narrator and reader scattered throughout this book illustrate the *power relations* that structure scripting activities. He directly identifies what is at stake in these relations: the capturing of the flows of desires and beliefs.

> Since I'm writing this for you, I must either proceed without your approval or give you what you want. And the fact is that you have a decided taste for love stories . . . All you've ever wanted since the day you were born was to gobble up love stories and you never get tired of them. You've been fed a steady diet of them and you'll be kept on it for a long time yet – men and women, old and young – and you'll never ever get sick of it.

Here, Diderot is expressing the dual relationship that constitutes an audience, or public. The narrator is subject to the tastes and expectations of the audience, to whom he must serve whatever fits into the framework of their pre-existing desires. In this sense, the author is the servant of his audience, just as Jacques is his Master's servant. But in return, the author who succeeds in capturing the attention of his audience by stirring their beliefs and desires reverses the initial relationship of domination by holding the audience subject to his narrative regime. The art of storytelling is all about capturing (pre-existing) desires and beliefs in order to attach them to oneself and bend them to one's own advantage. The whole focus of storytelling, then, is to *invent what the reader wants to hear.* Etymologically, 'invent' has a double sense which I want to play on here. It means 'creating' new ways of formulating and sculpting the reader's desires, but also 'discovering' (*in-venire*, 'arriving at' and engaging with what already exists) what the reader happens to desire a priori.

You want romance? You have got me under your thumb, reader, since my narrative will live or die depending on your paying attention. Well, that is where I am going to get you, too – by giving you an exemplary illustration of the power of human action, under the guise of a woman whose pride has taken a hit, and the revenge she exacts . . . The episode with Madame de La Pommeraye offers the novelistic equivalent of a scene filmed in slow motion, which would make it possible to analytically dissect every aspect and every level of a (properly) human act. For the scripting effort illustrated by this individual case has to do with *all* of our actions. We may lack her talents or her truly extraordinary foresight (which also ultimately falls flat). But we always strategise our actions according to the reactions we expect from others. We script little stories, which we hope will turn out to our advantage, and within which we try to meta-script the little stories that others tell themselves. Diderot's novel allows us to clearly stack up the different levels involved. At the lowest level (*level I*), a Marquis, fed up with his current lover, tries to ensnare a pious young woman; a poor girl strives to escape poverty and prostitution. In the first meta-scenario (*level II*), a virtuoso plotter, expert in foresight and machination, plays on these initial scenarios in order to redirect them towards her thirst for revenge. One level above these individual conducts, counter-conducts, and meta-conducts, is an 'up there' (*level III*) where for centuries legislators, priests, and moralists have written the general frameworks that guide these daily behaviours. Finally, at the upper limits, where the fictional world meets the author's own historical reality (*level IV*), the storyteller discusses with his audience the ways in which he is narrating this love story and its philosophical implications.

We have seen already that these various analytical levels may well be condensed, superimposed, and metaleptically crushed together even within our slightest gestures. In the early scene where Madame de La Pommeraye makes her false confession that her feelings have wilted, she is at once an actor in her attempt to catch out the Marquis (I), a meta-scripter of his behaviour (II), a moral reformer who hopes that her exemplary act of vengeance will induce men to be more respectful of women (III), and, as her plot is relayed by the inn's landlady, a storyteller who must bend to her audience's desires the better to recondition them as suits her intentions (IV). The 'up there' is constantly interacting with the 'down here'; the shifts between the different levels of power permeate each of the relationships between the various players, in an entanglement which is formally possible to analyse and yet practically inextricable. What remains constant within all these tangles of conducts, counter-conducts, and meta-conducts is that, in each instance, the *capacity* (potentia) *to act should be measured in terms of the power* (potestas) *of meta-scripting.*

The alienating and disturbing dimension of this power of meta-scripting tends, however, to be softened by the dialogues in which the (fictional) reader is staged by the (real) author. As you, the reader, are well aware, it is *not really you* who is speaking when 'the reader speaks'. Just as, in my scripts, my act turns into a *gesture*, and I as an agent into an *actor*, likewise when I am the target of someone else's scripts, it is always a *simulacrum* of my person that is meta-written by their machinations.

You as a (real) individual reader may have no special taste for romance. Diderot nonetheless manipulates your neurons, capturing your attention and making you follow, line by line, the progression of his narrative. You still keep a certain distance from the simulacrum of a reader he is staging – a distance that gives you a sense of what separates you from this simulacrum and of what brings you closer to it.

The essential difference that separates (inter-human) scripting from simple programming (by machines) depends on this distance, which can be infinitely modulated both by the scriptwriter and by the scripted. It is precisely because we are not puppets or Pulcinellas that we *meta-script* ourselves and one another (instead of merely *programming* the future, as if we were nothing but computers). This is the same reason why scripting activities are a matter of power (and not violence or constraint), since the irreducible metalepsis between the levels of narration always makes sure that the scriptwriter has a certain margin of freedom.

Jacques the Fatalist and His Master thus illustrates the conditioning power of scripting. Yet it never falls into the vulgar fatalism that would suggest we are impotent to act. It reverses the relationship between master and servant only to show us the limits of any claim to mastery. As a novel (story), it is indeed a machine for reconditioning our imaginaries – or, as Diderot said of the *Encyclopédie*, a machine designed to 'change the common way of thinking'. But this same definition also shows us that this book's aim is not just to programme our behaviour but rather to make us *think*. So, how exactly does scripting condition us to think? That is the question on which the next chapter tries to shed some light.

4

Attractors and Infra-Politics

We have said that the power of scripting relies on its ability to capture the flows of desires and beliefs. And we have also said that to do this, it must be able to attract the attention of those it hopes to influence, and then be able to retain that attention. The mobilisation of affects through storytelling and scripting activities thus involves the use of *attractors*, in order to bait an audience and retain it as the narration continues. In this chapter, we begin by distinguishing between two types of attractors, depending on whether their aim is simply to attract attention on a one-off basis or to plug that attention into a narrative sequence in a more sustained way. We will then ask what the effects of such connections might be and how they might help to redirect developments in society.

Hooks and plots

The first type of attractors, which we will refer to as *hooks* (*accroches*), aim to capture attention at the level of initial perception. The aim here is simply to make something appear in the field of perception, and to make the perceiving subject want to pay some attention to it, rather than just turning away. It may wrongly be assumed that simply being present is sufficient grounds to be an object of perception. But simply getting (someone's/something's) existence noticed is the object of efforts and struggles: in intensely mediatised societies with a plethora of informational supply, getting your existence noticed can be among the toughest of tasks. Indeed, this compels some desperate people to resort to the most spectacularly destructive acts in order to short-circuit a process of recognition whose normal channels they find impassable, full of obstacles, and intolerably long and uncertain. How can a new musician or a young novelist hope to reach an audience beyond their narrow circles of family and friends when so many countless albums and books are being released year in, year out?

The media field, by its nature, has an overwhelming excess of channels distributing content and a logjam of attention-seekers. For members of the public, then, a *presumption of indifference* is a condition of survival. The first goal of 'hooks' is to make themselves seen, rising above this wall of indifference. They must obviously do this in a way that attracts attention rather than prompt instant rejection – and that's even harder. One of the main stumbling blocks for certain types of performance, even when they do manage to push themselves into view against all odds, is to sound 'appealing' to the uninitiated. Certain types of music (free jazz, 'contemporary music') tend to trigger an almost automatic negative reflex in many who hear them, even when they do miraculously manage to get a hearing beyond their usual circles.

Strategies for grabbing attention using a hook are closely linked to the phenomena of genre and style. What we identify at first glance (whether it is music, a text, film, or performance) is not content, but styles of expression and communication. By conforming closely to the norms of a genre (a set of formal characteristics that can immediately be identified as a predefined block), a cultural object can hope to benefit from the channels of transmission that the genre has already carved out for itself with certain audiences. When I arrive in an unfamiliar town and sample the local radio stations, a certain type of generic sound formation (hearing certain instruments, harmonies, phrasing, production effects) will make me settle on a given frequency or not, within a fraction of a second.

The titles and covers of books and records perform the same function. The 'vocabulary' that defines a school of philosophy, the authors cited, and the tone of the argument play the same role in the field of discourse. When it comes to stories, we could settle for the initial announcement that this all went on 'once upon a time', or else this may be replaced by hooks relating to all the various aspects of the narrative. A soundtrack, a character type (the disillusioned detective), or a setting (a hospital ward) will, depending on the era and the social milieu in question, suffice to grab the target audience's attention.

In the case of Madame de La Pommeraye's script, everything seems to be based on a subtle variation on a look of pious devotion. during the first planned 'encounter' between the Marquis and Mademoiselle d'Aisnon, the girl 'looked quite ravishing in a simple dress which did not draw the eye directly but fixed the attention of the beholder on her whole person'.[1] Commercials – which have just a few seconds to capture attention and implant a brand name in the audience's minds – are obviously an especially important body of material for studying the use of 'hooks', reduced to their most primary function. Rather like the bait provided by Mademoiselle d'Aisnon's clothing, however, these few seconds are generally enough to cram in all the distinctive features of a story, a way of life and a high road to the Sovereign Good.

We might ask whether the very nature of hooks is based on a mechanism that is inevitably a matter of re-cognition, of identifying an *already-known* style – or whether our attention may also be drawn by the impression of encountering something entirely new. Can novelty generate anything other than a vague 'unease'? May this unease itself become the object of a deliberate quest?? Is the desire to be surprised (and potentially disappointed) our common lot, or the acquired privilege of a happy few? These are old questions – the seeds of which can be found in Descartes and Hume – but they are still central to any political thinking about a real economy of attention. In a world of plethoric supply, the success of the attention-grabbing operation is, in fact, an essential

1 Denis Diderot, *Jacques the Fatalist and His Master*, trans. David Coward, Oxford: Oxford University Press, 1999, p. 111.

condition for the dissemination of a story or an attempt at scripting in the social field.

Still, even if this is a necessary condition, it is not alone sufficient. A cultural object that merely hooks an audience, without anchoring this hook to anything beyond itself, will have little desirable effect. It may do no more than the pure and futile drawing of attention that seems typical of certain current media channels. The speeding up of average shot lengths, seen in both TV programmes and films since the final quarter of the twentieth century, is perhaps owed to the need to keep viewers' attention constantly engaged, even in the absence of any really compelling 'content'. We know that our sensory apparatus is 'wired' to perceive as a threat anything that suddenly appears or moves in our field of vision. As soon as the image stabilises, the perception of threat fades and the nervous system can relax a little. By adopting editing styles that cut shots every two or three seconds, the directors ensure that the viewer's attention is constantly drawn anew (and exhausted), as she is kept constantly on the alert. In this way, we have reached the 'degree zero' of hooks. For here, their effectiveness has nothing to do with either content or style, but is purely a somatic reflex triggered by the rhythm of segmentation alone.

The second type of attractors is more interesting and has more of a wealth of consequences, since it strongly connects forms with contents. Once our attention has been captured by a hook, another type of resonance comes into play, one that is no longer based on an isolated image, a block of sound, a style or a vocabulary, perceived in synchronicity. Rather, this is a resonance established between modes of concatenating actions.[2] We can use the term *plot* for this second type of attractors:[3] a

2 David Snow and Robert Benford have analysed the importance of these resonance phenomena to mobilisations by social movements. See their article 'Ideology, Frame Resonance, and Participant Mobilization', in Bert Klandermans et al., *International Social Movement Research*, vol. 1, London: JAI Press, 1988, pp. 198–9.

3 *Translator's note*: since this translation renders the French *scénarisation* by 'script', it will render the French *script* (which refers to this second type of attractors) by 'plot'. The activity of plotting can be seen as more focused on the sequence of actions, while scripting-*scénarisation* includes staging, acting, and directing (in the sense of meta-conducting).

plot provides a concatenation of narrative elements encapsulated within a story that carries the promise of a schematising *Gestalt* (an expansive form with a totalising function). Like Ricœur's narratives, plots provide a schema able to unite the variety of perceptual elements within a horizon of completeness that allows for meaning to emerge. In the plot come both a syntax specific to certain sequences of actions and a semantics which structures certain values between them.

Once Mademoiselle d'Aisnon's plain dress has caught the Marquis's eye, it is her 'tone of exud[ing] piety', her refusal to give her address or accept the Marquis's gifts, that capture him in the (toxically virilist) story of the libertine who sets out to storm an impregnable fortress of virtue. What sustains the Marquis's attention (and tension) is no longer a matter of the specific combination of a particular physical shape and a particular *imago* of desire (similar to the impulse that attracts the bull to the red rag waved in front of him), but a whole (largely pre-established) sequence of actions that itself lays out certain intended purposes, certain means to be mobilised, certain modes of operation, certain hopes, and certain foreseeable risks. It is within the unfolding of this plot of the libertine-seductor-of-the-ravishingly-pious girl that the attention of the Marquis (both scriptwriter and meta-scripted), as well as that of the reader, is captured.

The question of the need to recognise something already known (or, to put that another way, the possible attractive force of novelty for novelty's sake) arises not only for hooks but also for scripts. In the field of (political, commercial, or managerial) storytelling, it seems clear that a script's success depends on its being able to draw support from the spectator's already (partly) constituted sequencing habits. The plot will attract attention only as long as its syntax responds to the narrative grammar with which the recipient is operating. If the Marquis came across the pious girl drunk in a tavern on the arm of a porter, this non-grammaticality would be enough to make him disengage from the script in which he had been captured. Similarly, if the widow on the Île de Ré were photographed at the wheel of a Rolls-Royce with a gleaming Rolex on her wrist and a Louis Vuitton bag in the passenger seat, then the grammaticality of her story, as well as its meaning in terms of taxpayer justice, would be gravely undermined. Election campaign managers know how much this type of non-grammaticality – notably in the form of casting errors – can undermine the credibility of even the best candidate.

Without neglecting the share of rising novelties that can always be found in the production of plots, we need to give due weight to the notion of *attractor*. This concept refers here to all that attracts and holds attention. In its physical sense, an attractor tends to ensure the reproduction of the same thing, by treating 'differences' as mere 'variations'. In scientific observation, an attractor appears in the concentration of measured data around some mean statistical point, which subsequent observations tend to reinforce, as if the behaviour of the objects studied were 'attracted' to this point (without us necessarily understanding why).

But what would it mean to say that, to be acceptable, a plot or a hook must be based on what is already known? This is tantamount to setting forms of narration and plotting within a certain type of dynamic evolution, which proceeds by small progressive (incremental) shifts in relation to the statistical point where the attractor is located, rather than by bursts of absolute novelty. Insofar as the absolutely new escapes any identification (since identification always involves the phenomena of recognition), attractors always carry with them the inertia of past habits. The grammaticality of plots, which conditions their receptivity and their signifying virtues, always involves what economists call a certain 'stickiness' or 'inelasticity'.

When we conceive of power relations in terms of plotting and measure the role of attractors within these activities, we are not necessarily adopting a 'reformist' rather than a 'revolutionary' politics. Insofar as this opposition retains any relevance, we know that incremental changes often pass *thresholds*, where a modest quantitative addition gives rise to qualitative leaps that are truly 'revolutionary'. Just a few degrees' increase will make ice turn into water, and then, after a long flat calm (which is not even 'reformist') at another hundred degrees higher the water will suddenly evaporate without a trace.

Even so, an imaginary of power that centred its model of society's processes on plotting would surely be deeply suspicious of the notion of (political) 'action', which implies a break with the past. It would prefer to conceive of historical developments in terms of giving things a 'push': some plot, some concept, some movement for a demand pushes our social reality, which has a high coefficient of inertia or stickiness, in a certain direction (which we may either like or dislike). In this vision, social transformations are not so much the product of some decisive act. Rather, they result from a sum of small gestures, each of which in isolation is itself a micro-level push, even when they result in spectacular restructurings (that is, when all the micro-level pushes have succeeded in tipping a situation over a certain qualitative critical threshold).

Perhaps we ought to consider attractors in two distinct senses. They are, we know, the thing that makes it possible to draw spectators' attention to the story or object we are trying to get them to notice. But they are also the thing that tends to draw interpretations towards patterns inherited from the past, as an effect of 'sticky' social realities. This allows us to better describe the purpose of plotting activities meant to transform reality. They should be seen as attempts to *attract the attractors* that define the criteria of receivability endemic within a certain audience, in order to turn them in the direction of new perceptive configurations, new narrative grammars, and new semantic horizons better adapted to our needs or desires.

Plots that reiterate, plots that reconfigure

If we turn from the activity of narration to the activity of scripting, we find that the importance of plots is not only owing to their resonance with the sequences permitted by a narrative grammar which the spectators have already internalised. Rather, their importance lies above all in their ability to forge a path for the concatenation of different bodily affections (behaviours), according to a sequence that these plots make resonate. Telling a story, as we have seen, uses already forged paths, and this allows for the action sequences to appear grammatical. But it also adds emphasis to the paths which are thus revisited and sometimes helps make them deviate somewhat, preparing the paths that the subsequent action sequences will follow. When Madame de La Pommeraye (allusively) tells the Marquis the story of the trial which ruined Mademoiselle d'Aisnon and her mother, to emphasise the self-sacrifice with which the two women retreated from 'opulence' to the 'barest necessities', she is providing a piece of information which fits into the Marquis's narrative grammar. This allows him to see in the beautiful Mademoiselle both a woman of superior origin who has lucklessly fallen into poverty and a prey who will be driven by the 'necessities' of her new condition to accept his offers of assistance. The script's effectiveness relies both on resonance with analytical frameworks constructed in the past (girls from respectable backgrounds may fall into destitution) and on the prospect of future action (their poverty makes them easier prey to take advantage of).

While Diderot presents his protagonist Jacques as a 'fatalist', claiming with his Captain that 'Everything good or bad that happens to us here below is written up there', he also draws on a certain cliché – presumably part of the reader's own common knowledge – which leads him to expect Jacques's behaviour to be as resigned, submissive, and passive as expected from a servant. Yet, as the novel unfolds, we discover a cheerful and active-spirited character whose behaviour conflicts with this cliché. Instead of settling for an already-cleared narrative path, or even adding new emphasis to it and pushing further in the same direction, Diderot prompts us to reconcatenate our images of philosophical positions and existential attitudes in different sequences.

We might therefore be tempted to distinguish between two types of plots. The first simply *re-iterates* the pre-existing grammar with which they resonate in the spectator. When an eighteenth-century reader sees a beautiful girl in ruins, dressed as a pious young woman and accompanied by her mother, they will immediately have a certain number of expected narrative paths in mind. The young girl's repressed sensuality, her lack of marriage prospects, and her likely naivety make her the ideal victim for a seducer, who will have to start by getting her mother out of the way so that he can have a private audience. He will then charm the beautiful girl with gifts and flattery, give her a lesson in libertinism, and so on. Indeed, this is precisely the path which the Marquis sets along, falling fully into the trap set for him by his former lover. The stubborn resistance he encounters from both the mother and Mademoiselle d'Aisnon fits seamlessly into the framework of this traditional narrative grammar, whose rules the plot simply reiterates. This 're-iteration' should be understood in light of what the first chapter described in terms of 'facilitation': by 're-trodding' an already-trodden path, this type of plots deepens the attractive force of the predominant grammaticality.

The second type of plots, on the other hand, *reconfigures* the inherited syntax, so that originally ungrammatical sequences push to be accepted as grammatical (acceptable and meaningful). We see this when — in the middle of the 'part of the country that was never very safe' where the travellers are spending the night – Jacques suddenly decides to defy a band of ruffians by threatening, for no apparent good reason, to 'blow their brains out', after which he calmly goes to bed in the next room and leaves the inn the next day in no hurry, even though he feels the urge to escape from the riled-up brigands.[4] Here, he follows a chain of apparently incompatible behaviours, displaying an inconsistency that does not well 'fit the frame' of the common idea of the fatalistic attitude, or indeed of his own maxims of prudence. This is indeed one of the main tasks Diderot sets for his novel: to reconfigure the types of sequences of phrases and actions that we can expect from a 'fatalist'.

This distinction between two types of plots would account for the qualitative difference between the narratives found in an everyday soap opera and those found in a film by Jean-Luc Godard or Claire Denis. The sequence of phrases and actions in a soap opera tends to respect a syntax whose rules are generally predictable in advance (and fairly limited in number), based on a pre-existing combinatorial system that is repeated episode after episode. Conversely, the ones used in *auteur* cinema seem to take pains to trick our expectations (more or less ostentatiously), in order to exhibit concatenations that will surprise us and throw us off-balance. In the least interesting cases, this will simply produce an effect of uncertainty and disarray faced with fragmented elements which cannot be put back together in a way that seems meaningful. But in the most successful cases, the initial disarray soon gives way to the feeling

4 Diderot, *Jacques the Fatalist*, p. 8.

that the first contours of a different grammar are taking shape – one whose growing consistency will soon enable us to reconfigure the connections which we perceive between different aspects of our own reality.

Given all this, we may be tempted to see reiterative plots as the objective allies of the powers that be (whose modes of domination they strengthen by making them seem natural, effective, and unproblematic), while reconfigurative plots would seemingly be on the side of the critical, oppositional, or rebellious forces of change. But, rather than trying to classify plots into watertight, reassuring categories – on the one (right) hand, the 'bad' reiterative plots, the slumbering, mind-numbing accomplices of tyrants, and on the (left) other, 'good' plots that are reconfigurative, innovative, subversive, and progressive – we would surely better start from the hypothesis that every plot, while always forced to rely heavily on pre-established grammars, is always animated by a potential for reconfiguration (a potential that it is more up to its interpreter to realise than the scriptwriter as such). This is, moreover, what Paul Ricœur suggested when he made reconfiguration a constitutive virtue of narrative: on this reading, narrative has to capture attention both by mobilising pre-existing grammars and by subjecting them to certain (more or less strong) variations, which in turn inevitably leads to (more or less marginal) reconfiguration effects. Here, again, conceiving of power in terms of the interactions between scriptwriters and their audiences prompts us to observe transformations that take place on the margins, incrementally, less in the mode of upheaval than in that of pushes – more or less intense ones, acting in a direction whose angle is more or less divergent from the inertial force that leads societies to persevere in their present way of being inherited from the past.

Rather than reasoning in binary terms (reiterating or reconfiguring, conservative or progressive, commercial or *auteur* cinema, consensual or dissensual concatenations), it is more useful to ask in what precise direction a given plot pushes its audience at a given moment in its development. What connections between which actions or phrases will be corroborated, reaffirmed, and strengthened in the minds of which viewers by some particular episode in the narrative? Which cliché is shaken by another? What unusual concatenation between usually unconnected elements will be suggested by what twist in the plot? Just as a pragmatic approach to scripting, conceived in terms of 'pushes', questions the very idea of a political 'act', it likewise urges us to be wary of any gesture that would attribute a plot any one (all-encompassing) meaning. As we shall see in the next section, happy or unhappy endings produce quite specific effects on the scale of narrative totalisation. Yet the impact of narratives on our modes of behaviour, thought, and perception is more a matter of *micro-semantics* and *micro-ethics* (just as we speak of a *micro-politics* after having read Foucault).

Affective investment and re-elaborating values

Now we have got this far, it is worth asking again how the transition from narration to scripting takes place. In other words: how, concretely, can a narrative we read, see, or hear help us to mould our behaviour in the future? How can telling stories have the power to 'conduct conducts'?

We know from experience that a story can modulate our immediate behaviour by triggering reactions of laughter, tears, fear, etc. The power of scripting operates at a deeper level, however, through a delayed reaction: the stories I hear today condition the way I will react to something tomorrow, in a month's time, or twenty years from now. We have already tried to explain this conditioning in general terms in the section on 'facilitations'. The representations of sequences of actions that I get from the story give me the opportunity to establish or clarify, confirm or reconfigure the (causal) links between these actions, thus guiding the associations that I will mentally establish when I myself react to similar situations. My range of possible reactions to the states of affairs I face is thus broadened (compared with what my personal experience alone has enabled me to develop), depending on the quantity and diversity of the stories to which I have been exposed in the form of 'tertiary retentions'.

If we want to better understand how this widening of the range of possible reactions comes about, we need to refer to the *affective investments* that are necessarily involved in listening to a story once its plot has thickened enough to capture our attention. Of course, it is impossible to fully separate what comes under the realm of desires and what comes under the realm of beliefs – we desire what we believe to be good and, as Spinoza pointed out, we believe that what we desire is good. But it is also plainly apparent that narrative discourse mobilises our desires on a more mass-scale and in a quite different way than does reading a table of statistics or an administrative regulation. While we may engage our affects in all manner of activities of listening, reading, or interpreting, the way these affective investments are treated varies greatly from one type of discourse to another. Characteristic of narratives, from this point of view, is undoubtedly the complexity of the mechanisms responsible for modulating, channelling, dividing, superimposing, opposing, or combining our desires, our hopes, our fears, our loves, and our hates.

It is practically inevitable that anyone whose attention is captured by a narrative (or, say, by a sporting competition) will feel inclined to 'take sides' for or against a particular character, motivation, behaviour, team, or possible outcome. Without going into detail here about the rich analyses of narrative structures developed by the theorists of the past decades (Barthes, Greimas, Genette, Hamon, Baroni, etc.), we can draw some general conclusions from them.[5] These point to a mechanism (sketched here in simplified terms) which operates on at least five levels:

1. Any story can be seen to be structured by an *actancial model* and a *narrative programme* that structure the evolution between an initial condition and a final condition, according to a syntactic combinatorial system that can be modelled in terms of the gain or loss of a (generally immaterial) Object (love, glory, Graal, etc.) by a Subject.

5 See, for example, Roland Barthes, 'Introduction à l'analyse structurale des récits', republished in *L'Aventure sémiologie*, Paris: Seuil, 1991; Gérard Genette, 'Discours du récit', in *Figures III*, Paris: Seuil, 1972; Algirdas Julien Greimas, *Maupassant: La Sémiotique du texte, exercices pratiques*, Paris: Seuil, 1975; Groupe d'Entrevernes, *Analyse sémiotique des textes. Introduction, théorie, pratique*, Lyon: Presses Universitaires de Lyon, 1979; Raphaël Baroni, *La Tension narrative. Suspense, curiosité et surprise*, Paris: Seuil, 2007.

2. This actancial model generally appears to be polarised around *an antagonism* between the Subject (with their allies) and an Opponent (with their accomplices), which encourages the spectator to take sides with one of the two (or more) opposing camps.

3. This antagonism is expressed not only in conflicts, fights, and duels between characters, but also in opposition between *different value systems*. Above the fray of the characters and the conflicts among them, we can identify superior protector-figures – identified by semioticians through the actancial roles of the Destinator and the anti-Destinator – who send the Subject and the Opponent on their antagonistic missions, providing them with their means of action. In short, these are figures who 'destine' the characters to act towards certain goals, in accordance with certain principles, in the name of a certain definition of Good and Evil, plugging an *axiological* component into the heart of any narrative.

4. This whole actancial device, which structures the plot, is carried by one or several *narrative voice(s)* who relate the telling of this story. This narrative voice can modulate its (and our) attachment to the characters' viewpoint ad infinitum, aligning (more or less constantly) its perspective with one of them rather than others, relaying the information available to them, distancing itself from the values that drive them, etc.[6] The whole work involved in the narrative's discourse (the choice of words, comments, scenes, rhythms, images, framing, lighting, etc.) adds a top layer of more or less critical value-judgements on the desires and beliefs that drive the characters in the story.

5. Finally, as the reader/interpreter discovers the plot unfolded by the narrative voice, they are bound to project their own axiological sensibilities onto it. They may perceive as ridiculous not only the motivations of a given character, but also the values to which the narrative voice seems to subscribe. Likewise, their own personal history may lead them to empathise with the character whom the narrative structure, the

6 For the sake of simplicity, I am combining here under a single heading what Gérard Genette has aptly distinguished as belonging both to a narrative 'mode' (answering the question 'Who sees the story being told?') and to the narrative 'voice' proper (answering the question 'Who speaks?'). These two instances do not always overlap.

protagonist's viewpoint, and the narrator's voice all agree in presenting as a Villain to be reviled.

Through this complex mechanism, any (somewhat developed) narrative functions as *a reprocessing plant* in charge of updating and 'cleaning-up' the values that circulate in a society (*une usine de retraitement des valeurs*). As soon as my attention is attracted and held by a given narrative, through its particular hooks and plot, it begins to redirect the flow of my desires and beliefs. It does so by drawing them into the antagonism staged by its structure; by connecting them to the value systems which are portrayed in conflict; and by inviting me to take some stance of closeness to or distance from these value systems (those I was inclined to reject, as well as those I thought I could adhere to) according to the infinite modulations afforded by the play of the narrative voice. To pay attention to a narrative is to let one's sensibilities, affective complexion, and systems of valorisation be drawn into a machine that channels them and reprocesses their flows according to its own particular mechanisms.

Narrative activity thus reconditions our economies of affects. Insofar as most of the 'dramas' we witness in the course of our lives come to us in the form of tertiary retentions (films, TV series, short stories, novels, articles, performances, etc.), it is no exaggeration to claim that it is the narratives we consume on a daily basis that (constantly) fabricate the value systems which accompany and drive the evolutions of our societies. *Narrative machines are the site where we (re)evaluate the values in whose name we claim to direct our behaviour.*

Madame de La Pommeraye's bid for revenge also provides an exemplary illustration of the five levels outlined above. The plot of the trap designed to ruin the Marquis's reputation sets forth (1) a narrative programme (the punishment of a wayward lover), marked by (2) an antagonism between the manipulator and her victim. Behind this antagonism lies (3) a conflict of values between, on the one hand, a rigid cult of promises and faithfulness and, on the other, an acceptance of the fragility and mutability of human feelings. This conflict is staged not only by the very structure of the story, but also (4) by the values conveyed by the narrative voice – in this case that of the landlady of the inn where

Jacques and his Master have stopped off. The landlady not only presents the story from the viewpoint of the scorned woman but also casts her in a favourable light through her choice of words and characterisations. She (inevitably) expresses value judgements of her own, for instance pointing out that Madame de La Pommeraye 'did avenge herself, she avenged herself in the cruellest way, and her vengeance was highly publicized and it mended nobody's ways. Since then, women have not been any less vilely seduced and betrayed.'[7] All this setting up of conflicting value systems, which are superimposed but never exactly align with one another, nevertheless leaves each listener (5) a certain freedom to project their own judgements onto the narrative machine presented to them. Hence the Master himself passes a moral condemnation against Mademoiselle d'Aisnon: he 'did not see her protesting against her role throughout the whole ghastly business', even though the narrator (that is, the landlady) represented her as an innocent victim of necessity.

During his discussion with his reader, Diderot explicitly sheds light on the meta-narrative 'up there', which is the ideological battleground of every meaningful narrative.

> You foam at the mouth at the very mention of the name of Madame de La Pommeraye. You shriek: 'Oh, what a horrible woman! The hypocrite! The harridan!' Please, no shrieking, no foaming, no taking sides. Let's think about this calmly. Blacker crimes than hers are committed every day of the week, but they are not touched by genius. You may hate Madame de La Pommeraye, you may fear her, but you do not despise her. Her revenge was savage, but it was not contaminated by any motive of base self-interest . . . Her vindictiveness revolts you because either you are incapable of feeling vindictive on the same scale, or else place a very low value on the honour of women.[8]

Reading a narrative like this provides an opportunity to break new ground in defining the 'honour of women' or to make 'genius' a value

7 Diderot, *Jacques the Fatalist*, p. 104.
8 Ibid., p. 135.

that excuses the most 'savage' acts. The listener's beliefs, desires, affects, and values are invested in the story, and are then (marginally) reprocessed as they pass through the channels of the narrative machine.

It is worth making three short remarks here to clarify and qualify the role of narratives in this reconditioning of our affective economies and in this (re)production of our value systems.

1. It may be quite clear that a story that has happened to me 'in real life' will tend to leave a much deeper impression on me than a tale read in a book or an episode distractedly watched on TV. But the reprocessing of values which narratives perform is, in itself, independent of their fictional nature. The thing that counts, apart from the degree of attention which is actually mobilised, is the path of the channels through which my flows of desires and beliefs pass, even if the world represented in the plot does not correspond to any actual reality. Through the ability of purely fictional entities to shape the reality of our emotional economies, narrativisation offers the power of human self-affection an ontologically unique and potentially enormous field of action.

2. Just as we have contrasted two types of plots (the ones that tend to *reiterate* the grammar of actions, affects, and arguments we had before we plunged into them, and those that instead tend to *reconfigure* this grammar in unexpected ways), we may likewise draw a contrast between two types of reprocessing of values that narratives allow for. There are narratives that confirm, condone, and strengthen the value systems we were already operating with, in which case the 'reprocessing' in question merely consists in reviving colours that are a little outdated, but already assigned in identical fashion. On the other hand, we sometimes encounter narratives that tend to trick and gridlock our habitual valuations, potentially bifurcating them in new directions. In this latter case, the reprocessing consists in transforming the nature (and not just the intensity) of the affects that pass through the narrative machine, paving the way to other concatenations between them. This dichotomy may be 'crudely useful', for instance, to measure the mass-scale effects of the dominant positions occupied by certain types of narratives in certain media channels. But it would surely be fairer and undoubtedly more effective to ask, looking *within* each scene (of each narrative, each genre,

of each medium), precisely *what* is likely to lead to a confirmation of *which* values, and what specifically may tend to set in crisis which other values.

3. What best characterises the virtues of narratives is, most likely, the *complexity/subtlety* of their narrative construction. Christian Salmon's criticism of storytelling owes less to a rejection of narrative efficacy as such, and more to a denunciation of the simplicity of the narratives usually used by storytellers in advertising, managerial motivational speak, or political propaganda. If we were to speak of *narrative hygiene*, it should doubtless be gauged in terms of the multiplication of levels, the staging of contradictions, the nuances of expression, the cautiousness of description, critical retrospection, and axiological undecidability – in other words, in terms of formal complexity rather than ideological content per se.

The political issues at stake in narrative activities lie first and foremost in the work of *writing* (*écriture*), which refines (or does not refine) the sequencing of actions set out in the plot. On the one hand, narratives derive much of their merit from their ability for schematising and modelling – that is, for simplifying the heterogeneous and complex data of our lives and social relations. On the other hand, the most admirable narratives are the ones that manage to make this simplifying model more complex, to restore the integrating plot's tendency to escape any pre-set expectation, thus following the centrifugal dynamics of both writing and concrete reality.

Scripting from below and the power of equity

Having got this far, we can more readily understand why no one so far has successfully determined what a narrative can do. At the same time, we can also understand a little more about *the power of scripting that lies at the heart of storytelling*.

Our analysis of narratives as reprocessing plants in which a culture's values get sorted out resonates with the traditional humanist claim that 'the arts' help make the citizens more 'virtuous'. The power of scripting rests on an *ethical metalepsis* that deserves to be briefly discussed at this point of our reflection.

In a fine book on how humanist literature helped to write the history of its time, Timothy Hampton quite rightly centres his analysis on *exemplarity*. If an exemplar is indeed 'a kind of textual node or point of juncture, where a given author's interpretation of the past overlaps with the desire to form and fashion readers', then indeed 'the question of exemplarity involves the ways in which texts are public artifacts, documents designed to affect the political sphere'.[9] In starting his study with the case of Girolamo Olgiati, who joined in the murder of Galeazzo Maria Sforza in 1476 after feeling driven to tyrannicide by his (largely erroneous) reading of the pages Sallust devotes to Catiline, Timothy Hampton provides the extreme model of a gesture of application that he identifies at the heart of literary dynamics (in this following Gadamer and certain others). The power of scripting rests precisely on our tendency to 'apply' what we read of the past (or of fictional worlds) to 'similar cases' that we may identify in our own present or future reality. This application is always 'wrong', since no case is perfectly similar to another in all respects. At the same time, this application is always partly 'guided' (or at worst simply 'stimulated') by the indications that the interpreted narrative provides us with. As readers/spectators, we are moulded (or simply impressed) by public artefacts (tertiary retentions) that affect the political sphere by providing us with patterns of action to apply to our reality.

During the past decades, Richard Rorty and Martha Nussbaum developed several lines of argument based on this type of dynamic, in which they cast novelistic experience as a school of morality.[10] I think it is quite

9 Timothy Hampton, *Writing from History: The Rhetoric of Exemplarity in Renaissance Literature*, Ithaca, NY: Cornell University Press, 1990, pp. 3 and 5.

10 See, for example, Richard Rorty, *Contingence, Irony and Solidarity*, Cambridge: Cambridge University Press, 1989; Martha Nussbaum, *Poetic Justice: The Literary Imagination and Public Life*, Boston: Beacon Press, 1995; and in French, Sandra Laugier, ed., *Éthique, littérature, vie humaine*, Paris: PUF, 2006; and Jacques Bouveresse, *La Connaissance de l'écrivain. Sur la littérature, la vérité et la vie*, Marseille: Agone, 2008.

telling that this conception of literature as a formative ethical experience has been developed mainly in Anglo-Saxon countries, in legal cultures based on common law jurisprudence rather than the civil code. As against an imaginary that sees justice in laws enacted and codified by the parliamentary and administrative machinery of the State, imposing order through a reputedly centralising voice from up there, common law sees laws as being made up horizontally, through concretion, inflection, and gradual correction, as precedents are time and again reinterpreted. In systems based on the civil code, a judge is someone who applies a law drafted by a superior legislator. But in a system based on common law, the judge makes the law (of tomorrow) *at the same time as they apply it* today, drawing inspiration from similar cases their predecessors ruled on in times past. This jurisprudential imaginary provides the model for a system of *scripting from below*. Here, indeed, we are not dealing with some Big Brother or some Hobbesian or Rousseauian Legislator, who from the height of His superior rationality programmes subjects to become virtuous puppets. Rather, this scripting from below is a matter of many different thrusts and fumbling attempts, which amount to a pluralist ensemble. Through the solidarities and antagonisms scattered throughout the social fabric, this scripting will progress (or backtrack) one similar case to another, applying a law that emanates only from the inertia of previous applications.

Narrative experience provides the ideal terrain for exercising what Aristotle considered the supreme form of justice, that of *equity* (*epieikes*). He defined equity as the parallel recognition of the necessary universality of any law (which, in order to be just and equitable, must be applied uniformly to all similar cases) and the inevitable *singularity* of each case to which the law in question must be applied (so that although certain cases may appear, by simplification, to be 'comparable', they are never 'identical' nor indeed fully 'similar'). Narratives plunge us into tangles of relationships that have the relational density of concrete situations. For this reason, they feed the tension we mentioned earlier, between a simplification that schematises things and the nuances that bring greater sophistication. Since equity demands a 'correction of law where it is defective owing to its universality', it is also a call on all of us to become legislators. For 'where the legislator fails us and has erred by oversimplicity' it is our responsibility 'to correct the omission . . . to say what the legislator himself would have said had he been present, and would have put into his law if he had known.' Indeed, affective investment and the projection of values onto the narrative work rather like 'the leaden rule used in making the Lesbian moulding; the rule adapts itself to the shape of the stone and is not rigid.'[11] Here we are dealing with the ethics of 'care' (of attention, concern, and consideration) which emphasise the primacy of concrete relations between living beings rather than abstract and universal principles of justice.[12] Equitable judgement is applied based on our intuitions (which are informed by our critical knowledge of precedents) within concrete given relationships. We have to be able to adapt our 'leaden rules' to the contours of these relationships, through an

11 'All law is universal but about some things it is not possible to make a universal statement which shall be correct. In those cases, then, in which it is necessary to speak universally, but not possible to do so correctly, the law takes the usual case, though it is not ignorant of the possibility of error. And it is none the less correct; for the error is not in the law nor in the legislator but in the nature of the thing, since the matter of practical affairs is of this kind from the start. When the law speaks universally, then, and a case arises on it which is not covered by the universal statement, then it is right, where the legislator fails us and has erred by oversimplicity, to correct the omission – to say what the legislator himself would have said had he been present, and would have put into his law if he had known. Hence the equitable is just, and better than one kind of justice – not better than absolute justice but better than the error that arises from the absoluteness of the statement. And this is the nature of the equitable, a correction of law where it is defective owing to its universality. In fact, this is the reason why all things are not determined by law, that about some things it is impossible to lay down a law, so that a decree is needed. For when the thing is indefinite the rule also is indefinite, like the leaden rule used in making the Lesbian moulding; the rule adapts itself to the shape of the stone and is not rigid, and so too the decree is adapted to the facts. (Aristotle, *Nicomachean Ethics*, Book V, Chapter 10, trans. W. D. Ross, Kitchener, ONT: Batoche Books, 1999, pp. 88–9).

12 For an insightful characterisation of the contrasts between the ethics of care and the ethics of justice, see the first chapter of Grace Clement, *Care, Autonomy, and Justice: Feminism and the Ethic of Care*, New York: Westview Press, 1996. For a good introduction to these issues, see Sandra Laugier et al., *Qu'est-ce que le care? Souci des autres, sensibilité, responsabilité*, Paris: Payot, 2009; and the special issue 'Politiques du care' of *Multitudes* no. 37/38 (September 2009), pp. 71–141.

infinite effort of 'adjustment' – whose name itself displays an intimate link with the practice of justice.

Walter Benjamin lamented the disappearance of this function of jurisprudential deliberation and 'good counsel', as he predicted that the storyteller would soon die out:

> Every real story . . . serves, overtly or covertly, a useful function. This usefulness may consist in one case of imparting a particular moral, in another of offering a bit of practical advice; a third case may involve a proverb or a maxim – in each case, the narrator is a man of good counsel for his audience. But if the expression 'of good counsel' has begun to sound old-fashioned to our ears, that is due to the fact that experience is ever less communicable. That is why we ourselves are no longer of good counsel, neither for ourselves nor for others. Indeed, good counsel is less an answer to a question than a suggestion of how to continue a story (that is already in progress).[13]

We have spoken of the empowerment of each individual to legislate, which drives narrative life and the circulation of narratives within a society. This is part of the same form of dissemination we have already encountered in this chapter, down the countless branches of a horizontal, micro-level capillarity. The narratives that circulate within a population express, arrange, and rearrange the forms of life that emerge and are lived 'from below', among the multitudes. The integrating function of all narratives tends to set heterogeneous events within the horizon of some all-embracing concatenation of causes. Yet this concatenation is perceived in its *intensity*, starting from each node of existence, rather than in its total *extension*, as seen from up there. Attention to detail, care for the particular, and concern for the singular are the elements that fuel the dynamics by which narratives are generated, received, and propagated.

13 Walter Benjamin, 'The Storyteller', in *The Storyteller Essays*, ed. Samuel Titan, trans. Tess Lewis, New York: New York Review Books, 2019, p. 51. My thanks to Jean-François Perrin for drawing my attention to this text (and for enriching my thinking, through our stimulating and engaged discussions).

This also tells us something more about the power of scripting. It consists of *injecting* or *spreading precedents* across the social fabric, with the effect of inducing behaviour based on the application of these (historical or fictional) *exempla* to future real cases, insofar as these cases are perceived as similar to these *exempla*. This is, indeed, a question of 'power' (*potestas*), in that it is instituted by explicit and implicit norms (the ones that govern the economy of attention, interpretation, recognition of the 'similar', narrative syntax, or the compatibility or incompatibility of values). It is sanctioned by disapproval (booing, zapping, criticism) and reward (laughter, applause, recommendations, Oscars, literary prizes). But this power often remains extremely close to a *potentia*, insofar as both the ability for telling stories and the ability for interpretive application are endemic in human populations. Of course, governments may try (more or less brutally) to control 'from above' the stories that spread through a population, as well as the standard ways of interpreting and applying them in an acceptable way. Yet every speaking subject carries within herself the *potentia* to produce counter-conducts, counter-stories, and counter-interpretations.

Infrapolitical mythocracy

These dynamics of exemplarity and Aristotelian *epieikes* may now lead us to touch on an aspect of mythocracy that has remained unspoken in the preceding pages and chapters. In his fine work *Domination and the Arts of Resistance: Hidden Transcripts*, James C. Scott writes that we should 'distinguish at least four varieties of political discourse among dominated groups'.[14] At one end of the spectrum we have (1) the 'public transcript', corresponding to 'the self-portrait of dominant elites as they

14 James C. Scott, *Domination and the Arts of Resistance: Hidden Transcripts*, New Haven, CT: Yale University Press, 1990, p. 18. For related issues, see also Oskar Negt and Alexander Kluge, *Public Sphere and Experience: Toward an Analysis of the Bourgeois and Proletarian Public Sphere*, Minneapolis: Minnesota University Press, 1993; and the special section *L'Espace public oppositionnel* in *Multitudes* no. 39 (November 2009), pp. 181–217.

would have themselves seen' and which is 'designed to be impressive, to affirm and naturalize the power of dominant elites, and to conceal or euphemize the dirty linen of their rule'. At the other end of the spectrum, we have (2) the 'hidden transcript', a 'discourse that takes place "offstage", beyond direct observation by powerholders' and which consists of 'speeches, gestures, and practices that confirm, contradict, or inflect what appears in the public transcript'.[15]

This pushes against a simplistic understanding of the theory of 'hegemony', which holds that the masks the dominated have to put on in the presence of the dominant end up sticking to their face, to the point of merging with their own persons (with their 'spontaneous' feelings and thoughts). For Scott, the public transcript (what can be said within earshot of power) and the hidden one (what subordinates want to say but cannot say to its face) never coincide. Of course, his work focuses on situations of hard power, even terrorising ones, such as slavery, feudalism, or the caste system. But his conclusions can be extended to any power relationship. For each of us has our own little boss (foreman, supervisor, manager) to whom we dream we will one day get the chance to tell a few home truths.

In between the public transcript and the hidden one, Scott also helps us identify (3) a 'politics of disguise and anonymity' which is expressed in practice in 'rumor, gossip, folktales, jokes, songs, rituals, codes, and euphemisms' used to denounce the iniquities of our rulers in a roundabout way, as well as through underground insubordinate behaviour such as pilfering, poaching, sabotage, and shirking our responsibilities. Finally, the last variety of political discourse concerns (4) 'the Saturnalia of power': moments of 'the rupture of the political cordon sanitaire between the hidden and the public transcript'. Such 'moments of challenge and open defiance typically provoke either a swift stroke of repression or, if unanswered, often lead to further words and acts of daring'.[16]

Indeed, Scott invites us to imagine the infrapolitics he is discussing in the dynamic terms of *pressures* and *thrusts*:

15 Ibid., pp. 4–5.
16 Ibid., p. 19.

> Systematic subordination generates pressure of some kind from below . . . For any subordinate group, there is tremendous desire and will to express publicly what is in the hidden transcript, even if that form of expression must use metaphors and allusions in the interest of safety . . . Infrapolitics is . . . always pressing, testing, probing the boundaries of the permissible. Any relaxation in surveillance and punishment and foot-dragging threatens to become a declared strike, folktales of oblique aggression threaten to become face-to-face defiant contempt, millennial dreams threaten to become revolutionary politics. From this vantage point infrapolitics may be thought of as the elementary – in the sense of foundational – form of politics.[17]

As we reach the end of this chapter, we can now complete the model of power outlined in Chapter 2. If we conceive of power as arising from the circulation of flows of desires and beliefs, what we then understood to be *points of leverage with multiplier effects* (institutions) now turn out to qualify the *attractors* (hooks and plots) defined above. An institution can function only insofar as it is constantly fed by the flows of desires and beliefs (yearnings, fears, hopes, hatreds) of the human beings it is dealing with. It can mobilise these flows of desires and beliefs only insofar as it succeeds in attracting them with some desirable and credible story. Such stories may be based on hope: work hard and one day you just might get rich, and maybe even famous. They can be based on terror: if you do not answer 'Yes, master' to every demand made of you, then you will be mercilessly whipped. These stories, which are always myths, are usually based on a complex mix of promises and threats, which draw our desires and beliefs towards a certain respect for the institutions in question.

Consideration of the hidden transcript and infrapolitics, as defined by James C. Scott, allows us to take a further step. It enables us to account for the strategic nature of the capture of flows of affects, for the conflicting nature of the plots around which institutions coagulate, and above all for modulations in the forms of utterance (*énonciation*) through which

17 Ibid, pp. 164, 186, 200–1.

these narratives may (or may not) manifest themselves in a more or less roundabout way. Scott writes that the interplay of infrapolitical pressures and counter-pressures constitutes 'the elementary form of politics'. This is because the structures governing social life result from a power struggle (*rapport de forces*) between the constant pressure exerted by the expressions of the hidden transcript, and the no less constant efforts to hold back these pressures and keep everyone subjected to the place allotted to them by the public transcript. The disguised (euphemised, roundabout, anonymised) expressions of the hidden transcript push 'up toward the top', in the opposite direction to all the (petty or mass-scale) forms of oppression validated by the stories that make up the public transcript. The differential between these two forms of pressure is what decides, from one day to the next, the placing of the frontier that separates what may and may not be said (told, narrated). Moreover, this frontier also coincides with the one that separates – on the scale of society as a whole – the thinkable from the unthinkable, the normal from the unacceptable, the regrettable from the revolting. For Scott, 'the frontier between the public and the hidden transcripts is a zone of constant struggle between dominant and subordinate – not a solid wall . . . The unremitting struggle over such boundaries is perhaps the most vital arena for ordinary conflict, for everyday forms of class struggle.'[18]

If our diagram of power has any insight at all, then we can only conclude that this is the same frontier which, through an incremental exchange of pressures, maintains institutions as they are or allows for their form to be changed. For institutions cannot function sustainably unless they manage to attract the affects of the human beings whose behaviours they modulate.

The historical examples studied by James C. Scott throughout his book generally relate to an oppression based on terror; they could, therefore, be read as entirely counter to our previous chapters and the roles that they ascribe to 'soft power'. Yet even in the most extreme cases, the whip and gallows martyred only the bodies of a few unfortunates, for the sake of spreading messages of submission in the minds of the (direct or

18 Ibid., p. 14.

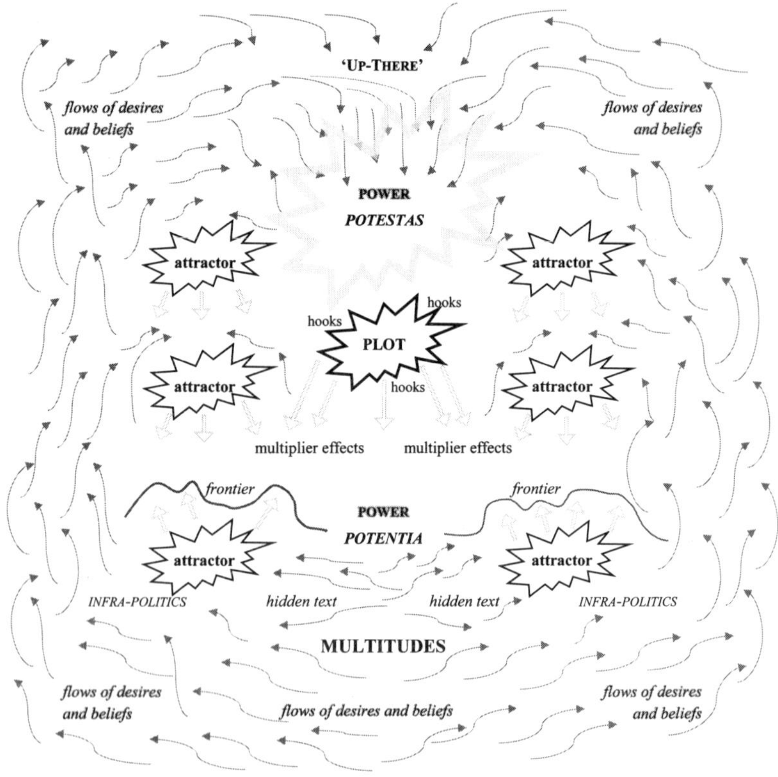

Figure 4. Completed diagram:
power, attractors, and infrapolitical frontiers.

indirect) audience to these punishments. Here, too, the stories that are told (or which we tell ourselves) hold us in chains, much more often than metallic chains worn around the ankles. Indeed, in physically restraining us these latter also prevent us from being really useful to our exploiters (who may remove such constraints, if they find other more effective ways to conduct our conduct).

If infrapolitical analysis also applies to our societies of control, this is partly because, as we pointed out in the introduction, not all power is 'soft': in our liberal democracies there are always clubs to beat demonstrators' heads, employees losing their jobs for insubordination, 'things that shouldn't be said' unless we want to expose ourselves to the many forms of repression unleashed on individuals suspected of terrorism, paedophilia, fanaticism, emotional instability, chronic bad temper, or simple laziness. Sure, a propensity for televised confessionalism can mislead us into too readily believing that anything – starting with the worst things – can be said, indeed all the more proudly the further we head into prime time. It would be naive, however, to think that the imperative of 'expressing yourself' that has invaded much of the media has really abolished all forms of censorship and all boundaries of what can and cannot be said.[19]

Some 'transcripts' remain 'hidden', not because it is formally forbidden to utter them, but because they tend to go missing amid the plethora of discourses that saturate our social environment. The challenge of infrapolitics in societies of control would, therefore, push forward these transcripts which get 'lost' in the noise of overabundant mass of communication. At the same time, infrapolitics tends to take forms that may be described as '*intra*-political' insofar as the frontier between the public and hidden transcripts is increasingly to be found at the heart of my thoughts, my ambivalences, and my internal cleavages. The less explicit violence there is in the forms of domination, the more likely it is that the mask will cling to the face (without ever fusing completely with it). In this case, the frontier of political struggles will run through the stories that I tell myself in order to justify the intolerable or else to alert myself to its horror. Each of us – alternately dominated and dominant, depending on the complex tangle of power relations knotted together within us – is torn between different plots that pull us in contradictory directions.

19 In an interview which appeared as the afterword to the French translation, James C. Scott makes clear that his analysis also applies to more 'modern' forms of government: 'Liberal societies have their hidden transcript in the immense inequalities and glaring differences in equality of opportunity (with huge inheritances, the virtual monopoly that certain privileged classes have over higher education, etc.) that cannot easily be justified or defended publicly . . . What I have written also has to do with the lives of contemporary citizens, who spend most of their day under forms of political or professional tyranny, in other words in social contexts that are fundamentally undemocratic' (*La Domination et les arts de la résistance*, Paris: Éditions Amsterdam, pp. 251–2).

An examination of infrapolitics – among those who suffer the most extreme forms of domination, or those with the privilege of living under less violent regimes – enables us to identify the power of myth, storytelling, exemplarity, and scripting across a range of situations, from those that seem dominated by the most savage constraint, to others where the individual appears to 'freely' consent to oppression. The precarious boundary that separates the hidden transcript from what can be heard and said (in public or to oneself) represents the sensitive zone where scripting strategies have their most important effect in shaping societies' future. The disguised words and secret acts of insubordination in which the dominated indulge are constantly working to reconfigure this frontier – and so, too, are the gestures of authority or appeasement which the dominant use in response. The stories that get told when the boss, the teacher, the policeman, the examiner, the bureaucrat are far enough away that they can no longer hear what's being said about them all put pressure on this boundary. This same frontier is also redrawn by our (apparently) solitary efforts not to lie to ourselves, in the stories we tell ourselves.

It is in this frontier zone that mythocracy – understood as the power of myth-story and the power of enchanting words (*thelktêrious muthous*) – appears in its most vivid form, in its emerging status. We could cite countless examples from across the world and all manner of eras to illustrated how true it is that 'the first public unveiling of the hidden transcript frequently sets in motion a crystallization of public action that is astonishingly rapid' and that 'its mobilizing capacity as a symbolic act is potentially awesome'.[20] Scott uses the term 'Saturnalia of power' to describe the moment when 'the frontier between the hidden and the public transcripts is decisively breached', allowing a whole section of society to step into the breach thus opened.[21] 'Saturnalia' refers to the annual festivals celebrated in honour of Saturn in ancient Rome, during which slaves were momentarily free to put their obedience on hold and openly criticise their masters. The choice of this term clearly illustrates

20 Scott, *Domination and the Arts of Resistance*, pp. 223, 227.

21 Ibid., p. 202.

the continuity between the stories (of the overthrow of power) that we tell ourselves in the form of myth (at carnival time) and the transformations that can be imposed on a society's history on account of the myths which a sizeable enough part of the multitude believe in.

Scott resists the idea that carnivalesque moments merely serve as 'safety valves' that allow the existing order to contain dissatisfaction by allowing it to express itself through intermittently authorised channels – thereby neutralising any 'real' resistance. He instead suggests that the carnivalesque reversals of the established order of things open new avenues of demand, increase the pressure that the hidden transcript exerts on the public transcript, and push the frontier between them as far as possible. Indeed, this may sometimes even have the effect of transgressing all frontiers and turning the theatrical rebellion into a true theatre of revolution.

If the term 'Saturnalia' refers both to the annual myth of an imaginary revolution, and to episodes of real revolt, this is perhaps because the force of myth also plays a central role in such episodes. In fact, it often happens that the simple voicing of insubordination marks the first breach in the frontier separating the public transcript from the hidden transcript. These insubordinate words will take on the apparently magical virtues of *thelktêrious muthous* only insofar as the legend of them spreads in the form of a myth among a population that sees in this the sign of a fatal crack in the wall of silence and domination. It seems to the participants in such events that the 'spell' of subordination has suddenly been broken – and it is broken by the opposite spell of an act of bravery which is instantly endowed with an invincible 'charisma'.

One of the most original dimensions of Scott's work is that he shows that the source of this charisma never really lies within the individual themselves. Of course, every Saturnalia has its herald, whose single act of bravado and bravery triggers a process that makes them into a hero. But it is mythocracy itself that makes the difference – that is, the *power of myth* as a collective reality constituted by the convergence of flows of desire and belief. Emphasising 'the importance of the hidden transcript for the social production of charisma', Scott points out that the charismatic figure's role 'is to a large extent scripted in advance offstage by all members of the subordinate group'. They prepare this script through the recriminations, grievances, hopes, and dreams that they had initially only dared to express among themselves out of the earshot of power, or in disguising them in indirect, anonymous, roundabout, or allegorised forms of utterance. Hence for Scott, 'the powerful emotional valence of the charismatic speech or act for subordinate groups – their sense of elation, joy, release – depends, I think, on it finding this resonance within the hidden transcript.'[22] The bearer of the event is the myth itself, as a resonant story which acts by means of the charismatic individuals who happen to bring it onto the public stage. This myth is, moreover, inseparable from the network/community already formed among the many individuals whom it electrifies; it draws on the heightened tension of this network/community as a trans-individual ensemble (rather than any one of its members).

At the heart of the most intense moment of infrapolitics is mythocracy, as Sun Ra defined it. If, for Sun Ra, mythocracy is 'what you never came to be that you should be' – something which you can only dream about at the same time as you submit to an oppressive domination – then Saturnalia, in their revolutionary eventmentality as in the carnivalesque forging of new paths, represent the moment when you *actually become the myth that you should be.* Is it any wonder that Sun Ra could break through racist domination and develop an art of creative resistance only thanks to the force of a myth that had him born on Saturn – the planet of the god of Saturnalia?

22 Ibid., pp. 221–2.

5

New Demands for Equality

The last chapter emphasised that everyone plays their part in a collective power of imagining, inventing, and affirming various forms of life. In this sense we represented the power of scripting as a fundamentally *endemic power*. This should not obscure – of course – the considerable structural inequalities that mark the individual actualisations of this power in our age of mass media–dominated communication. If the question of equality was briefly eclipsed during the three-decade rise of neoliberal ideology, this question will certainly return in the decades to come. As philosophical claims and sociological studies have long asserted – and as certain (not necessarily radical) economists are beginning to rediscover for themselves – the societies that pay most attention to questions of equality are not the weaker performers. Rather, these societies are more stable, more secure, and more fulfilled: in other words, they are 'richer', so long as the wealth of nations is not reduced to the restrictive terms of GDP.

Within this context, what is to be said about (in)equalities in the power of scripting itself? Is this power inherently egalitarian, insofar as anyone can take part in it? Is it structurally unequal, since not everyone can be equally 'famous'? Should this type of (in)equality be treated at the level of legal and political regulation, or that of individual modes of behaviour and resistance? This is the type of question that Chapter 5 seeks to address.

The social production of charisma

Frédéric Lordon rightly points out that

> the potentate is not at all a demiurge through his own power, which is in fact entirely borrowed. He is merely an opportunist. That is why tearing down the man in power does nothing to remove the structures of power, the structures of 'intermediated' or 'instrumented' verticality, as we might call the *mediated* self-affection of the multitude, the *captured* potentia multitudinis.[1]

Given that power is always 'borrowed', insofar as it derives from the circulation of flows of desires and beliefs, and considering that scripting is based on the differentials between distinct levels, a 'left-wing' reflection on inequalities in scripting power must face up to three simultaneous challenges.

On the one hand, any inequality in a power (*potestas*) which is 'borrowed' from the common power (*potentia*) by opportunistic appropriation appears illegitimate. More than that, it seems precarious. For the other participants in the 'web' always retain a certain degree of control over this common *potentia*, which is indeed inalienable given that it resides in their own capacity to see, interpret, reason, and imagine things for themselves. The first challenge is, therefore, to recognise (1) the common nature of the power (*potestas*) borrowed from the power (*potentia*) of the multitude, (2) the fragile status of its private appropriation, and (3) the degree of participation through which individuals lend

1 Frédéric Lordon, 'Derrière l'idéologie de la légitimité, la puissance de la multitude. Le *Traité politique* comme théorie générale des institutions sociales', in Chantal Jaquet, Pascal Séverac, and Ariel Suhamy, eds, *La Multitude libre. Nouvelles lectures du* Traité Politique *de Spinoza*, Paris: Éditions Amsterdam, 2008, p. 118.

themselves (often for good reasons) to 'borrowing' operations that sometimes seem more like a robbery of their own property. Nobody is putting a gun to TV viewers' heads to force them to watch an interview with some celeb – instead of reading Spinoza, composing songs, or doodling a comic strip. So, at this early stage of reflection, the inequalities in question seem both unfounded and easily reversed.

On the other hand, because 'power structures' are necessarily *vertical*, they are necessarily based on the inequalities between different levels. As we saw in previous chapters, scripting strategies and counter-strategies always seek to meta-script the scripting developed by their opponents, in other words to place themselves on a higher level of scripting. This is well illustrated by Madame de La Pommeraye's position, as she meta-scripts the Marquis's own seductive scripts. It would therefore be futile to demand a 'flattening' equality that simply aims to 'put everyone on the same level'. So, the second challenge is to recognise that inequality is the lifeblood of the script. Instead of seeing this as an insult to an idyllic 'natural right' in which all of us are 'born equal', we can recognise – without betraying the traditional ideals of the 'left' – that (1) that we are all 'born different', in circumstances which necessarily give us different powers to act (from both a qualitative and quantitative point of view), whose actualisation will necessarily be unequal, (2) that the demand for equality is both a postulate (the 'equality of intelligences' promoted by Jacques Rancière) and an institutional aim that must be asserted against the inequalities of what is originally given, and (3) that the inequalities between different levels, as long as they are organised in a way that emancipates rather than enslaves us, are part of the common construction of a 'verticality' that enables human societies to overcome their original limitations.

The third challenge, then, is to build institutions in which the inequalities between different levels make it possible to *mediate the self-affection of the multitude in the direction of a common and egalitarian empowerment*. This is not about accepting the given inequalities (their unacceptable aspects), nor of seeking to flatten all inequalities between different levels (which would be neither possible nor desirable), but of arranging the structures of power, the 'structures of verticality', in such a way as to make them 'the mediation' or 'the instrument' of an increase in our common and individual powers to act. In other words, the harmful or threatening thing is not the inequal levels of meta-scripting per se, but rather certain directions in which they push us.

These formulations may seem a little abstract, so let us illustrate them with an example: the particular case of education. The teaching relationship is structured by an inequality between different levels, that is, between teachers and students. The aim of this verticality is to help the latter to overcome some of their own limits, and thus rise to a superior mastery of certain knowledge and skills. However, we may conceive of the students' 'elevation' (*élève* = pupil) in very different ways. The teachers may speak from a position of authority, which radically separates them from the common lot of their pupils, by casting themselves as the bearers of a superior knowledge which the pupils cannot hope to reach directly. Such teachers heighten the structural inequality inherent in the classroom and push their pupils towards blind (or terrified) submission to authority, even if this is done in the name of creating more equal positions in future. Through their attitudes, their modes of intervention, and the hopes and fears which they spur in their students, such teachers script the pedagogical relationship as an experience of obedience and one-directional transmission. The effect is that the horizon of emancipation is constantly deferred.[2]

Other teachers may push the inequality inherent in the classroom situation in a different direction. They may present their knowledge and power (*potestas*) as 'borrowed' from a common intellectual power (*potentia*), of which they are not the privileged bearers, jealous guardians, or sacred initiators. Rather, they strive to realise the properly common nature of this knowledge by seeking to enrich it with students who also fully contribute to it, in their own way. These teachers will

2 The reader will of course recognise in these three paragraphs the argument set out in Jacques Rancière's fine book *Le Maître ignorant. Cinq leçons sur l'émancipation intellectuelle*, Paris: Fayard, 1987 (*The Ignorant Schoolmaster: Five Lessons in Intellectual Emancipation*, Stanford, CA: Stanford University Press, 1991). See also Charlotte Nordmann, *La Fabrique de l'impuissance 2. L'École, entre domination et émancipation*, Paris: Éditions Amsterdam, 2007.

indeed be in a position to meta-script the teaching relationship: they do so by giving their students assignments, or by guiding their intellectual behaviour in certain directions that they have sought to predetermine. But they will also script the teaching relationship as a shared endeavour, which concretely teaches the practical modalities of sharing in the space of the classroom itself, and which does not settle for dangling an external and ever-deferred horizon of sharing. In a sense, there surely is an inequality between they (the teachers) who choose the focuses of learning and who hand out the assignments and correct them, and then those (the pupils) who take part in a shared experience that has already been preframed for them. There may even be a relationship of obedience established within this structural inequality. But this scripting leads the participants to recognise a fundamental 'equality of intelligences', asserted as a postulate and as a practical condition of social interaction, starting with the actual relations established in the space of the classroom (one always teaches more by what one does than by what one says).

Madame de La Pommeraye made the Marquis her victim and her inferior by playing a (confidante) role that concealed the reality of her scheme (for revenge). The authoritarian teachers play a role that denies and contradicts in their concrete practice their supposed aim, the (ever-deferred) intellectual emancipation. Unlike Diderot's heroine, they certainly do put their cards on the table: *I know, you don't know*, they tell us. But this game begins with the cards distributed in such a way that the students cannot really win what they are being promised (intellectual emancipation). The emancipatory teachers, those who have learned from the reflections of Joseph Jacotot and Jacques Rancière, will also lay their cards on the table. But what is different is that they strive to distribute these cards in such a way that the students may begin, without delay, in putting into practice and learning to master the gestures of the intellectual emancipation for which they say they are training them. These two attitudes may each claim to belong to a certain 'left-wing' tradition, insofar as they both have egalitarian aims. However, it is clear that they reflect two imaginaries of power, and two ways of practising power, that are likely to clash. Indeed, they come into conflict not only in abstract philosophical debates, but as soon as decisions have to be made about how to listen to and speak to each other in the concrete space of a classroom.

In this respect, the practice of scripting, which is clearly at the heart of the educational relationship, deserves (at least for the higher levels of the school curriculum) to be the subject of specific reflection and transformation which is openly identified as such. As we have seen in previous chapters, the power of scripting is both a skill universally shared by all human beings and a set of techniques that can and should be the subject of institutional training.

Everyone can tell (themselves) stories: narrative activity is a shared ability to string together sentences, thoughts, and actions. This is an ability which each human being, as a human being, necessarily has some share in. However, not everyone tells their stories with the same talent: some storytellers captivate our attention even before they open their mouths, and manage to keep it alive for hours. Others will have a hard time getting to the end of a joke without making us yawn. In 1936, Walter Benjamin lamented the imminent disappearance of this talent: 'The art of storytelling is dying out. Encounters with people who know how to tell a story properly are becoming ever rarer . . . It's as if a capacity we had considered inalienable, the most reliable of all our capacities, has been taken from us: the ability to share experiences.'[3]

Still, the resurgence of the arts of the spoken word in recent years seems to contradict this gloomy prognosis. It illustrates both the marvels of the ever individual and inexplicable charisma that characterises each virtuoso storyteller and the possibility of institutionalising the promotion, transmission, and production of this type of talent (through festivals, courses, workshops, and schools). As we saw when we were discussing James C. Scott's book, 'charisma' is best seen as part of 'social production'. There need to be special testing grounds where emancipatory speech can be tried out, which will give rise to 'networks' and 'heralds' and allow for 'hidden' transcripts and stories to take shape on the public stage. In continuity with pedagogical developments underway

3 Walter Benjamin, 'The Storyteller', in *The Storyteller Essays*, ed. Samuel Titan, trans. Tess Lewis, New York: New York Review Books, 2019, p. 48.

in recent decades – but counter to the reactionary forces that have taken hold of school curricula in recent years – a 'left-wing' policy will thus be one that strives to encourage the emergence of these spaces for subaltern speech, as well as to develop educational institutions that explicitly and practically value the ability to narrate, to capture the attention of an audience, to construct innovative scripts, to deconstruct the scripts of others, to counter-script, and to meta-script.

These are the same skills cultivated each time we learn to organise our thoughts in the form of an essay or an oral presentation. Current teaching, however, places excessive emphasis on argumentative logic – in part, at least, a mystifying choice. This has led to an underestimation of the powers of rhetoric, storytelling, dramaturgy, and scenography. We might wonder whether the current popularity of the performing arts among French university students does not in fact reflect their own keen awareness of how important it is to learn scripting techniques. Perhaps some small proportion of these students may harbour the hope of pursuing the career of their dreams (becoming a famous director, running a national theatre, putting together the arts section for some major periodical). But their course choices undoubtedly also reflect a perception of the central role played by the dynamics of scripting and of performing in the way that society is developing – a central role that has recently surfaced in the struggles of temporary workers in the performing arts, which are anything but marginal.[4]

Infrastructural inequalities and symbolic 'stickiness'

The inequalities of skills and education, with regard to scripting, are real enough (and could in part be remedied). But we can also see these inequalities in a more relative view, just as Rousseau does with regard to the inequalities present in his state of nature. The really damaging factor is not so much the inequality among individual capacities, but the

4 On this point, see Antonella Corsani and Maurizio Lazzarato, *Intermittents et précaires*, Paris: Éditions Amsterdam, 2008.

disproportionate consequences that our social institutions attach to this inequality. The power to script is measured much less in terms of talent, skill, or virtuosity, than in terms of position within a certain structure of circulation of words, ideas, and images.

Here, we get to the major difference between the ability to tell stories and the power of scripting. Narration captures the flow of desires and beliefs in function of the particular virtues of the storyteller and her narrative (her hooks, her plot, her syntax, her resonances within different environments). Scripting, for its part, captures the flow of desires and beliefs in function of its access to an audience's attention. For narration, the relevant questions are about how to tell a story effectively. For scripting, the relevant questions revolve around who is reached and affected by what is being told.

If we want to understand the realities of scripting power, we therefore need to map the system of channels that govern, in moment X, the flows of attention circulating within the different publics that make up a given society.[5] This is the inextricably material and symbolic infrastructure of the 'public sphere', at the crossroad between the physical realities of bit flows, the legal realities of property rights, and the economic realities of investments and buyouts.

We can now look at the two extremes of these infrastructural inequalities, which are material in nature. On one end of things, there is the talented storyteller who spends a night out making their friends smile without ever going outside their own narrow circle. At the other end is the Berlusconi syndrome. The billionaire controlled most of the media and broadcast networks of a country of 60 million inhabitants (and even if this was not absolute control, it was remarkably direct). The case of Berlusconi illustrates both an extreme concentration of multiple types of power (from economic to political and media power) and the inherent limits of a power that relies on capturing the beliefs and desires of a public.

5 Here it is worth looking at Philippe Boisnard's fine work in developing these channels into dynamic visual diagrams, which appear (among other places) in various issues of *La Revue internationale des livres et des idées*.

Berlusconi and his henchmen had many ways of getting a hearing, through their speeches, their press organs, their radio stations, and their TV channels. Through these, they could, of course, feed the beliefs that direct the frustrations felt by part of the Italian population – faced with economic, social, and political processes that leave them in a vulnerable position – against certain categories of foreigners. It is also true that this involved an essentially unilateral control of how these networks were used: the likes of Berlusconi can decide at any time to close down their companies or redirect their activities to something else. But not even Berlusconi could impose every whim and taste on an amorphous mass of hypnotised TV viewers. Had some angel persuaded him to broadcast only religious hymns on his radio stations, evangelical sermons in his newspapers, and edifying films on his TV channels, his media conglomerate (and its scripting power) would have melted in a few weeks.

If we do not want to overestimate the inertia of such infrastructures, then we need to learn – as Éric Macé invites us to do – to get a better sense of how permeable they are to the *scripting strategies* that clash in the political arena. Our media cultures' characteristic conformism is 'unstable'; and so, the question of what 'the news' will talk about is itself resolved by often volatile conflicts between rival scripting strategies:

> The information that is broadcast does not reflect the 'reality' of the 'facts', nor all the points of view that make up the definitional conflicts that animate the public sphere. Rather, it reflects different actors' ability to constitute facts as 'events' and to impose them on the media-political agenda through communication strategies that simultaneously provide their own desired interpretative frameworks. To put that in other words, the information produced by the mass media is the relatively unstable result of a generalized conflict between social actors, whose object is the definition of the reality of the social world and its 'problems'. This observation allows us more easily to understand why the democratic question is not a matter of deploring the lack of objective information or of denouncing the corruption of politics by the media. Rather, it is a matter of increasing subaltern actors' and counter-publics' capacity to constitute themselves as sources of information, agenda setting

> and framing (and the numbers who can do so), in order to limit the now-routine hegemony of certain social groups and interpretative frameworks within the public sphere.[6]

Certainly, scripting capacities depend on the economic, political, and legal power that determines the material control of distribution and broadcasting infrastructure. But at the same time, these capacities should also be measured in terms of the opportunities for access that go together with *symbolic recognition*. A name or, to quote Naomi Klein's famous arguments, a logo (of a celebrity, of a brand, an institutional authority) can constitute a form of power just as considerable of the material possession of the networks of mass dissemination.[7] This logo is so valuable because it condenses many already forged paths, of which it becomes the vehicle as soon as it begins to circulate within these networks. Showing the face of a famous actor like George Clooney offers a hook that will give you a head start in capturing the attention of a broad audience. But it also allows you to mobilise a whole series of virtual scripts condensed in his image: Clooney the activist for humanitarian causes, Clooney the doctor from the emergency, Clooney the producer of political films, etc. It can be used to publicise a political cause in need of more media coverage, or to sell coffee machines.

Here, we get to the Schwarzenegger syndrome. It is emblematic of the type of power condensed in a logo (name/image), as it provides an example of the spectacular translation of the power of symbolic recognition into directly political power. We are in this case both very close to and very far from the case of Berlusconi. True, the Italian businessman-politician cultivated a star image, also via a great deal of cosmetic surgery and media stunts. But, under the table, he still retained economic control of the material networks for disseminating forms and content, as well as a degree of political-legislative control which allowed him to use ad hoc

6 Éric Macé, *Les Imaginaires médiatiques. Une sociologie postcritique des médias*, Paris: Éditions Amsterdam, 2006, p. 96–7.

7 Naomi Klein, *No Logo: Taking Aim at the Brand Bullies*, London: Picador, 1999.

decrees to keep a lid on his crimes. In the case of the Austrian-American actor – just the latest in a long line of entertainers to invest their media image in the pursuit of a political career (Ronald Reagan, Jesse Ventura, Noël Mamère) – we are dealing with a pure product of the power of scripting. It was essentially through the pre-established celebrity of his image, shaped by successful film scripts, that Schwarzenegger managed to channel the flows of confidence, hopes, and fears that raised him to the California governor's office. What won election in 2003 and 2006, thanks to the support of the funding and the networks tapped by the Republican Party, was an essentially fictional mix of muscular virility, irresistible strength, superhuman police officer, and slightly naive good intentions. Such a mix, it seems, has all the same weaknesses as the myths which it drapes itself in, but also the full power of the common affects which identify with these same myths. Far from a quirky exception (as befits the homeland of Disneyland), the case of Schwarzenegger reveals the both superficial and profound reality of all political personification in a mass-media democracy. In such systems, what wins election is always a condensation of credibility (around some logo/name/image), and what is in competition are always different mixes (in varying proportions) of lived reality and fictitious projections. In this sense, any democracy is a mythocracy.

For a long time now, media studies have analysed the symbiotic effects that develop between broadcasting channels and the logos that circulate on them. We watch a particular channel because we know that a particular celebrity often appears on it; a particular actor becomes a celebrity because he is frequently featured on a particular channel. Such mechanisms are developed through feedback loops that temporarily stabilise around a few attractors, due to the stickiness inherent in the flow of beliefs and desires. This stickiness, on which the logo's power of attraction is based, is more generally related to the phenomena of styles, genres, and filters that were discussed in Chapter 4. Insofar as a broadcasting channel is built around what suits its audience, it tends to make a selection of forms and content that 'naturally' fit into the framework of the conventions (of acceptability) that define it.

In between material infrastructure and symbolic 'stickiness', we should therefore recognise that inequalities in scripting power stand at the intersection of questions which concern both (1) access to the nodal points of the networks of dissemination and (2) the acceptability of certain logos to certain audiences. More than a century ago, Gabriel Tarde's sociology set out to identify the parameters characterising the multiplier-effects that condition the impact of a scripting activity within a given population. Once we begin to ask ourselves who is affected by what we say, we must then at least take into account (1) the *number of* people whose flows of affects the scripting efforts will have some effect on; (2) their *social weight*, depending on their status, function, prestige, notoriety, and everything else that determines the capacity of their behaviour (as 'decision-makers') to *influence* the mass behaviour of the public; and (3) the *intensity* and *precision of the conditioning* effected by the scripting.[8]

These multiplier effects are generated indifferently by certain points in the infrastructure (appearing on the TV news, on the *Tonight Show*, during the half-time of a World Cup final, making the front page of *Le Monde* or the *New York Times*) and by certain promotional vehicles (drawing on George Clooney's fame). In both cases, the power of scripting depends on access to a place or a celebrity capable of giving visibility to the story you are trying to spread, by multiplying its dissemination. It's easy to see the different vertical levels on which these inequalities of access are built, from family conversations to the White House press conference, via local radio stations, regional newspapers, popular websites, and national broadcasters.

At this point, we can identify at least three factors that determine the (always provisional) outcome of the struggles between scripting strategies in a mass-media mythocracy. These are (1) the *scarcity of access to the Archimedian points* of the broadcasting infrastructure; (2) the *filtering restrictions* operated by the conventions of acceptability that favour already open paths at the expense of new ones and those running in the opposite direction; and (3) the *constant need for renewal* that feeds the

8 See, for example, Gabriel Tarde, *Psychologie économique*, Paris: Alcan, 1902, vol. 1, p. 64.

instability inherent in media cultures' own conformism. The dynamic of mythocracy thrives on the – fundamentally unpredictable – interaction of these three contradictory factors. This is how the frontier between hidden and public transcripts is redrawn on a daily basis: a boundary that, as we have seen, conditions the very shape of the institutions that govern us.

Regulation or disintermediation?

A 'left-wing' (*dirigiste*) policy might consider regulatory measures to combat the current structural inequalities in access to scripting power. The welfare state has established a set of tax measures meant to redistribute income and thus keep a lid on the wealth inequalities produced by market forces. In France, there are regulatory measures to rein in Hollywood's domination of TV and cinema programming, to protect French-language artists, or to actively promote innovative films and music. Taxing advertising activities, with a strongly progressive scale corresponding to the budgets involved, could be used to redistribute financial resources towards cultural products that less directly obey (and profit from) market imperatives.

In the current calamitous state of the media sphere, which is dominated by the competition for revenue streams from advertising, such measures would surely be useful, despite their inevitably byzantine nature. But we can also imagine another 'left-wing' policy that could go in parallel with – or be an alternative to – such *dirigiste* measures. This policy would be designed to thwart the predominance effects that today govern the infrastructure of scripting power. It is hardly certain that the current hierarchies among the various levels of dissemination, or among the different multiplier levers, will continue as they are for any long time to come.

It is a cliché by this point to note that the transformations linked to the rise of the internet have brought about a major restructuring of the media landscape, modes of dissemination, and regimes of visibility. The circular logics of notoriety, generic norms, and the mimetic dynamics of convergences of desires are, of course, also exercised through digital media. But these media also have the (salutary) property of short-circuiting some of the dominant filters and the mass homogenisation processes produced during the era of megahertz broadcasting. Under the name of *disintermediation*, a new era has been much celebrated as allowing everyone and his brother-in-law to 'become-media'.[9] While this has had, and still promises to have, very beneficiary effects on the redistribution of the power to script, a number of limits have been reached, which could already be observed in certain forms of disintermediation already performed within broadcasting media. Reality TV, talk shows, and *vox pop* sequences can illustrate such shortcomings.

When a TV presenter's hands stretch out the microphone to some passers-by to ask them what they think of a strike, a scandal, a politician, we could greet a fine effort at mediatised 'demo-cracy', in the literal sense of foregrounding the power of the people to express themselves. This foregrounding is represented by the citizen in the street, who is accosted all of a sudden so that she can share her humble opinion with an entire nation gathered in front of their TV sets or computer screen. A similar foregrounding seemed to happen in highly successful TV programmes where families were brought on to pour their hearts out about their private dramas, washing their dirty laundry in public. In a more dignified way, everybody is welcome to contribute to common knowledge by proposing an entry to be included in Wikipedia, just like anybody can launch her own YouTube channel. In all such cases, we seem to be dealing with popular expression 'from below': each of us, as a *quidam* – a somebody who is nobody – can tell our own little story and thus influence our audience by widely sharing our feelings and thinking. Voices coming from 'little people' bypass the traditional mechanisms of authority, with their gatekeepers and inhibitions constitutive of the 'public transcript'. Such newcomers on the media scene do not speak from the heights of a position of authority (institutionally corroborated by some

9 On these issues, see Laurence Allard and Olivier Blondeau's excellent book *Devenir média. L'Activisme sur internet, entre défection et expérimentation*, Paris: Éditions Amsterdam, 2007.

title, some expertise, some claim of rationality). Rather, it is often because they are not 'somebody' but *quidam*, because they bring a 'direct' perspective from 'below', that they get a hearing.

This is where the distinctions between freedom of speech, access to media, and the power to script become crucial to understand. Despite their apparently similar status, the contributions that the *quidam* makes on Wikipedia and in a vox pop are radically different, if we judge them from the point of view of their scripting power. The difference is owed to the relationships that each of these mechanisms establishes between scripting from below and meta-scripting from above. In the case of Wikipedia, the contributor can write their article according to the temporality of their own thoughts. They can bring in elements of information and stories that they choose themselves, correcting whatever has been introduced by other contributors, on the same level as them, which they identify as unsatisfactory. In the case of the vox pop, the interviewee is generally caught unprepared, in a situation where he can say nothing other than the first banality that comes to mind. Even if they do manage to articulate a slightly complex and coherent analysis, their performance will be subjected to the scissors of an editor who will only retain a sentence cut according to needs and logics that are completely beyond the interviewee's control. Whereas in the first case, meta-scripting (from above) only intervenes at the margins, in the second, it is meta-scripting that controls and orients the production of words (according to the question put to the 'man in the street'), the public's access to them (according to the cuts made in editing), and their ultimate meaning (according to the position that the passer-by's reaction is supposed to illustrate within the logic of the report as a whole). The passer-by's best efforts at scripting are thus almost completely neutralised by the meta-scripting device.

It may be admitted that the vox pop represents an extreme case of meta-scripting violence – mitigated somewhat in the 'new' forms of media participation where I can fully control the production (editing, length, choice of guests) of my own personal video channel. But even in this case, the product presented to the public is fashioned not only by my sovereign free will, but rather by an interplay of scripting and counter-scripting that takes place between participants on the same level as each other – under conditions of competition that (unintentionally) meta-script a lot of what I can do and say if I want to find an actual audience. This is precisely the challenge posed for the digital media sphere: it will, indeed, be essential to devise post-media devices of a new type, which will allow scripting from below to collectively pull itself upward (through the vertical self-transcendence discussed in Chapter 2) rather than being caught up in twentieth-century televised vulgarity contests where whoever stoops the lowest wins the jackpot.

The media-delivered outpourings of pathos that invaded the airwaves at the end of the last century were, in general, dismaying. And yet they may turn out to be symptoms of something more encouraging. What they were capturing (and reducing to the tawdriest level) is a thirst for more open and egalitarian access to the power of scripting, which goes hand in hand with a fairly healthy mistrust of any discourse that assumes the privileges of authority. The fact that 'anyone could go on TV' (if possible, at prime time) could be seen as an important achievement. Provided, that is, that everyone is given the means to have something interesting and substantial to share (which is of course by no means always the case). The problem, then, is not one of access, but of empowerment – that is, of conquering a steady capacity to express ourselves from below with a reflexive grasp on an actual power to script our social transformations.

As long as our societies don't move in this direction, they will be haunted by the pathological forms of the 'Erostratus syndrome'. This is named after the Greek who, with no aim other than becoming famous and preserving his memory for posterity, set fire to the temple of Artemis in Ephesus. This is undoubtedly the syndrome that lies behind many of the 'desperate acts' that make the TV news headlines, from Columbine-style school shootings and the presidential assassination plots illustrated by *Taxi Driver* to suicide bombings carried out for political/religious ends. Each such case has, obviously, its own characteristics and motivations. But all of them present the greatest possible differential between an initial lack of access to media channels and the maximal scripting power achieved through the short-circuit of spectacular violence.

The 9/11 attacks were immediately counter-scripted and meta-scripted by a Republican Party which was impatient to tighten the screws on US society. But the perpetrators of the attacks did manage to impose (snippets of) their own script, across all the obstacles that barred their access to media visibility. Like a bumblebee flying through the spider's web that was supposed to imprison it, a gesture of this nature meta-scripts a media reaction that cannot fail to speak to an act of this magnitude. Beyond the very real horror experienced by the victims of this act of destruction, it is as a gesture of scripting that its power, scale, and significance must be measured. These 'terrorist' events themselves – sadly – illustrate a *takeover of scripting power from below*, even if, as we have seen with the Patriot Act and its twin brothers in European securitarianism, established frames are sometimes reconstituted with renewed force and an intensified grip.

Whether they explicitly serve a political, religious, or narcissistic cause, these violent scripting gestures, imposed from below, are not at all just the product of the (post-)mass-media era. Erostratus was already doing this in 356 BCE, Ravaillac in 1610 (with his assassination of Henri IV), and Damiens in 1757 (slashing Louis XV with a pen knife). Behind the horror, the human tragedies, and the harmful consequences of these acts, we need to learn to recognise the logics particular to the power of scripting that helped fuel such actions.[10] It is, likewise, important to identify, earlier on in the chain, the inequalities of access, the shortfalls of representation, the frustrations, the forms of hope and despair that might push young men to blow themselves up with suicide vests, to attack their former high school with a machine gun, or to assault passers-by with a knife while screaming *Allahu Akbar*.[11] And it also needs asking, further along the chain, what types of media scripting are liable to feed and exacerbate this type of behaviour, and what other reactions would be best able to resolve them.

10 On this subject, see the book by the Retort collective, *Afflicted Powers: Capital and Spectacle in a New Age of War*, London: Verso, 2005.

11 On this, see the insightful texts collected in John Berger, *Hold Everything Dear: Dispatches on Survival and Resistance*, London: Verso, 2016.

How can we use, bend, and arrange these logics in order to make subaltern discourses heard? How can we shift the frontier between hidden and public transcripts? How can we push its boundaries in the direction of achieving institutions and forms of life that are more sustainable, less unequal, more fulfilling, and fairer? These are some of the questions to be solved by a clearer understanding of our common power to script.

Literary Interlude

From Interrupted Myth to Epic in the Making

There is a tension running throughout this book, one that makes its references to narrativity and scripting unstable and perhaps sometimes confusing. On the one hand – drawing on quotations from Paul Ricœur and theories of storytelling – we focused on how narration can integrate our heterogeneous experiences into the finished horizon of the 'classic' unfolding of a story. This leads us, according to Aristotle's false truism, along the thread that runs from the 'beginning' of the story through its 'middle' and its 'end'. On the other hand, phenomena such as Wikipedia, advertising, and the public broadcaster's evening news programme are cited as references for the power of scripting – though, in each case, their 'narrative' character is at least questionable, at best enigmatic, and at worst indefensible. This tension, which may appear to be the result of a certain clumsiness in our argument, in fact (also) owes to deeper causes. These are worth explaining through a brief literary interlude, before we reach our conclusion.

The history of literary forms – rather snootily ignored in the preceding chapters – in the second half of the century saw the erosion of the (constantly reworked) narrative conventions that had gradually established themselves over the previous three centuries. If Ancien Régime literature had a quite considerable variety of modes of narration, hardly reducible to the canonical model of the Balzacian novel, our dominant vision of 'narrative' is still marked by models which, from *La Princesse de Clèves* and *Manon Lescaut* to *Les Misérables* and *La Recherche du temps perdu*, can be (more or less) easily summed up as a 'plot' with a beginning, middle, and end.[1] The structuralist appropriation of Aristotelian definitions, the examples of the *Iliad*, the *Odyssey*, and some medieval novels convince us (all too easily) that 'narrative' constitutes an autonomous and self-sufficient category within discursive forms, and that it is only through 'transgressive practices' or (secondary) 'hybridisations' that it can become contaminated by other, rival discursive functions. But we could easily write an alternative literary history, in which the isolation and standardisation of the narrative function would be the exception: from Herodotus to the present day, via Abbé Bordelon and all those whom literary tradition has condemned to the status of 'novelistic monstrosities', 'stories' have always been a battlefield on which narrative interminably has crossed swords with factual and informative elements, commentary, political protest, philosophical reflection, encyclopaedic temptations, or moral satire.[2] Resituated in such a battlefield, the comparisons made in the preceding pages between Madame de La Pommeraye, the Widow of the Île de Ré, Wikipedia, advertising, and the TV news do not seem so incongruous. By establishing a rivalry between narration and explanation, Walter Benjamin did more to mark out this common battlefield than to separate discourses into watertight categories:

> Every morning, news reaches us from around the globe. And yet we lack remarkable stories. Why is this the case? It is because no incidents reach us any longer not already permeated with explanations. In other words: almost nothing occurs to the story's benefit anymore, but

1 On this point, see the collection of articles edited by Marc Escola and Jean-Paul Sermain, *La Partie et le Tout. Les Moments de la lecture romanesque sous l'Ancien Régime (XVIIe–XVIIIe siècles)*, Louvain: Peeters, 2010.

2 On this point, see Mathieu Brunet's excellent book *L'Appel du monstrueux. Pensées et poétiques du désordre en France au XVIIIe siècle*, Louvain: Peeters, 2008.

> instead it all serves information. In fact, at least half of the art of storytelling consists in keeping one's tale free of explanation.[3]

Rather than a separation, there is a constitutive tension between information, explanation, and narrative. As we have seen, a piece of information or an explanation takes on a concrete meaning for us only insofar as we can insert it within an essentially narrative schema of action (*I do this, and, as a consequence, this or that will happen, for better or worse*). On the other hand, any narrative is the bearer of an exemplary sequence of actions, which is capable of acquiring an informative and explanatory virtue, as in the classic connection between temporal unfolding (*post hoc*) and causal consequence (*propter hoc*). If the art of the storyteller consists in 'keeping one's tale free of explanation', this is not because narration is allergic to explanation as such, but, rather, because it is linked to it too closely. When the bad storyteller brings in an (explicit) explanation, they will only limit the open number of (potential) explanations that the narrative by its own virtue entails.

The power of scripting operates precisely within the constant exchanges that take place, at every level, between informative narratives and narrativised explanations. It is (partly) because 'left-wing' forces have failed to appreciate the full extent of these exchanges that they have allowed the worst 'right-wing' narratives to occupy the political and media battlefield:

> The idea that ideologies had died out brought with it the idea that it was enough to relate the facts – that the facts were enough to mobilise people. Well, ideologies may be dead, but people still need frames, value frameworks to read reality with. If we don't work on that and let the right do it, people will go out and vote utterly against their own interests – as long as they can elect someone with those frames . . . We need symbols, myths. If you let the right create them (from the top down) and you abandon that terrain and limit yourself to saying

3 Walter Benjamin, 'The Art of Storytelling', in *The Storyteller Essays*, ed. Samuel Titan, trans. Tess Lewis, New York: New York Review Books, 2019, p. 35.

> 'There was 10% unemployment, now it's 12% and payroll taxes were at 15%, now they're at 11% . . .', you're not going to warm people's hearts! You think it's all about offering a series of numbers: but you're giving abstractions, when we need to be capable of constructing stories.[4]

'We need to be capable of constructing stories': this phrase perfectly expresses a historical necessity, experienced in the mode of an impotent lament. In fact, this 'need for myth' is not simply a call for politicians to hire professional storytellers to get their 'message' across. We need a certain mythopoetic voluntarism, but so, too, a better understanding of how myths circulate in order to produce stories that have real impact. Myths that bring new kinds of emancipation can only arise in synergy with desires, beliefs, and stories that are already circulating, in a diffuse state, among the multitudes. These are the desires, beliefs, and stories that the storyteller will manage to bring together and to condense (as in the etymology of the German word designating the poet as a *Dichter*).

> Myth cannot be conjured up artificially, just like that, just because someone calls for it. It has to emerge from reality, from below. There has to be a moment of spontaneity. The shared narratives that always emerge in social movements have never been projected from above – and if they are, they are just propaganda tools. They take form because they emerge from a social reality and someone has been able to work on them.[5]

There is, then, a tension between the unifying power of myths and the disjointed fragmentation of the 'latest events on the face of the earth' (which cannot be enrolled under crude ideological banners without thereby imposing a mutilating violence on them). This should lead us, in

4 Wu Ming, 'Wu Ming: La Narration comme technique de lutte', trans. G. Pascon, interview, *Politique. Revue de débats*, no. 56 (October 2008); available online at wumingfoundation.com.

5 Ibid.

the first instance, to base the production of stories on a game of listening, calling, and responding that takes place among a multitude of storytellers/information givers. Insofar as this collective interplay is beyond the control of any individual storyteller, those who set out to provide our present with the emancipatory myths it so desperately needs can only feel the sense of helplessness implicit in an awareness that 'We need to be capable of constructing stories' in tune with the multitude's aspirations. To avoid the paralysing effects of this impotent necessity, we can revisit the remarkably fine diagnosis made by Jean-Luc Nancy in his great 1986 book *La Communauté désœuvrée* (*The Inoperative Community*). Instead of deploring it, he saw our lack of myths as an opportunity to redefine literature and, in parallel with it, community:

> Whether one laments that mythic power is exhausted or that the will to this power ends in crimes against humanity, everything leads us into a world in which mythic resources are profoundly lacking. To think our world in terms of this 'lack' might well be an indispensable task.[6]

This lack of myth seems at first to have dramatic consequences, since, 'just as there is no new mythology, so there is no new community either, nor will there be'.[7] However, this assertion loses its despairing character once the new form of community we are called upon to constitute is no longer really a classic 'community', defined by a fusional, productive, operative project, or by an organic unity, but a community that 'assumes the impossibility of its own immanence, the impossibility of a communitarian being in the form of a subject'.[8] This means, indeed, an *inoperative* community, made up of irreducible separate singularities, which nevertheless live out their individuation on the horizon of the common that nourishes them all. Rather than a 'lack' of myth, Jean-Luc Nancy

6 Jean-Luc Nancy, *The Inoperative Community*, Minneapolis: University of Minnesota Press, 1991, p. 47.

7 Ibid., p. 57.

8 Ibid., p. 15.

focuses on the inevitable *interruption of myth*, which would open up the possibility of a new definition of community:

> The interruption of myth . . . disjoins myth from itself, or withdraws it from itself . . . In the interruption of myth something makes itself heard, namely what remains of myth when it is interrupted – and which is nothing if not the very voice of interruption, if we can say this. This voice is the voice of community, or of the community's passion.[9]

It would be tempting to see, in the countless interruptions of Jacques the Fatalist's account of his love affairs, a prefiguration of the 'interruption of myth' which is here presented as constitutive of both a new way of being-in-common and a certain definition of literature (and writing). Indeed, Diderot's work has often been read as an anticipation of the boldest experiments in the novel form that would mark the twentieth century. Through it, and far beyond, various aspects of the literary creation of the last fifty years become really meaningful when they are read as 'what remains of myth when it is interrupted'. Whether they are written against the grain of the Balzacian model of narrative, like the Nouveau Roman; written against the myths of Empire, Femininity, Conjugality, or Prosperity, like the authors of subaltern literature; written drawing on the words of the voiceless, or setting themselves apart from the advertising slogans or instructions to be happy that so pervade our lives – the richest literary endeavours of recent decades have developed through the combination of a 'voice of interruption' and a 'passion for community'.

> 'Literature' (or 'writing') is what, in literature . . . interrupts myth by giving voice to being-in-common . . . Thus, once myth is interrupted, writing recounts our history to us again. But it is no longer a narrative – neither grand nor small – but rather an offering: a history is offered to us. Which is to say that an event – and an advent – is proposed to

9 Ibid., pp. 61–2.

> us, without its unfolding being imposed upon us. What is offered to us is that community is coming about, or rather, that something is happening to us in common.[10]

Such a definition of literature perfectly illustrates a certain tension which we already considered during Chapter 4. This, we said, was a tension between the simplifying modelling inherent in the work of the *plot* and the escapist power carried by the dynamics of *writing*. This definition of literature is not confined to a contradiction between opposing and incompatible demands – far from it. Rather, it exacerbates and transcends the tension that is constitutive of contemporary forms of scripting power, insofar it makes it impossible to draw any clear distinction between the narrative and the event. The 'voice of interruption', heard in the aborted syntax of Jean-Luc Lagarce's characters, as in the suspended slogans of Hugues Jallon's novels, succeeds in making apparent the impossibility and harmfulness of myth, in making us feel the need for another form of community, and to tell our story without giving us the comfort of a grand narrative or even a lesser one.

What we are presented with is, indeed, a matter of 'events', just like on the TV news bulletin. Unlike the latter, which imposes a pre-scripted sequence on us and sets factual information against a backdrop of 'explanations' (which are generally both superficial and implicit), the story offered to us by such literary works proposes a happening to which we are invited as participants (and not just as spectators). Even if the story is told in the past tense, the work of writing makes it an event that 'is today happening to us in common'. This, because we are called upon to react to it within the horizon of a 'community that is coming about', and, indeed, because it is in the very nature of the event that it takes on a meaning only through the interpretations, care, and loyalties to which its traces are subjected.

There is today a literary enterprise which, I think, embodies this interruption of myth, and which strives – with varying degrees of success – to make this same voice of interruption resonate in the contemporary

10 Ibid., pp. 63–4, 69.

world. This is a group of Italian writers, first registered under the collective identity of Luther Blissett, then in 2000 joining together under the name (or literally, 'no name') Wu Ming. They condense a series of practices, stances, and theories that provide an excellent platform for reflection on the status of stories, myths, communities, and scenarios at the dawn of the new millennium – offering a rich springboard for (literary) forms of scripting that are still to be invented.[11]

By abolishing author names, the creators coming together in Wu Ming are practising the 'interruption of the myth of the writer' of which Jean-Luc Nancy spoke, and indeed do so as a central dimension of the interruption of myth which characterises our broader historical situation. In a context where a whole series of writers are 'experimenting, in literature, with collaborative arrangements between authors, between writers and the public', they constitute – to use the term proposed by Félix Guattari – 'collective assemblages of enunciation' in variable combinations.[12] They compose certain narratives together, by various techniques of collaboration, writing other texts solo (published under the code names of Wu Ming 1, Wu Ming 2, etc.), but often invite each other to insert notes, remarks, or various interventions in their writings. As Jean-Luc Nancy put it in 1986, they embody 'thinking, the practice of a sharing of voices and of an articulation according to which there is no singularity but that exposed in common, and no community but that offered to the limit of singularities'.[13] It is the articulation between the singularity of all writing and the commonality of a multitude, from which this singularity comes and to which it must return, that represents 'a voice that could never be the voice of any subject, a speech that could never be the conviction of any understanding and that is merely the voice and the thought of community in the interruption of myth.'[14]

11 See the collective's website at wumingfoundation.com.

12 Wu Ming, 'Wu Ming: La Narration comme technique de lutte'. My thanks to André Gattolin for helping me discover Luther Blissett, and Maurizio Vito for familiarising me with the different focuses and issues involved in Wu Ming's work.

13 Nancy, *The Inoperative Community*, p. 80.

14 Ibid.

This collective assemblage of enunciation opens itself up to a proliferation of works that develop under no outside control. Their overabundance, diversity, and heterogeneity undermine the notion of 'The Work' even more radically than does any ascetic-type 'inoperativity'. Each book released by Wu Ming is part of a community and a transmediality in the making, since it

> is potentially surrounded by a quantum cloud of homages, spin-offs and 'lateral' narrations: stories written by readers (fan fiction), comic strips, drawings and illustrations, songs, websites, and even networked or tabletop games inspired by the books, role-playing games with characters from the books and other contributions from 'below', to the open and changing nature of the work and the world that lives within it.[15]

As soon as we consent to interrupt the myth of the writer, it appears that, as Jean-Luc Nancy had it, 'the myth communicates itself' of its own accord, through proximity and contagion, along the model of the Saturnalia.

The writing practices proposed by Wu Ming, in their effort to produce narratives that are 'complex and popular at the same time', may seem to lag behind (or to exceed) a certain formal rigour imposed by other contemporary literary endeavours.[16] But I think that their main strength

15 Wu Ming 1, *New Italian Epic: Memorandum 1993–2008: Narrative Literature, Oblique Point of View, Back to the Future*, trans. E. Paint. Available at wumingfoundation.com; translated here from the Italian original at carmillaonline.com.

16 Wu Ming makes a conscious effort to enact a 'hidden' subversion of language and style: 'Many of these books are also stylistically and linguistically experimental, but the experimentation is not noticeable if you read the pages in a hurried or distracted way. Often it is a *concealed* experiment that aims to subvert from within the linguistic register commonly used in *genre fiction*. From the outset, the style seems simple and flat, with no peaks or troughs, and yet if you slow down your reading speed, you can perceive something strange, a series of echoes that produce a cumulative effect. If we pay attention to the sequence of words and sentences, we gradually discover a "swarming", a set of small interventions that alter the syntax, the sounds and the meanings. One example of a "hidden" intervention: stripping out an indefinite adjective from a text (e.g. "each", "all"), or adverbs with the inflectional

lies in the renewal of the epic genre, which they explicitly set on their theoretical horizon:

> These stories are *epic* because their subject matter is historical or mythic, heroic or in any case adventurous endeavours: wars, inland expeditions, journeys of initiation, struggles for survival, always within wider conflicts that decide the fate of classes, peoples, nations or even humanity as a whole, against a backdrop of historical crises, catastrophes and social formations on the brink of collapse . . . The epic provides a vast perspective. It allows us to tell stories where there are multitudes, where there are conflicts, where there are complex dynamics.[17]

It is easy to see what Wu Ming is here thumbing its nose at. There is a whole critical discourse on the transition from the epics of ancient times – taken for expressions of primitive communities – to the modern novel, contemporary with the emergence of possessive individualism. Clearly, Wu Ming does not agree that this evolution is necessarily a one-way street. Claiming to be part of a new (Italian) epic genre is to reassert the anchoring of narrative activity in the movements and flows that animate the multitudes. This is, on the one hand, because Wu Ming's stories emanate from a collective body, in constant connection with listening to social movements and being a relay for them. But, as well as that, the chains of actions represented in these stories are themselves carried by collective agents (artistic movements, classes, peoples, nations, or humanity as a whole).

The community described by Jean-Luc Nancy stems from the impossibility of establishing a fusional (organic, operative) community. And,

---

"-ly", or even pronoun particles ("me", "you", etc.), even where they are unavoidable, like in reflexive verbs. A British reviewer of our novel *Q* [i.e. by Luther Blissett] was struck by "a tendency to drop verbs in descriptions of fights in a not unsuccessful attempt to convey the confusion and speed of the action" ' (Wu Ming 1, *New Italian Epic*).

17 Wu Ming 1, *New Italian Epic*; and Wu Ming, 'Wu Ming: La Narration comme technique de lutte'.

likewise, the new epic practised by Wu Ming makes no attempt to describe the triumphal march of a people guided by a tutelary hero towards the founding of a nation with the mission of world domination. This new epic is out of step with the old genre in at least three ways: it focuses on *eccentric* heroes, on moments of *contingent* bifurcation, and on communities driven to retain their *minority status* (central European peasants, Laotian guerrillas, Iroquois tribes, Irish, Scots, Canadians, free jazz musicians), and sometimes driven to *extinction* (rather than promised a glorious future). 'The epic hero, when there is one, is not at the centre of everything, but indirectly influences the action. When there isn't one, his function is fulfilled by the multitude, by things and places, by context and by time.'[18] The chain of actions which these collective characters are swept up in resists forming a thick plot, and manifests itself rather as an (unpredictable) 'event': the knots of structural necessities and local indeterminations that make them tipping points are loaded with enormous consequences, even though they emanate from the most fragile and apparently least inevitable coincidences. Turning Walter Benjamin's thinking on its head, the new epic informs us of events that have *not* occurred on the earth's surface, through 'alternative histories and potential uchronies': 'what would have happened if the failure of event to happen (for example: Napoleon's defeat at Waterloo, the attack on Pearl Harbor, the counter-offensive at Stalingrad) had produced a different course of History?'[19]

Following the example of Herodotus, these 'histories' take the form of *investigations*, in which the narration reintegrates politics into an ethnographic perspective. This reveals History to be a construction site, which is constantly being ransacked and reinvented, rather than a series of monumentalised triumphs. Between the events in the making and the aborted futures glimpsed through counterfactual uchronies, between, on the one hand, a great work of historical research, a constant effort at political theorising, the invention of scripts conducive to being both complex and popular and, on the other hand, writing that practises a

18 Wu Ming 1, *New Italian Epic*.
19 Ibid.

'hidden' subversion of stylistic codes – this new epic represents a remarkably coherent scripting project. It steers the tension between information and narrative in an original and promising direction – one that ought to make its mark on the TV news, and not just in the bookshop windows.

The plots of these new epics tend to depict warlike situations; and Wu Ming 1 asserts that 'literature must not, must never, must never believe itself to be at peace'. But this scripting project is more a declaration of contingency and freedom ('literature *must* never') than a declaration of war. It starts from a keen awareness of the strategic nature of power relations and scripting practices (neither literature nor the achievements of past emancipation struggles 'can ever believe they are at peace'). But, far from making us dream of winning crushing victories, it is based on a principle of each and every one of us participating in the activities of narration and scripting. It is a shared site for the construction of the common good, by virtue of the collaborations between *quidams* – anonymous nobodies – that it helps our imaginations to forge. 'What remains of the myth when it is interrupted' are, perhaps, the voices of fragile minority epics that teach us to live in an eternal construction (and destruction) site. Which is to say, a site alien to the peace of final achievements (which no doubt overly resembles the peace in a cemetery) but remains ever-open to the rearrangements that might be imagined by our power for scripting.

6

Renewing Left-Wing Imaginaries

'The left' needs to tell (itself) more inspiring stories – and to gain hold of the means of spreading them as widely as possible. Countless novelists, playwrights, filmmakers, singers, and series developers already produce myriads of emancipating stories. What's often missing are the relays between these great plots and effective political traction, translated in terms of electoral victories and political thrusts. The previous chapters have offered a few models in our exploration of mythocracy.

In his narrativising machinations, Apollo threw Orestes into the arms of Athena, while also gifting him with precious, enchanting words – in so doing, helping to establish Athenian democracy. Sun Ra imagined himself as having come from Saturn, built the community of the Myth-Science Arkestra around himself, and paraded his extraterrestrial carnival around the four corners of the Earth. In so doing, he pushed back the boundaries of what could be said and heard, in his struggle against racism and in the cause of artistic creativity. Wu Ming is today piecing together a collective identity and inventing a new Italian epic in order to give a shared voice to the interruption of the communalist myth. In so doing, Wu Ming is laying the groundwork for a 'literary communism' which has freed itself from any dictatorship of the proletariat.

Faced with the difficulties that 'the left' (in France) today encounters in devising a myth able to serve as its foundation, we will suggest one first avenue to be explored. This particular avenue also has the advantage of requiring only the smallest spark of imagination. Why not start, modestly, from the latent fear that we feel building up, both all around us and within ourselves – the fear of sinking into a hole? And what if the most immediate means of responding to the interruption of myth was to forge ourselves a (little) *myth of interruption*?

The tale of the *Maladroite* fairy

Once upon a time there was a nation carried at breakneck speed by a vast machine racing towards the abyss. Everyone aboard was busy making sure that the craft kept going as fast as possible, convinced that to slow down even slightly would allow other crews to take the lead in the race for Growth. They showed no mercy as they lashed their whips against those on the outside, who gripped onto the doors as they tried to clamber on to the wagon of prosperity. Those on the inside did suspect that in some distant future – albeit one growing closer each day – the road, and the myth, would suddenly be interrupted. For the crews working hardest, this portended a catastrophic collapse. But, curiously enough, few of the passengers bothered to draw out the full consequences of the threat that was now bearing down on them.

Everyone's attention was captured by the rivalry between four fairies, who each hankered after the privilege of laying their hands on the steering wheel. The Resentful fairy blamed the clandestine passengers – the ones who gripped onto the outside doors or had even managed to sneak into the craft – for the sometimes-violent jolts suffered by those who did have valid tickets, acquired (it was said) at great sacrifice. As for the Industrious fairy, it skilfully fanned the flames of resentment, but was also aware that these clandestine passengers were among the ones making the most direct contribution to the machine's onward progress. It exhorted the others to work even harder, to gain even more of these famous Growth numbers. The Proletarian fairy, who rather missed the stability of the good old days (of heavy industry and colonisation) sharply denounced (and not without reason) the highly unequal distribution of the cushions within the craft: for this meant that while a privileged minority barely felt the bumps along the road, most of the other passengers' behinds were put hard to the test. As for the Sweet-Talking fairy, constantly torn between its old complicity with the Proletariat and its acknowledged dependency on Finance, it resorted to the most outlandish (and least convincing) slogans in a desperate bid to reconcile the ogre of market competitiveness with the hobgoblin of social fairness.

After the machine had suffered a series of shocks a little sharper than the previous ones – a Growth 'crisis', they kept saying – it resumed its breakneck advance, having barely modified its course. The four fairies immediately returned to their competition, seeking to devise the most ingenious ways of rallying as many passengers as possible under their own leadership. The Resentful fairy did marvellously at spreading baseless alarmism and harsh calls for vengeance; the Proletarian fairy used the very finest deductive reasoning to demonstrate that the State remained the only guarantor of a common prosperity for all; the Industrious fairy offered ever more bonuses and incentives to stimulate each individual to push the limits of excellence; the Sweet-Talking fairy dusted off the most hackneyed slogans, picked out from all corners, as it sought to give them a new lustre. All four were proud of their perfect mastery of their briefs, their seriousness, their weightiness, their competence, and their expertise.

Anyone who bothered to look out of the front of the machine would already have seen the first unmistakable signs of the abyss immediately ahead of them. And one day a fifth fairy, with a dodgy haircut and a growling voice, started to speak. No one had ever paid attention to it being there before, or its previous attempts to intervene. It was suspected of being another ticketless, likely jobless, intruder, one of these 'welfare scroungers' living at the Republic's expense, whom everyone was busy trying to put back on the sacred course of paid work.

How they laughed when they heard it present itself as the Maladroite fairy![1] They barely even cared to shrug when it stammered out its programme, which even it hardly seemed to believe, and which came down to just one point: to make the sharpest possible left turn, without delay and even without calculating it in advance.

The Industrious fairy made a condescending display of compassion as it learnedly explained to the Maladroite fairy what 'a folly' such a left turn would be – all too obviously, such a move would risk the machine tipping over. The Sweet-Talking fairy thought it rather witty to add that it was no surprise that a Maladroite fairy would suggest such a catalogue of gaucheness.[2]

Everyone grinned for a moment, before they got back to work again, more industriously than ever. Reassured by the consensus among so many experts in matters of security, they continued full tilt along the unyielding line of accelerated Growth.

Interrupting the myth of King Growth

This book makes no claim to provide recipes which can be used to concoct 'left-wing stories' able to mount an assault on our media cultures. It is clear that a party of 'the left' cannot hope to win the next elections by spinning a tale like the story of the Maladroite fairy. My goal in this final chapter is not to 'solve' the many difficulties that 'left-wing' politicians face – whether on the terrain of theoretical elaboration or of communicating through the media. It is simply to make clear some of the conditions that would allow them to make a *real* turn to the left, at the level demanded by the social transformations that are now underway, and with the intellectual boldness that makes up the real tradition of progressive thought.

1 *Translator's note*: The French is a pun on *maladroit* ('clumsy', 'awkward') and *mal à droite* ('uncomfortable on the right', 'sick on the right').

2 *Translator's note*: *Gauche* means 'left' as well as 'clumsy', 'awkward'; 'gaucheness' [for the French *gaucherie*] should be understood as a mix of 'clumsiness', 'uneasiness', and 'leftism' [*gauchisme*].

When it comes to the contents of this turn, some of its main axes are obvious already. To identify as on 'the left' today means – as the previous chapter suggested – reframing political discourse around the question of *equality*. We are heading towards the abyss at full speed – but this abyss has to do not only with the deterioration of our natural environment, as a 'surface-level environmentalism' invites us to think. As deep ecology and ecofeminism emphasise, it also has to do with the deterioration of our *relations* with our fellow humans, and with other living beings. Worsening inequalities threaten the human relations on which our mental state depends, just as much as mounting global warming or the risk of nuclear contamination threaten the conditions of our biological survival.

After decades of false alternatives between (capitalist) liberty and (socialist) equality, a genuine turn to 'the left' must be based on the assertion of the fundamental inextricability of these two ideals. Étienne Balibar has aptly proposed that they be combined in a single demand for equaliberty.[3] As against the illusions promoted by individualist ideology, the emancipation processes regarding each of us as individuals (the freedom to become what I feel I should be) cannot be separated from the modes of egalitarian participation in the common goods on which our futures depend. Whether we are talking about the power of money or the potential force of the human mind, wealth is inevitably impoverished by its contact with poverty: the price of insecurity, of fear, of vulnerability, of isolation, of the feeling of iniquity – each the toll of situations of extreme inequality – always overwhelms the exclusive benefits that the privileged seem to enjoy.

To say that you are on 'the left' today, of course, also and above all means interrupting the myth of King Growth.[4] This remains necessary,

3 See Étienne Balibar, *Equaliberty: Political Essays*, Durham, NC: Duke University Press, 2014.

4 Dipesh Chakrabarty makes a proposal within an apparently very different perspective, with which I would nonetheless like to make my own argument convergent. He suggests that we conceive capitalism's globalising developments in terms of the interaction between two types of History, one of which *interrupts* the other. There is *History 1*, the history of a 'universal and necessary' logic of capital, whose own

even though this myth is today the object of a consensus embracing the whole spectrum of discourse from the Front National to the encrusted residues of the French Communist Party – passing via the large majority of the institutional 'left's' official representatives.

A stance at odds with such a consensus means not just taking the fruits of GDP growth and 'distribute them more fairly', but rejecting GDP as *the* measure of the sovereign Good and quantitative growth as the main yardstick of 'progress'. Whether they come from an old working-class tradition or they were more recently borrowed from neoliberal governance, a whole parade of slogans and demands today raised by 'the left' deserve to be pulped. Let us take in a brief overview of some of these.

The thing we should be fighting for is *not* purchasing power. After all, the (average) purchasing power of the (statistically defined) European household increases each time a company offshores production in order to profit from low Chinese wages and allow us to import consumer goods at indecently low prices. The world economy is thus made 'more efficient' and global growth 'boosted'. Far from it needing to be increased yet further, our (aggregate) purchasing power as consumers in wealthy countries is already unsustainably overheated. We are overindulging not only in poverty wages – the meagre amounts paid to producers subject to untrammelled competition – but also in energy resources (wood, coal, oil, gas, uranium). Currently, we are paying only a fraction of these resources' real cost, because their price takes no account of the trail of

---

movement poses the conditions of its expansion and intensification; this is plagued (and potentially threatened) by *History 2s*, 'which always modify and interrupt the totalizing thrusts of History 1'. These History 2s are made up of reflexes, customs, collective practices, relations with other living beings that make us *something other* than mediations of the reproduction of capital – music lovers and not just piano makers, Bengalis and not just workers, Hindus and not just entrepreneurs. 'The idea of History 2 beckons us to more *affective* narratives of human belonging where life forms, although porous to one another, do not seem exchangeable through a third term of equivalence such as abstract labor . . . What interrupts and defers capital's self-realization are the various History 2s that always modify History 1 and thus act as our grounds for claiming historical difference.' Dipesh Chakrabarty, *Provincializing Europe*, Princeton, NJ: Princeton University Press, 2000, pp. 63, 66, 71.

destruction brought by environmental damages. Far from demanding an increase in purchasing power, the European 'left' ought to be putting on the agenda *a* fairer distribution of this purchasing power *on a world scale* – which could also entail a real *reduction* of this purchasing power across wide, currently privileged, layers of our populations.

A 'left-wing' politics needs to *shake off the whole pro-work imaginary* of waged employment indexed to the production of quantifiable goods. For decades, feminists have been fighting for the recognition of the work carried out in the home, which is excluded from all GDP figures even though it represents a creation of wealth equivalent to a third of the total.[5] It is time that they were not only listened to, but their demand generalised: whether men or women, occupied in breastfeeding, hoovering, shopping for an elderly person, making dinner for friends, helping an asylum seeker, or putting on a play, all of us are co-producers of a common, transindividual social fabric which constitutes the material and affective infrastructure of all our existences. A stable, guaranteed income remains an essential demand, of course. But it ought to be decoupled from a wage-form (fetishised by a certain traditional 'left') which integrates individuals into the productive fabric only through its simultaneous operation as a vector of exploitation (through the constraint of the wage relation to which the worker is subjected) and as a factor of exclusion (through the stigma attached to the status of the 'unemployed').

The fact that neoliberalism does its best to erode all forms of common good –indeed, suicidally so – does not impose the need for an a priori defence of *the State* apparatuses that administer these common goods. Allowing itself to get caught in the trap of the alternative between State and Market, the French 'left' has blinded itself to the radical-democratic, 'autonomist' tradition – notwithstanding the life which this tradition breathed into 'the left' across the last two centuries. A politics of 'the left' should define itself both against the competition generalised by the Market, and against the disempowering bureaucratic apparatuses of the

5 See Matxalen Legarreta Iza's fine article 'Le *temps donné* dans le travail domestique et de care', *Multitudes*, nos 37–38 (2009), pp. 106–12.

State (and of large firms). Even in the knowledge that it cannot bypass either of these modes of regulation entirely, it must cultivate a radically critical attitude towards each of them.

Aside from these traditional warhorses of the historic 'left' (purchasing power, the centrality of work, Statism), another thing to be avoided are all those apparently attractive watchwords attached to the idea of '*good governance*' – with its inherent but concealed subservience to the quantifying fetish for GDP. To accept the need to promote 'competitiveness', 'excellence', 'transparency', 'efficiency', and 'balanced books' – in the manner of many leaders eager to give 'the left' a renovating, modernising, enlightened, responsible, undogmatic tone – is the most insidious betrayal that the movements they claim to represent can suffer (and the one which costs the highest price in terms of the political damage it causes).

Even if just as a provocation, it should be insisted that today the very idea of 'managing' a pre-given reality should be considered the main enemy of all progressive politics. Of course, that does not mean that it is pointless, and still less blameful, to strive to manage the given situation. For any form of life, it is vitally necessary to make calculations (which can be more or less formalised or intuitive) regarding the best use of potentially scarce resources. From this point of view, the often-thankless work of administrators at all levels is doubtless to be considered valuable. Even so, this work is not itself 'left-wing' – or, more precisely, the one thing that today ought to define 'the left' is the impulse to denounce *the radical insufficiency of managing the given.*

A short history of left-wing gestures

To grasp the implications of such an impulse, and its specific character, we need to take in a rapid overview of the different phases in the history of 'left-wing' demands, looking back to the French Revolution, which seated the deputies closer to the old royalist regime on the 'right' of the assembly's hemisphere, and those who most radically criticised it on the 'left'. We can thus briefly distinguish between *four orders of rejection* which have successively emerged in the discourse emanating from the left wing of politics over the last three centuries.[6]

The eighteenth century saw the coagulation, among certain intellectual elites, of a *rejection of the Divinities* which were supposed to regulate human affairs. This involved a rejection of the mediators (priests) and institutions (ecclesiastical apparatuses) in charge of communicating with (illusory) transcendental powers. In this we can again see the foundational move at the basis of the imaginary of power we sought to outline in Chapter 2. Contrary to the Pauline doctrine which had dominated Western thought for over a millennium, in this imaginary, power does not descend from some divine origin but emanates from the immanent potential force of the multitude.

Independently (or not) of religious and metaphysical beliefs, 'left-wing' forces also expressed themselves through the *rejection of Sovereigns.* Once power was conceived as resulting from an appropriation of the potential force of the multitude, there was no lack of voices questioning the way in which sovereigns managed the (common) power with which they were invested. From the anti-absolutist heirs to Hobbes, to those who denounced the Hungarian, Czech, and Polish *nomenklatura* – passing, of course, via the French, Russian, and Chinese revolutions – a constitutive act of 'the left' was to question, or push into crisis, the top of a State apparatus accused of not administering the people's common goods according to the people's common interests.

In more or less close connection to these first two, a third move characteristic of the demands raised by the left wing of the political assemblies which convened over the last two centuries was a *rejection of Appropriations.* The illegitimacy of political power and the hollowness of religious mediations was often all the more starkly apparent to multitudes whose urge to fill their empty stomachs drove them to challenge the distribution of material goods. In this case, what aroused indignation was not the abusive oppression exercised by the representatives of

6 I sought to expand upon this point in 'De la voyance à la contre-scénarisation', in Alain Jugnon, ed., *Une révolution nécessaire, laquelle?*, Villeurbanne: Golias, 2009, pp. 119–40.

political power but rather an intolerable inequality or a revolting injustice in the appropriation and distribution of goods and services. Here, 'the left' demanded that the propertied render unto the exploited part of what they monopolised by unjustly dispossessing their labour. Such a demand could take different forms, from demands for higher wages to 'proletarian appropriation' – including the looting through which the exploited took back what had been stolen from them by the system of exploitation (as humorously portrayed in Dario Fo's marvellous *Non si paga!*).[7] The main challenge for today's 'left' (in the West) is to reject the current modes of appropriations *at the planetary scale*, and not only within the borders of any national entity.

These three types of rejection certainly do remain pertinent in this early part of the twenty-first century, depending on the particular context of each political situation. But it is also important to take note of a fourth move. If this latter was long associated with the other three in latent fashion, it is now taking on a force of its own, in the form of a *rejection of the Given*. Unlike in the previous case – the challenge to existing forms of appropriation, to demand more for the most deprived – this is not a matter of wanting to lay our hands on something we think we have every right to. Rather, it is a matter of refusing something which is apparently given (the *datum*, hence *data*), refusing to swallow what we are fed up with already. This rejection adopts the perspective of anorexia, abstentionism, and absenteeism, constituted as political acts: 'Your data, your hamburgers, your electoral circus, your stress bonuses, I don't want them, I can't take it anymore!' Contrary to the simplistic interpretations which some psychoanalysts fall into in their explanations of anorexia, we are not 'missing' lack itself. It is much more that what is given to us does not suit us, that we feel a growing disgust towards it, to the point that it ends up no longer being acceptable at all.

This is no longer the same context as a crisis of subsistence, such as would demand the redistribution of scarce resources shared out too unfairly. Rather – in sharp and all the more revolting contrast with the

7 Dario Fo, *We Won't Pay and Other Works*, New York: Theatre Communications Group, 2001.

very real forms of hardship and artificial indigence forced upon the underprivileged even in the wealthiest countries – we are in a situation of over-abundance in which the plethora itself becomes oppressive. We can identify this move with the example of activists who smash shop windows but have no intention of looting what is inside, as in the case of anti-WTO and anti-G8 demonstrations. Here, it is not a matter of taking that of which we have been dispossessed but of destroying a shameless surplus which is indecent for the privileged to adorn themselves with. If such a gesture were to be vested with a 'revolutionary' dimension, it would have much less to do with the fact of attacking a luxury boutique, as with the *refusal to take what we are supposed to want*.

This rejection of the Given involves a dimension of auto-affection. Indeed, it presupposes that a certain alteration (intentional or otherwise) takes place *within me*, before it has consequences for power-structures or the prevalent logics of appropriation in the outside world. The rejection of the Given is based on a *self-refusal of my own sensibility*. Recognising this allows us to get a better understanding of what separates this last type of move from the previous three. While these others had to do with opposing external and objective characteristics of reality (the power of priests, and what they say, the actions of a government, the principles underlying the distribution of goods), this fourth move consists of fighting against one's own self (hence the dimension of *self*-refusal), against one's own habits, some of one's own desires, one's spontaneous emotions, one's likes and dislikes. Before they can result in demands concerning the social structures which organise our interactions, these (self-)refusals, at first sight, appear to remain at the surface of our contact with the things that surround and constitute us: they do not overthrow any visible target, but settle for making us feel or think differently.

At the same time, we understand that such alterations of our sensibility are both a *precondition* of traditional revolutionary movements and their most profoundly important result. To tear down the statues of idols, to refuse to obey a king's command, to find more joy in smashing a window than in stealing a handbag, we must *first* have transformed our perception of the idol, the king, and the handbag; we must have come (individually and collectively) to no longer see the idol as divine, the king as legitimate, and the handbag as desirable. We must have broken the chains that we bring into the stories that we tell ourselves, even when our feet are not shackled. If the revolutions of the past did bear lasting fruits, they did so insofar as they had the consequence of 'changing the common fashion' of feeling and thinking (to again take as our own the purpose that Diderot ascribed his *Encyclopaedia*). What is at issue here is the transformation of the way that the members of a population allow themselves to be affected by their surroundings. Cutting off the heads of statues and kings is nothing but a way of cutting off the *belief* in the power of gods and kings, in the minds of those who witness this spectacle.

So now we can get back to the provocation that we just made, which cast the administration of the given as the main enemy of all progressive politics. In light of this fourth move, a thought or an activity that settles for managing what is given – *such as it is given* – neutralises in advance the very possibility of a real social transformation. Whether we oppose 'politics' to the 'police', in the manner of Jacques Rancière, oppose 'loyalty to the event' to 'knowledge of the state of affairs', in the manner of Alain Badiou, or oppose 'a situation's particular virtualities and potentialities' to the 'present power relations', in the manner of Maurizio Lazzarato, in each case the constitutive gesture of a 'left-wing' thought is based on a refusal to keep within the framing in which the existing information (objectively, empirically) appears. To reject the Given (data), to 'smash clichés' (Deleuze), to 'reconfigure the distribution of the sensible' (Rancière): the whole labour of reflection (and explanation) incumbent upon 'the left' consists of showing that *given facts are never given by reality itself*, but only by certain questions posed to it, within certain thought-schemas which are themselves maintained by certain practices and power relations (which they, in turn, perpetuate).

What ought to be rejected is not so much the Given per se as the presuppositions on which basis the Given has been produced – presuppositions that became inherent to it as soon as it appeared to us as 'given facts'. Percentage points of GDP growth or the results of this or that opinion poll really do correspond to certain (objective, empirically observable) characteristics of 'external reality' – precisely the characteristics that the continued existence of clichés feeds upon. There is no need to deny that. The struggle, rather, is to assert the possibility and the need to pose other questions, to bring into view other characteristics of the same reality, to produce other givens. In Deleuzian terms, the simple management of the given threatens to suffocate the *emergence of the virtual*, the advent of a possibility that must first be *imagined* (like a dream) before it can be *envisaged* within the existing state of affairs, so that it might finally be *realised* through the transformation of this state of affairs. Without doubt, care for the virtual today defines the essence of 'left-wing' politics in the most concise fashion.

To speak of a rejection of the Given also helps to explain the accusations of 'a lack of realism' often advanced by 'the right' (which, as it happens, includes almost all of France's Socialist Party) in its opposition to any suggestion of a turn to the left. Indeed, not only is it easy to accuse 'the left' of 'not wanting to face reality', but such a claim is partly justified. For 'the left' is characterised precisely by its unwillingness to settle for administering the currently given state of affairs, as it instead strives to *imagine possibilities for its radical transformation*. This is not a matter of utopianism, blindness or autism – except, that is, insofar as we sometimes do need to shut our eyes in order to have any hope of beautiful dreams, allowing us to draw out myths worthy of inspiring others.

Even so, the examples of the unstolen handbag and anorexia clearly show that there is a problematic aspect to identifying the gesture of refusing the Given with a 'left-wing' imaginary. For these 'deluxe' revolts and illnesses are associated with images of bourgeois 'self-indulgence', much more than with proletarian activism. This does not, of course, mean to suggest that the efforts to gain hold of a more adequate (empirical) knowledge, or struggles for more egalitarian or fairer appropriations, are now to be left in the past. The disgust at and rejection of certain Givens – and the fight against them – combines with the three earlier forms of demands, without in any way overcoming or neutralising them. Even in the West, most rioters still loot the shops they break into, often because they cannot make ends meet with what they are legally 'given'. This fourth level in 'the left's' array of gestures nonetheless takes on particular importance in those societies which – we saw in Chapter 1 – can be characterised in terms of the new power of publics.

Perhaps some will still remember that, only a few months before May 1968, Herbert Marcuse proclaimed the 'end of utopia'. He made this claim in light of the fact that the main obstacle to the realisation of emancipatory life-forms no longer lay in the limits of material reality (the objective impossibility of satisfying all our needs), but rather in the problem of our (subjective) desires remaining bogged down in false needs, in which our main sources of oppression, misery, and self-mutilation now resided.[8] The fact that Rousseau and the whole Stoic tradition long before him had already drawn the same lesson does nothing to take away from the present-day relevance of this conclusion, or from the novelty of the historical conjuncture in which it takes its place. For indeed, as we have seen, the different forms of power have never so immediately depended on the variations in our beliefs and our desires, across the various publics of which we are part.

The way I am affected by the given facts (and the clichés) which reach me as a member of these publics thus becomes ever more important, in the renewal or reconfiguration of power relations within our mass-mediatised societies. Even before we get to the question of my (active) habits – and even if I am just a drop in the vast river network of highly unequally structured mediaspheres – the positions of power on which today's priests, governmental figures, marketers, and stars try to maintain their hold are precariously dependent on my desires, my likes and dislikes, on my appetites and the things I vomit out (as well as those of millions of others). So, while the rejection of the Given is present at the foundation, in the core, and on the horizon of any process of social transformation, it now more than ever appears as *the* privileged place where 'the left' must direct its efforts.

8 Herbert Marcuse, *The End of Utopia*, 1967, available at marxists.org.

Sun Ra and the mythocracy of the virtual *quidam*

Heroes, leaders, and representatives live off the limelight that makes their individuality, their names, and their celebrity shine out for all to see. As for publics, they generally remain in the shadows, anonymous. They are made up of *quidams* – nobodies, just anyone. Sketching out a myth of the interruption of myth thus doubtless requires that we take *quidams* as our (anti-)heroes. This is, indeed, what the previous chapters have already done. In terms of social hierarchies, the valet Jacques is less than no one; Sun Ra the jazz musician, the Black American born in Birmingham, Alabama – the city subject to the harshest segregation in the whole United States – rotted in the shadows in jail (where he was sent for conscientious objection) before the originality of his music confined him to the underground. Both of them together offer the perfect image of the *quidam who counts all the more because he counts for nothing.*

To conclude, I would like to suggest that this figure deserves to become the emblem of a 'left-wing' sensibility – and that the myth of the virtual quidam may be best able to interrupt and counter-narrativise the myth of King Growth. Let us set these two myths in direct comparison so that we can better bring out the contrast between them.

1. *Recounting without counting.* Both Jacques and Sun Ra are constituted as bearers of a myth that transcends them and grants them a counter-narrativising power beyond all measure with their original status among 'the dominated'. Both count for nothing in the society in which they are born; each gives without counting what they are giving, whether that means an act of charity towards a poor woman who has broken her jug of oil,[9] or finding themselves touring through Egypt with their band without enough money to make it home.[10] As against a myth of King Growth, which suffocates and blinds us by making us

9 Denis Diderot, *Jacques le fataliste et son maître*, ed. Pierre Chartier, Paris: Livre de Poche, 2000 (1780), p. 130.

10 John F. Szwed, *Space Is the Place: The Lives and Times of Sun Ra*, New York: Da Capo Press, 1998, p. 294.

want to submit everything to the laws of accounting, the virtual *quidam* who recounts and gives without counting reminds us that all that is truly valuable is bound to slip through the net of quantitative measurement.

2. *Myth against reality*. Jacques the Fatalist never had a flesh-and-blood body; and although Sun Ra was born on 22 May 1914 under the name Herman Poole Blount, he was quick to invent himself a birth on Saturn and an extraterrestrial identity. Both of them committed to an ostentatious guise as fictitious beings, as myths, even though one of them, at least, could boast of some of the credentials of 'real' existence. As against the discourse of King Growth, which draws its authority from an objective (scientific) understanding of reality and condemns its 'left-wing' rivals in the name of economic 'realism', the virtual *quidam*, through his gesticulations expressing his fictional nature, in fact offers the very model of a much higher level of realism, for he explicitly recognises his (real) mythical status, where the myth of Growth (fictionally) pretends to reflect reality such as it really is.

3. *The virtual, as against the already-given*. Sun Ra defined mythocracy as 'a magic world, that makes things to be'.[11] There could be no finer definition of the virtual. As against a myth which, in pushing us to seek endless growth, in reality tends to imprison us within the limits of the already-given, the *quidam* summons up a mythocracy which, through the joys of storytelling, introduces possibilities into our existence such as the quantifying rationale could never have suspected. In both the case of Jacques (a character in a novel) and that of Sun Ra (fiction incarnate), the inspiring force of example opens up the paths of the virtual, as it allows myth to transform reality.

4. *Should-be, as against could-be*. In making mythocracy 'what you never came to be that you *should* be', Sun Ra indirectly indicates another way the myth of Growth is found wanting.[12] This myth feeds an infinite

11 Cited in Aurélien Tchiemessom, *Sun Ra: Un Noir dans le cosmos*, Paris: L'Harmattan, p. 232.

12 Graham Lock, *Blutopia: Visions of the Future and Revisions of the Past in the Work of Sun Ra, Duke Elligton and Anthony Braxton*, Durham. NC: Duke University Press, 1999, p. 61.

expansion of *could*-be: the accumulation regime set in place by capitalism, measuring everything by the yardstick of market profit, indifferently advances in all the directions of development which promise good returns on investment. This indifferent approach towards all that could be (profitable) may have some virtues in cutting away and emancipating us from certain traditionally repressive taboos. But it also pulls us into an unbridled rush towards the environmental and relational abyss. After all, for the capitalist machine oriented by short-term profit, it is a matter of total indifference if our descendants are going to be subjected to calamitous climate change, nuclear radiation, or internecine warfare. As against a directionless growth of our *could-be*, indifferent to what will become of future generations (whether they turn out to be prosperous, starved, or flooded), the mythocracy of the virtual *quidam* puts back in place the demand for a *should-be*. This, even though it still leaves it up to each of us to discover the particular nature of this should-be within our own individual and collective becoming. However much one might want to hear a second-person plural in the mythocratic invitation to become 'what you never came to be that you *should* be', if 'the left' is to be able to reorient its political agenda, its starting point must be an intimate feeling for what links the individual becoming of each person to the fate of those around them.

5. *Happiness in the present as against deferred prosperity*. While the myth of Growth, heir to the Protestant spirit of capitalism, barely ever lifts its gaze beyond short-term profit, it never ceases to defer the moment of enjoyment. Despite the new record levels of (both private and public) debt being reached, the right always promotes the same message of 'belt-tightening today to ensure prosperity in the future'. If we believed this story, wages will only be able to increase and free time become more extensive when the deficits have been drawn down, when inflation has been put in check, when we have finally overcome a 'crisis' – a fiscal 'rigour' and an austerity that have now become permanent. (All the while, capital gains and dividends have never reached higher summits.) As against these endlessly deferred promises, the *quidam* from Saturn makes mythocracy a way of immediately attaining happiness: 'I would say that the synonym for myth is happiness, because that's why they go

to the show'.[13] For the storyteller as for the musician and the spectator, this activity is not an opportunity to accumulate the (monetary) means of finding happiness: it is, in itself, happiness. The 'left' would do well to relearn the virtues of this short-circuit, which fuelled the most inspired moments of its own history: taking power without waiting for it to be granted us, redistributing wealth without waiting to be given the crumbs, and imposing paid holidays, health insurance, and mutualised pension funds without first waiting to get out of the crisis or end the budget deficits.

6. *Free time, as against pressed-for-time.* The Growth race pressures each of us to work ever more quickly (Time Is Money), constantly compressing our temporalities under the weight of an ever more omnipresent stress. Conversely, the virtual *quidam* invites us to reverse the established terms of the problem: following Marcel Duchamp's motto, we should recognise that 'My capital is time, not money'.[14] The main demand of the left – itself a traditional demand, dating back to the struggles over the length of the working day in the nineteenth century – must focus on control over and the liberation of time as a 'source of change, metamorphosis, and the creation of the possible', that is, as a condition of the emergence of the virtual. To demand a protection against stress, to benefit from 'calm and pleasant' working conditions: these are doubtless the new frontiers – necessarily 'utopian' ones by the yardstick of the givens of the present-day situation – which distinguish 'left-wing' politics.[15]

7. *Ambivalence, as against arrogance.* The tyranny of King Growth,

13 Szwed, *Space Is the Place*, p. 315.

14 Cited by Maurizio Lazzarato, *Experimental Politics: Work, Welfare, and Creativity in the Neoliberal Age*, Cambridge, MA: MIT Press, 2017, p. 174. He explains (pp. 173–4): 'We require time as the initial primary material needed to create something, whether a theatrical piece, a film, a way of life, or a political action. Empty time, time suspended and ruptured, open time, and time for hesitations, which are the conditions of all artistic, social, and political production, are the kinds of time that neoliberal policies empty of their power of metamorphosis.' The race for growth means that 'time is regulated in order to homogenize and make uniform subjectivity. The impoverishment of subjectivity is first and foremost an impoverishment of time as a source of change, metamorphosis, and the creation of the possible.'

15 This is Magali's demand in Jean-Luc Godard's 1982 *Passion*, as she quits her subaltern job in the filming of the movie: – 'What does she want?' – 'I want it to be calm and pleasant' – 'There is no pleasant work!'

flanked by his lieutenants – namely, the blackmail to work, the constraint of the wage relation, and the 'scientific' sanction of econometric data – tends to adopt political stances characterised by twin forms of arrogance: the arrogance of the manager and that of the expert. Each of them, backed up by the 'reality' of the figures duly processed by the numbers analysts, speaks *as if they knew*. They do not get carried off by stories: their decisions or their recommendations may well acknowledge a certain measure of 'uncertainty', but it would never occur to them that these might be 'myths'. Even if they may sometimes have some niggling doubt over one of their forecasts, they sign their reports and their contracts as full and responsible persons, under their officially registered names. This is also the model of the 'right-wing' politician (a term which embraces the near totality of today's political class).

By contrast, the virtual *quidam* from whom the 'left' can draw inspiration in reconfiguring its political image (or imaginary) appears as less than a person: a (fictional) character, a mask, a visionary disguised as an extraterrestrial. Any 'left-wing' politician must necessarily be affected by an irreparable internal divide: insofar as they bid to take up positions of responsibility, they must show at least some minimal mastery of the management of the given facts (or data). Insofar as they do not give up on being of 'the left', they must constantly self-challenge their own administrative decisions. They are thus traversed by a deep ambivalence, between the (official) administrator character which they are forced to play, and the (extraterrestrial) *quidam* in search of virtuality, which they strive to remain. In this there is nothing to puff them up with arrogance; rather, all the conditions are there to incite them to humility (when they recognise the difficulty of their position) and, at the same time, a measure of farce (when they do not want to deceive their base as to the fact that their public persona is a mask).

8. *Plural meta-scripting as against individualist mastery of the sovereign self.* One of the pieces that Sun Ra had his Arkestra singing began with the questions: 'If you're not a myth, whose reality are you? If you're not a reality, whose myth are you?'[16] While the myth of King Growth feeds on the

16 Sun Ra, 'Myth versus Reality', on *Out In Space*, Berlin, 7 November 1970 (MPS Records, 1971).

illusions of the Individual-as-King, the myth of the virtual *quidam* knows that our realities and our myths are never simply our own, but always have to do with a tangled multiplicity of *other* nobodies.

The ambivalence of mythocracy does not only owe to its ambiguous status, made up of both a hypnotised torpor and suggestive dreams. It is a rejection of the I as a sovereign: it owes to my never truly knowing who dreams my dreams, or who sleeps in my sleep, or – as we have already seen – *who it is that tells my stories*?

But, against the backdrop of such uncertainties, mythocracy does grasp one fundamental truth: myths and realities are always *someone*'s myths and realities. In other words: in whatever scenario I happen to find myself living, I always have to ask *who is in a position to meta-script it*. This awareness of our common state of existential meta-scripting is an object of anxiety only for the adepts of individualist self-mastery and those who fetishise intellectual property. For the virtual *quidam* as for an imaginary 'left-wing' politician, there is no particular scandal in knowing that one is traversed and affected by clichés, visions, torpor, dreams, sleepwalking, and shared myths that circulate from one mind to the next. If mythocracy is that which 'you never came to be that you *should* be' – with your real becoming lagging behind your virtual possibility – this owes more to the inertia of your individual evolution or the insufficient richness of the myths that have thus far passed through your mind, rather than any kind of 'alienation' deriving from conspiracy-driven meta-scripts. Mythocracy formulates matters clearly on this point: it is precisely through immersion in a suggestive myth that one can hope to gradually draw closer to what one should be.

It little matters that the myth of King Growth is the myth advanced by 'Big Capital', by an advertising mega-machine, or by a political spectacle 'perverted' by tele-cracy. The question that needs to be posed to myth is not so much a matter of its origins, external to our own subjectivity, or of its greater or lesser (but necessarily partial) adaptation to reality, or even of the particular agents and agencies that meta-script us through this myth. Rather, the question is about *what this myth is making us become* and *where it is leading us*. Towards a better distribution of wealth, or towards aggravated inequalities? Towards a real improvement of our living conditions, or towards a material enrichment coming at the cost of the impoverishment of subjectivities? Towards new spaces of freedom, or towards the ecological abyss?

Leftism and gaucheness

Reading the previous sections, the thought will surely have emerged in some readers' minds that 'the left' we are talking about here was long ago baptised with a much more suitable name, one that does not need any scare quotes: *gauchisme* ('literally, leftism, but used pejoratively to mean 'ultra-leftism'). The more sensitive parts of all progressive movements are tormented by this 'infantile disease' of political organisation, which constantly destabilises it, pushes it into 'irresponsible' acts, and threatens to kill off in advance any institutional (and thus real, realistic, and effective) translation of its ideas.

The accusation of *gauchisme* is directed against those considered to be too far out to the left. In parallel to this, many of us today struggle to identify with a 'left' which is not left-wing enough. The systematic use of quotation marks around the term 'the left' in this book is an expression of this discomfort: the *left-wing imaginary* some of whose traits this chapter has sought to sketch out is situated precisely in the problematic interval separating that which is usually accused of '*gauchisme*' and that which officially, institutionally presents itself as the 'left' – it being impossible directly to identify with either.[17]

So, should we commit to a political space demarcated by a purely negative definition: neither 'infantile ultra-leftism' nor 'the official left', but the fluctuating and unstable space in between? Perhaps this negativity does provide the basis for thinking through electoral

17 In France, the appeal *Nous sommes la gauche* marked out this political space in 1997. This appeal was republished in issue 8 of *Revue internationale des livres et des idées* (November 2008) and on its website. Jerôme Vidal shrewdly analysed the ongoing relevance of this appeal in *La Fabrique de l'impuissance 1. La Gauche, les intellectuels et le libéralisme sécuritaire*, Paris: Editions Amsterdam, 2008, especially pp. 15–35 and 118–28.

strategies: in that case, those who find themselves maladroit amid the ambient right-wing drift would be the ones *gauche* enough to be considered 'the left'.

Yet we could also draw inspiration from this minimalist definition to attribute positive value to a political consciousness characterised precisely by being maladroit (clumsy, awkward). In the interval between leftism and *gauchisme*, we could try to make gaucheness a property whose risks any non-arrogant politics must learn to embrace, the better to lay claim to its virtues. In a recent book, Michel Vanni invited us to do precisely this. Developing a responsive approach inspired by the German phenomenologist Bernhard Waldenfels, he calls for the recognition of an awkwardness, a gaucheness, inherent to any political act. For such an act is constituted as an (always-already committed) response to a perceived prompt – it never being possible precisely to determine to whom this prompt is addressed:

> Here I propose to speak of an essential awkwardness [*maladresse*] in the response or in responding, in the sense of an uncertainty over the direction in which the response and the query that inspires it are addressed, as well as an essential fragility of the very act of responding, a certain form of 'gaucheness' in all acts. Uncertain of its legitimacy, the act of response already advances, fragile and awkward, within a conflicting array of queries which it never manages to fully satisfy, but which maintain it in a perpetual imbalance – which is but another name for the capacity for reinvention and fruitfulness.[18]

Tellingly, Vanni makes the naming-operation itself ('the left'? '*Gauchisme*'? '*Gaucheness*'?) a crucial moment of this awkwardness:

> Precisely this approach to responding has led us to cast a light on the awkwardness of naming as a site of genesis and social creativity. It has made us conscious of the power-mechanisms that revolve

18 Michel Vanni, *L'Adresse du politique. Essai d'approche responsive*, Paris: Cerf, 2009, p. 79.

> around this naming of the event and the control over the attention which is at play therein. It is thus necessary to resist the external imposition of categories or names, which aprioristically inscribe the agent and his acts within framings that pay no heed to the novelty of the event, and which fatally stifle the potential force of displacement and invention.[19]

Michel Vanni further urges us to reject the binary oppositions (politics vs. police, event vs. state of affairs) within which Jacques Rancière and Alain Badiou set our perception of political realities. In this sense, the awkwardness in giving things a name is related to the whole molecular fabric of our everyday interactions, and not only the great traumatic events that define whole eras (for example, was 9/11 'fanatical terrorism' or the 'resistance of the subaltern'? Was the 2008 financial crash a 'self-correction' or a 'crisis of neoliberalism'?). The 'novelty of the event' – faced with which the essential awkwardness of giving things a name serves to open up a space of reconfiguration – can crop up in any kind of occasion, even the most insignificant and everyday. What, then, is this thing on my plate? 'Beef'? A 'pound of flesh hacked off the body of an animal'? 'The product of an agroindustry that has tormented this animal and generated enormous environmental damage, while also adding to the scandalous division of food resources among human populations'?[20]

As we can see, as soon as we even begin to scratch at the surface of the most banal names for things, a dizzying tangle of unposed questions and already-given answers emerges. It takes only the slightest uncertainty to reveal a 'conflicting array of queries', which threatens to 'perpetually imbalance' whoever does not stick to the 'external imposition of categories or names' that belong to ready-made 'framings'. Already in Chapter 3, we saw plenty of evidence that these names for things come to make sense only within (generally implicit) narrations, which are always-already scripted. Hence the word 'meat' conveys the image of a

19 Ibid., p. 260.

20 On this example, see Fabrice Nicolino, *Bidoche. L'Industrie de la viande menace le monde*, Paris: Les Liens qui Libèrent, 2009.

hat-wearing chef armed with a sharp knife, skilfully stringing together the actions of cutting, seasoning, and stirring the sauce, along with a whole imaginary of colours, sounds, and smells. Conversely, the word 'agroindustry' stirs up the image of animals confined in cages, fed on chemical sludge, packed into trucks, serially massacred on a production line, hung from hooks and hacked apart in sterilised halls where the only people working have to wear masks. The narrations implicit in such commonplace words are not only scripted in advance but they write scripts of their own: if someone promises me 'meat' I will pick up my knife, gulp down a mouthful of red wine, and cut myself a slice of bread; if someone talks to me about 'agroindustry', it will bring a frown to my face as I ready myself to explain that my butcher is supplied by an organic small farmer from the same region or (if I am a vegetarian) that 78 per cent of farmland worldwide is taken up by meat production.

Other than the fact that this would rapidly lead to paralysis, it would certainly be considered rather gauche to feel called on to answer all the 'conflicting array of queries' swarming around both the meal on my plate and my fellow diners. In promoting an 'awkward and fragile vision of the political', Michel Vanni rightly takes into account the fact that we cannot respond to these questions in a satisfactory way, or even know for certain that they are questions, or if they are really addressed to us.[21] It is the *uncertainty of the address* which makes some people pay attention to the question marks they see as being raised by animals, the hungry, or the environment, and thus decide to stop eating meat, while others feel perfectly at ease tucking into their bleeding steak.

As well as the ambivalence which is often its counterpart, gaucheness is inevitable faced with such uncertainties. Since no one can escape this, the decisive thing is the relationship one maintains with this awkwardness. Vanni proposes a restructuring of the field of the political ethos by counterposing 'two different subjective "postures": loyalty to the constitutive awkwardness of responses, and, on the other hand, the denial of this awkwardness'.[22] We can illustrate and radicalise this spectrum by

21 Vanni, *L'Adresse du politique*, p. 309

22 Ibid., p. 257.

placing in the one corner (the top right) the model of the fully self-assured fascist leader, hammering out his both assured and reassuring claims and shouting slogans with a magnetic pull on the fascinated crowds. And, in the opposite corner (the bottom left), the Maladroite fairy who stammers out her proposal for a sharp turn without herself being entirely convinced that this will not end up tipping the machine on its side, but despite everything considering it (perhaps) better to take this risk, or at least to discuss it, given the multiple uncertainties of the situation. The whole range of political scripts is situated in between these poles – scripts to which we could attribute varying coefficients of gaucheness, even if we make no claim to rigorous quantification.

'To militate for uncertainty or for awkwardness' implies the quest to (permanently) reform institutions, in order to seek greater flexibility in the invariably ossified (bureaucratised) responses they give to the requests coming from their participants and their users. The coefficient of gaucheness would here be measured using the yardstick of 'institutions' degree of openness regarding the awkwardness of their own responses'.[23] But, as Vanni himself suggests, this gaucheness also has to be addressed in terms of a 'subjective posture'. Instead of being defined mainly by certain ideological contents (being against privatisations, for the taxation of large fortunes, etc.), the 'left-wing imaginary' doubtless ought to be characterised by certain modes of utterance (*modes d'énonciation*). A subjectivity is (at least somewhat) 'left-wing' when it finds itself in an awkward position when it is alongside the manager playing the master, or the expert imposing scientific truths without opening the door for other perspectives to carry other (no less scientific) truths. When we feel the need to 'fight against a whole mythology of skill and effectiveness, which enjoys a far-reaching dominance in the age of globalised capitalism', the enemy is not of course to be identified in the expert or the manager themselves, who are doubtless responding as best they can to the 'conflicting array of queries' they find themselves wrapped up in.[24] If there is an enemy, it should instead be located in certain

23 Ibid., pp. 268, 309.
24 Ibid., p. 258.

authoritarian ways of staging and performing the act of response and the utterance.

For example, the habit of using ever more quotation marks – and it will not have escaped the readers' attention that this book makes that sacrifice to a caricatural degree – could provide a measure of this coefficient of gaucheness. Through the distance they introduce between the subject of the utterance and the names he cites, quotation marks bring the uncertainty and the fragility of these names right to the surface of the text itself. Each set of quotation marks points to the underlying myths wrapped up in the terms used. This typographical awkwardness also has a counterpart in the realm of oral communication, in the habit of the (generally Anglosphere) academics whose arms are almost constantly aloft throughout their lectures, so often do they place two fingers above their heads to make air quotes. It is an annoying, ridiculous tic – and one that marks out their – our – gaucheness . . .

When will we veer towards Saturn?

The gaucheness promoted here is, therefore, really about a certain kind of scripting, a certain way of distributing the roles (present and future) of those who are brought together by the stories they are telling. To conclude, let us try to imagine what one of its scripts might look like. Let us conjugate it in the future tense and describe its agents as the mythocrats that Sun Ra is calling us to become. He is, indeed, already blazing its tortuous path, through the deliciously awkward titles of his compositions populated by dancing shadows, intergalactic quests, tapestries from the asteroids, calls to all demons, and musicians busy travelling through space, from planet to planet, hoping that fate will be in a pleasant mood and that they'll have time to call planet Earth before rocket No. 9 takes off for the planet Venus . . .

The mythocrats called upon to script left-wing policies will present themselves as *quidams* who, despite the charisma they may have, will strive to speak from a position of non-sovereignty. Resisting the arrogance of stardom, they will act as if their name were *nobody* (Wu Ming 1,

Wu Ming 2, Wu Ming 3, a farmer in Larzac, a postman in a posh suburb like Neuilly, a 'non-intellectual'), or a *persona*, a borrowed mask (Luther Blissett).[25] Those who have the misfortune not to have been born female will at least try as they can to rein in their effluvia of testosterone, damaging to all true gaucheness.

To express their uncertainty in the face of what is presented to us as the given reality, they will refer to it by foregrounding the use of inverted commas, that is, by asking (themselves) in each moment *whose* reality we are talking about (*whose reality are you?*).

Faced with the given, questioned by the uncertain requests that seem to emanate from it, and unarrogant about the precarious answers they can think of, these *quidams* will strive to become extraterrestrials (recently arrived from Saturn) to encourage the emergence of *virtuals* by imagining other possible worlds. Self-proclaimed mythocrats, they will start by asking (themselves) what we *should* become, before looking into how we can enrich ourselves. Without hastily disqualifying the myths that may seem to be blinding others, they will be content to ask (briefly) *whose* myths these are (*whose myth are you?*). Then, they will try above all to catch a glimpse of the kinds of futures these myths are leading us towards.

The greatest challenge, in this effort to script political gauchness, is that of learning how to turn their clumsiness into a performance endowed with its own persuasive force. As they become 'apostles of clumsiness', they will have to learn to make their gaucheness the object of a virtuoso practice, and to establish the 'confidence in awkwardness' (*confiance dans la maladresse*) sketched out in the final pages of Michel Vanni's book.[26] It is worth noting, however, that the deceptive self-confidence shared by the vast majority of today's politicians – this 'mythology

25 It seems that it is through a similar gesture of 'quidamisation' and an interruption of the myth of the intellectual that Jérôme Vidal calls on 'the left' to recognise itself in the figure of the *non-intellectual*, '(you, me, anyone) whose action . . . works to undo in thought and in practice the privileges associated with intellectual difference and contributes no less actively to the production and development of a collective democratic intellectual' (Vidal, *La Fabrique de l'impuissance 1*, p. 132).

26 Vanni, *L'Adresse du politique*, pp. 262 and 302.

of skill and dexterity' which imbues their public interventions with a 'denial of their answers' constitutive clumsiness' – could well be the remnant of a traditional rhetoric, out of step with the (not so) new technologies of political communication. It is easy to understand why, in an agora or a forum or on a battlefield, and even in a stadium with ample sound systems, the speaker can hardly expect to communicate with the crowd by way of wry smiles. Now that three or four cameras are multiplying close-ups of the candidate's face, the nuanced expression of uncertainty and hesitation can be the subject of much finer scripting efforts. These open up the possibility – historically unprecedented in a democracy – of convincing without having to shout, or in other words, of governing without having to gesticulate like a *Duce* or *Führer* or other such sovereign Leader. Numerous recent reversals of public favour, in response to intimate confessions or apparent signs of weakness, suggest that a completely different script for political discourse can be imagined, though its resources have yet to be tested.

The last great feature of these virtual (gauchiste) *quidams*, the bearers of a renewed political imaginary, will be their essentially experimental conception of scripting. Experimentation can be used here as a synonym for gaucheness. Like clumsiness, even when it can determine precisely what it is looking for, it is never certain of what it will achieve. It, too, is based on a fragility that is well suited to neutering any arrogance, as well as many of the criteria related to efficiency and effectiveness. The figure of experimentation allows us to put our finger on the paradox of Michel Vanni's 'awkward and precarious vision of politics': how can we imagine that people will ever elect leaders whose first property is not to reassure them by parading their own competence, skill, and effectiveness?

We could, of course, answer that there are very different ways of 'reassuring' people: for most of us the little guy with the moustache shouting from the podium in a stadium is not especially reassuring. It may be more reassuring to see someone weigh up their ambivalent attitudes, rather than invest their entire faith in dubious military adventures or growth plans that will launch us towards the abyss. In other words, it is always myths (the myth of the leader, the myth of efficiency, the myth of moderation, the myth of radicalism) that give political speech its reassuring (or troubling) character. Working to establish a certain confidence in a certain form of gaucheness is no more 'impossible' than it was impossible in 2008 – contrary to many predictions – to elect a black man to the White House.

Translating gaucheness into the terms of *experimentation* raises another crucial question. Experimentation generally takes place in laboratories. Procedures are put in place to ensure that what takes place there does not contaminate the surrounding environment. Experiments are conducted on mice or chimpanzees, whose suffering leaves us indifferent. But surely no one would be foolish enough to expose themselves and fellow humans to life-size experiments in which they are the guinea pigs!

If resistance to political experimentation seems even stronger than resistance to any potential 'apostles of clumsiness', we can, nevertheless, see more precisely at which points we could break this resistance. On the one hand, we could stress that – troubling as this may sound – *all* politics is, by its very nature, experimental. The sorcerer's apprentices who lull us into the myth of King Growth have launched our carriage into motion, in a race whose future episodes no one can imagine – let alone calculate: they gamble on our lives (and countless future generations'). In the short term, the drastic left bifurcation suggested by the Maladroite fairy is certainly riskier than sticking to a straight line, continuing right on. Yet sticking to the same course is itself an experiment, in seeing how close we can get to the abyss before we fall in, which isn't necessarily much safer. The main problem is that the political right presents its policy (keep on straight ahead!) in such a way as to deny that it is indeed an experiment, conducted under the greatest uncertainties, by sorcerer's apprentices who are not particularly skilful or reassuring (as we were well reminded of by the bank runs and the State-applied sticking-plasters of 2008). Capitalism's next big financial crisis is not a matter of *if* but of *when*.

At a deeper level, the question of how much confidence we should place in experiments is based on a highly unscientific assessment, which has much more to do with the tales that circulate among us than with the (highly uncertain) accounts that the experts try to enlighten us with. This infinitely complex assessment can be summed up in a simple question: *When will we believe we have more to lose by continuing in a straight line than by making a left turn?* Such a question is, of course, part of a long tradition in the left-wing 'imaginary'. The last words of Marx and Engels's manifesto made this the wellspring of the communist revolution: 'The proletarians have nothing to lose but their chains. They have a world to win.'

Here too – indeed, above all on this note — the 'left-wing' imagination needs to be drastically updated. In the face of threats such as climate change and the build-up of nuclear waste, there can be no question of waiting until we have nothing to lose. For the basic conditions of human life on Earth are now at stake. Have we any hope of winning another world before we are reduced to having nothing to lose – in other words, before we are so close to the abyss that we are bound to plunge into it? This is the ultimate challenge facing mythocracy in the twenty-first century: to create myths that will enable us to interrupt the Growth myth before it drives us into the abyss. This is the function of the myth of Saturn (and the Saturnalia). Contrary to what some billionaires would have us believe, this is not a question of 'leaving planet Earth behind', thanks to new technologies, financed by new NASA programmes. No Rocket no. 9 will ever be able to take Earthlings to live on the planet Venus, once they are done transforming their habitat into an unliveable dustbin. The bifurcation towards Saturn (and towards the Saturnalia), as a myth, does not call for a flight into space, but for a change of perspective. As this book has tried to show, *shifting points of view* is precisely what a narrative can do. Through their myths, ordinary people and the multitudes they form *can* move towards another 'up there', which gives them a more distant, more fine-grained, and sharper view of what really matters in our lives on Earth. This is about doing the same thing that Sun Ra did: looking at our world from a Saturn(al)ian viewpoint, one that allows us to spot the abysses all around us, but also and above all to discover the mountains that we could hope to climb. Indeed, we could see these peaks through the left-hand window, if we didn't have our eyes fixed on the motorway of Growth.

This is how Sun Ra describes mythocracy: an experimental form of politics. It is something we now have to try out, after having tried, with mixed success, democracy, theocracy, the dictatorship of the proletariat, the nationalisation of land, or the deregulation of the banking system. This experiment is about the way we see our world and the way in which we can put into myths – into *stories* and into *enchanting words* – the demands made on us, the beliefs that run through us, and the desires that drive us. Precisely the power of such myths is that they enable us to reach other possible worlds: a non-racist world on Saturn, which fuels our dreams, but also, through it, a creative and festive world of Saturnalia, anticipated and already realised by the (real) concerts of the Astro-Infinity Arkestra, through the costumes, masks, rhythms, refrains, and dances it spread across the four corners of the planet. Insofar as artistic creation always far exceeds the threats and the oppression to which it is a reaction, the mythocracy theorised and illustrated by Sun Ra above all makes it possible to activate the desire to win a different world, not because we are cornered by the desperate imperatives of survival but under the impulse of how we feel we ought to live. This is the true significance of the quotation at the beginning of this book. So, let us hear again Sun Ra at the conclusion, too: 'I'm telling people that they've tried everything, and now they have to try mythocracy. They've got a democracy, theocracy. The mythocracy is what you never came to be that you should be.'

Afterword

Mythocracies and Conspiracies

This translated edition of *Mythocratie* brought only minor edits to the text of the 2010 French edition. No attempt has been made to update the examples drawn from political or media life of the time, nor to complete the footnotes with the numerous references published over the past fifteen years on related issues. The theoretical effort made a decade and a half ago is obviously dated, but it hopefully still speaks to our current situation. It would often have been easy to substitute Trump's name for Berlusconi's, to refer to TikTok instead of reality TV, to deride Boris Johnson's histrionics instead of Nicolas Sarkozy's, the myths of Brexit instead of those of French Sovereignty.

Here is not the place to draw a balance sheet of the pathetic failure of François Hollande's presidency, which totally discredited the little amount of trust and hope still vested in the 'left'. In direct opposition to the daring bifurcation (negotiated with a self-assumed gaucheness) advocated in the closing chapter of the book, the Hollande–Macron sequence managed to associate a total submission to the Given with a perfectly arrogant form of authoritarianism. Worldwide over the past decade, the (re-)elections of Putin, Erdoğan, Modi, Duterte, Bolsonaro, Bukele, Trump, Netanyahu, Orbán, Wilders, Meloni, and the like seem to demonstrate that the far right has been much more adept than anyone else at navigating the seas of mythocracy.

One relatively recent development, however, deserves to be revisited in this afterword in light of the analyses presented in the preceding chapters: the current surge in debates about the threats of conspiracy theories. Just as *Mythocratie* attempted in 2010 to mobilise some technical tools and hermeneutic gestures borrowed from literary studies to reassess the potentials of storytelling and the power of scripting, similarly, it may be politically relevant to revisit conspiracism in a literary perspective – a perspective which has been systematically neglected among all the social sciences supposed to account for this present danger. So, rather than attempting to update the framing of mythocracy sketched in the previous chapters, this afterword will be entirely devoted to pursuing the same investigation in an attempt to understand why and how conspiracist stories shape our worlds.

Beliefs? A brief analytics of conspiracist mythocracy

The *prima (im)materia* of the diagram through which this book attempted to model mythocracy was made of 'flows of desires and beliefs' (Chapter 2). The debates around conspiracy thinking provide a good opportunity to question more in depth the puzzling nature of the three terms linked in this formula. First, how are we to understand a *flow*? The Latin etymology of 'conspiracy' answers this question in a very suggestive manner: a flow of desires and beliefs is something we 'breathe in and out' (*-spirare*) 'together with' other people (*con-*). To conspire, first and foremost, is to share the same air, the same atmosphere, the same myths. What better definition of a public – that of a musical group, a periodical, an influencer, or a TV channel – than the fact that its members breathe together, in and out, the same jingles, the same news, the same ideas, the same suggestions, the same images, the same stories, more or less at the same time?

More specifically than this minimal definition of conspiracy, the common uses of the term refer to the idea of *plotting* some (evil) deed together. Here again, however, mythocrats are on familiar ground. A great deal of Chapter 4 was devoted to clarifying the role and the importance of plots, defined as assertive ways to concatenate actions in tight relation with imputations of causality. A quasi-synonym to conspiracy is *complot*, referring to a covert coordination of malevolent actions purposefully geared towards the harming of its target.

Valentina Desideri and Stefano Harney have revisited with joyful brilliance the necessity to conceive of 'conspiracies without a plot' in order to make room for the possibility of 'breathing-together' (in solidarity) without being caught in the traps of 'plotting-against' an enemy (who has already partially won the fight by the moment we become obsessed with them).[1] For the sake of clarity, we may follow their cue by hardening an analytic distinction between the mere breathing-together of conspiracy and the more offensive plotting-against of complot – even if this abstract distinction cuts across concrete realities that mix the two. What distresses political commentators in the current conjuncture is a certain tendency to interpret all our states of affairs as affairs of State: whatever happens in the world that doesn't agree with my interests or my whim gets loudly denounced as the result of a complot.[2]

From here on, we can follow the path trodden by familiar friends of ours, the Italian mythocratic collective Wu Ming (discussed at length in the 'Literary Interlude' between Chapters 5 and 6). In a sum which delineates the most convincing reflection on conspiracism to date, Wu Ming 1 articulates a distinction between two rather different imputations of *complot*. The '*phantasmagorias of complot*' are unresearched allegations

1 Valentina Desideri and Stefano Harney, 'A Conspiracy without a Plot', in Jean-Paul Martinon, ed., *The Curatorial: A Philosophy of Curating*, London: Bloomsbury, 2013.

2 The following books on the topic are particularly interesting: Anonymous, *Conspiracist Manifesto*, Los Angeles: Semiotext(e), 2013; Michael Barkun, *A Culture of Conspiracy: Apocalyptic Visions in Contemporary America*, Berkeley: University of California Press, 2003; Luc Boltanski, *Énigmes et complots. Une enquête à propos d'enquêtes*, Paris: Gallimard, 2012; Gérald Bronner (ed.), *Les Lumières à l'ère numérique*, Paris: Présidence de la République, 2022; 'Conspiracy Thinking', special issue of *Social Research* 89, no. 3 (2022); Russell Muirhead and Nancy L. Rosenblum, *A Lot of People Are Saying: The New Conspiracism and the Assault on Democracy*, Princeton, NJ: Princeton University Press, 2019; Katharina Thalmann, *The Stigmatization of Conspiracy Theory since the 1950s: 'A Plot to Make Us Look Foolish'*, Abingdon: Routledge, 2019.

based on poorly documented imaginary machinations supposed to establish a universal control over all aspects of social life; '*hypotheses of complot*', by contrast, formulate a hypothesis about a limited set of malevolent coordinated actions, a hypothesis that either results from a serious work of investigation or can lead to a properly documented fact-finding inquiry.[3]

In light of this distinction, it becomes clear that simply using the accusation of conspiracism to discredit a certain assertion is misguided at best, oppressive at worst. We all know that there *are* countless cases of conspiracies, where breathing-together leads to acting-together, and where acting-together involves some forms of plotting-against. Economic life and political life are made up of just that: people who are not content to breathe the same air, but who undertake to turn their common breath into organizations, more or less formalised, capable of taking advantage of opportunities, thanks to the strength of (partly covert) coordinated actions.

The idea that Bill Gates is inoculating people with subcutaneous microchips disguised as vaccines in order to inform Microsoft of our every move, or that the world is being ruled by a clique of cannibalistic paedophiles, is undoubtedly phantasmagorical. But how are we to describe the campaigns set up to get Western consumers to buy electric cars? National governments and the European Union put in place legal machinery to ban the sale of new combustion engines by 2035 and subsidise the purchase of electric vehicles. Car companies multiply their advertising machines to convince us that we're saving the planet by buying a green SUV. Meanwhile, Aurore Stephant and the SystExt association meticulously investigate the current practices of metal extraction and make convincing calculations to show that the simple substitution of (heavy) electric vehicles for current thermal vehicles, without rethinking our transportation policy, will lead to mining disasters scarcely less damaging than climate disruption.[4] Are far-right parties conspiracist

3 Wu Ming 1, *La Q di qomplotto: QAnon e dintorni. Come le fantasie di complotto difendono il sistema*, Rome: Edizioni Alegre, 2021, p. 141.

4 Association SystExt: systext.org.

when they denounce such a green deal as a scam? Shouldn't we see the collusion between business interests and government policies as the symptom of conspiracies (they breathe together in the same growth-oriented direction at all costs), machinations (they put forward selected quantitative figures, while leaving other important factors in the dark), or even complots (the decisions of CEOs and ministers are taken by players who consult and lobby each other regularly, coordinate their actions, and often swap roles)?

As Wu Ming 1 suggests, hypotheses of complot generally contain precious 'kernels of truth' out of which further investigation may draw important information. But the relations between truth and conspiracist mythocracy are more complicated than that. Whether phantasmagorical or empirically documented after a fact-finding investigation, conspiracists are storytellers. They do not simply reveal facts: they construct narratives that often have the power of myths. Assessing the truth-value of these myths is made particularly difficult and conflictual because it takes place on a battleground between two very different definitions of 'truth'.

The authoritative debunkers that Wu Ming 1 portrays as 'ratio-supremacist' operate with a *punctual* definition of truth, which focuses its attention on facts: an assertion is true or not depending upon the asserter's capacity to document the factuality of what is asserted. What irrefutable evidence can one show about an actual meeting (or a transfer of funds) taking place between Volkswagen's CEO and Ursula von der Leyen in the days preceding the promulgation of EU's directives on electric cars? This punctual definition of truth is the one that holds weight in the judicial system, in order to check the veracity of punctual allegations. Of course, it is essential to defend and enforce it, not only in courts but more broadly in journalism, scientific inquiry, and administrative reporting.

There is another conception and practice of truth, however, that is orthogonal to the previous one, but no less important and respectable. This second, *integrative* definition considers something as true insofar as it provides a big picture on the background of which punctual facts can be 'figured out' and assessed. Whereas the first conception was a matter of reference and of proving, this second one is a matter of relevance and of making sense. I can't prove that Ursula von der Leyen was bribed by anyone, and I don't think she was, but that's not the point. The sum of partial information I have absorbed over the years suffices to convince me that conservative politicians and business leaders are systematically in cahoots to scratch each other's back at the expense of the more general good. A hypothesis is not only true when it is corroborated by well-established facts, but also when it fits within a meaningful pattern (*Gestalt*), a certain 'figure' emerging out of a 'background'.

Let us remember the phrase used by economists to explain potentially surprising data: 'we have a story for that'. As we saw, this is the power of myth: it provides us with a narrative concatenation of events that organises them within an integrative explanatory frame. This concatenation goes beyond the particular facts considered in this singular instance. It works as a model that can apply to a whole range of other comparable situations. When this explanatory process of 'figuring-out' rises in generality, it ends up resembling what used to be called, a few decades ago, an *ideology* – a system of ideas and representations that is internally coherent enough to offer an integrated perception of the different aspects of our lives, articulated to a system of values capable of orienting our actions.

Even if ratio-supremacist debunkers are perfectly justified to question and denounce phantasmagorias of complot that are deprived of factual evidence (or that go directly against factual evidence), they may be misguided in disqualifying as 'pure myths' hypotheses based on the need to make sense of reality through the 'figuring-out' relevance of a big picture. What is at stake in these orthogonal definitions of truth is a double experience of belief. It is very different to believe in the sensory evidence that happens to be within sight at the present moment (a cat is sitting on a chair in front of my desk) than to believe in the explanatory power of a causal scheme (capitalism is responsible for global warming). While believing in what one perceives with one's eyes becomes more and more problematic – as it is mediated by screens increasingly permeated by generative AI expert in producing deep fakes (more on this later) – the traditionally reflexive experience of belief takes place when one asks oneself if this or that assertion actually fits with one's overall understanding of the world (that is, with one's ideology), not with one's current sensory data.

As we saw in the diagrams of Chapter 2, flows of beliefs are constantly reconfiguring themselves and each other, according to generally minor (but exceptionally dramatic) clashes with contradictory evidence: narratives provide an open playground where such readjusting can take place under safe conditions. Far from being exceptional, or exceptionally dangerous, conspiracy thinking appears as mythocracy-as-usual – no more (but also no less) dangerous than your average ideological struggle. It may be because ratio-supremacist debunkers, often operating in the positivist fields of political theory or cognitive sciences, have forgotten the category of ideology that they are so prompt to denounce the speck of conspiracy in their adversaries' eye, rather than the plank of ideology in their own.

But what our analysis of storytelling has suggested with more insistence is that beliefs held are a very different thing than beliefs *stated*. The difference between the two rests in our intuitive awareness of the power to script. While flows of beliefs are very hard to access, what floods our public sphere and social media are flows of blabber about beliefs. There seem to be many more people believing in an invasion of flat-earthers than people who actually believe that the earth is flat: it has become a cliché to repeat that a third of (young) Americans are mystified to the point of seeing the earth as a pancake, whereas a 2018 YouGov poll got only a few percentage points (between 2 per cent and 4 per cent) of them saying so – a few more percentage points prudently stating their cautious 'doubts' about the whole thing.[5] The crucial question, however, is that such a poll does not implant a captor inside people's brain, but triggers them to make an *utterance*. And it is not hard to imagine what might prompt a surprising response: to sound clever, to piss off the system, to

5 Craig A. Foster and Glenn Branch, 'Do People Really Think Earth Might Be Flat?', *Scientific American* blog, 21 August 2018, scientificamerican.com; and Signe Dean, 'No, One-Third of Millennials Don't Actually Think Earth Is Flat', *Science Alert*, 4 April 2018, sciencealert.com.

give a stupid answer to a stupid question, to test how far the joke can go . . . What Boris Groys has persuasively flagged as 'the obligation to self-design' seems much more decisive than adherence to factual reality when assessing statements of beliefs or conspiracist build-ups: the democratisation of our access to social media leads to a situation where we all feel called upon constantly to design (and redesign) our public persona – that is, where the *duty of scripting our self* takes precedence over all other tasks.[6]

While paedophiles and complots *do* actually exist in factual reality, and while numerous carriers of phantasmagorical conspiracist rumours *are* the victims of cynical manipulations orchestrated 'up there' by the Republican Party or the Putin government, a good number of conspiracy theorists may be much more intuitively savvy in communication pragmatics and self-scripting strategies than your average cognitive scientist. Spreading a world-view that portrays decision-makers of the 'deep state' as sucking the blood of innocent children may need to be assessed according to its oppositional virtue, rather than its truth content. It may express the refusal of a government that spends billions of dollars to establish democracy in Iraq and Afghanistan (with the success we know), while telling me there's not enough water left to irrigate my golf course. Which big picture can I turn to in order to explain such budget priorities? Which myth will better express my rejection of such systemic aberrations? Whose myth am I attacking by retweeting a climato-sceptic post? Who will 'like' me if I do? These are the questions to raise in a mythocratic approach to conspiracism. To give us the tools to answer them, we need to sketch an all-too-brief energetic view of conspiracist mythocracy.

Desires? A hurried energetics of conspiracist mythocracy

What flows of desires fuel statements deemed conspiracist in the current state of our mythocracies? The following pages summarily identify

6 Boris Groys, *Going Public*, London: Sternberg, 2010.

eleven dynamic principles to be taken into consideration in order to do two things at the same time: on the one hand, combat the toxic effects of a far-right conspiracism that undermines the very possibility of holding empowering democratic debates, and on the other hand, shed light on some of the debunkers' blind spots that lead them to fuel the fire they pretend to extinguish, or to disqualify potentially emancipating movements.

1. *Motricity precedes sensoriality.* What taps on a keyboard, reacts to an image, swipes on a screen, or relays a story is the human body, driven by vital needs (food, shelter, the ability to pay bills). What the body perceives in its surroundings, what it sees, hears, absorbs, remembers, is a function of what it needs to notice in order to put itself in a position to satisfy these vital needs (as well, of course, as a host of other derived desires). Strictly speaking, then, one's perceptions and one's 'emotions' are 'motivated' by the 'movements' one's body makes to satisfy these needs.

In his lectures on *Imagination and Invention*, French philosopher Gilbert Simondon suggested that the shape of the mother's breast, and the shape of the lips that enables it to be sucked, constitute an 'a priori image', prior to any perception of an external object – an image in which 'motricity precedes sensoriality'.[7] If we didn't come into the world with an internal aspiration to suck on something round that could fill our mouths, we wouldn't live beyond a few hours. This obviously has psychoanalytic implications: all we aspire to, through all our subsequent desires, including when we listen to a story or relay a conspiracist myth, is try to find the original satisfaction of suckling. The more general implication is that our world-views are drastically filtered by the practical perspective of our daily behaviours.

Our habits have taught us that our life-forms depend on certain movements. To persist in our existence, these movements seem indispensable, rightly or wrongly. If my livelihood depends on keeping a job located thirty miles from home, and there's no public transportation to

7 Gilbert Simondon, *Imagination and Invention*, Minneapolis: University of Minnesota Press, 2022.

get me there, my car and the fuel to run it seem as obviously essential to my well-being as air and water. Any speech advocating a significant hike in the price of gasoline sounds like a vital threat to me, no matter how justified it might be from an environmentalist perspective. As Upton Sinclair wrote in 1934, 'it's hard to make someone understand something when his salary depends on his not understanding it'.[8] The same goes for water-saving policies that would imply the closure of the golf club around which my social life revolves.

This primacy of motricity over sensoriality structures a large part of our relationship with 'the truth'. Our expectations precondition our attentions. We can therefore subscribe to a conspiracy delusion, despite its implausibility, as long as it is closely aligned with our vital needs. At a time when so many daily habits of middle-class Western consumers would need to change if people are not to render large proportions of the planet uninhabitable, conspiracist myths conveniently disqualify inconvenient truths that one's 'salary depends on not understanding'.

2. *Perception is controlled hallucination.* As Andy Clark showed in *Surfing Uncertainty*, our orientation in our daily environment is based on processes of 'projective predictions':

> Naturally intelligent systems do not passively await sensory stimulation. Instead, they are constantly active, trying to predict (and actively elicit) the streams of sensory stimulation before they arrive. Before an 'input' arrives on the scene, these pro-active cognitive systems are already busy predicting its most probable shape and implications.[9]

My eyes are not content with being merely open, to passively receive luminous fluxes that they would a priori treat in an egalitarian manner, only gradually to allow the shape of this or that object to be composed. My perceptual system operates from a stock of expansive forms (*Gestalts*)

8 Upton Sinclair, 'I, Candidate for Governor and How I Got Licked', *Oakland Tribune*, 11 December 1934, p. 19.

9 Andy Clark, *Surfing Uncertainty: Prediction, Action and the Embodied Mind*, Oxford: Oxford University Press, 2016, p. 52.

already constructed according to what my bodily movements need me to identify. This is the case of the innate rounding of the baby's mouth ready to suckle but, most often, these are figures constructed through our perceptions and our previous practices.

Scanning the visual space, my eyes constantly project these figures onto it, based on an anticipated holistic correspondence that they attempt to recognise (rather than discover). We only (sometimes) correct these anticipated predictions at a later stage, when the sensory data prove to be (too) incompatible with them. Andy Clark summarises this principle with a striking formula: 'Perception is controlled hallucination.'[10] This implies, among other things, that hallucination precedes perception. The expectations projected by our myths generally pre-empt the careful observation of what lies before our eyes. We do not have an originally pure, inductive, objective perception that dark, malicious manipulations would then pervert and divert from the truth. We begin by hallucinating our lived world, and we never really stop doing so. We live in hallucinations and myths until they become too damagingly incompatible with the responses we get from our environment. I can believe that the earth is flat or that Democrats suck the blood of babies because it doesn't make much difference to my daily actions. No conspiracy, however, will convince its supporters that by cutting off one finger a day, they will become virtuoso pianists in a week.

In plain language: we are all born suckers. Certain political myths operate as pacifiers: their primary effect is to shut our mouth around an illusory and ephemeral satisfaction, as they are incapable of nourishing our real needs in the longer term. Other myths and ideologies, however, pre-configure our attentions to identify opportunities or threats that would take years or generations to be inductively constructed through costly trials and errors.

3. *Sociality trumps factuality*. We don't suck and hallucinate on our own. Seeing this reality or believing this myth rather than those other ones does not so much depend upon their more or less probable character as on who sees or believes them among the people we know (and tend

10 Ibid., p. 14.

or need to trust). Twentieth-century psychologists have multiplied experiments showing to what extent I will come to see very different things in the same image depending on what my peers seem convinced of finding there. What applies to the size of parallel lines on a sheet of paper also applies, a fortiori, to much more abstract objects of thought, such as freedom, merit, or justice.

Myths and conspiracy thinking draw a large part of their power from the fact that sociality trumps factuality. We need to believe, and we always believe *with others*. Believing with others sometimes proves more important than adjusting our beliefs to the specific evidence of the facts. Even though I know that water shortages may worsen, the convivial weekends I spend with my golf buddies push me to endorse their climate-denialist convictions.

Informal sociality has been neglected by the mainstream 'left' over the past decades. During much of the twentieth century, the French Communist Party managed to weave a strong community life maintained between the different electoral cycles, a life made up of routines (meetings, campaigning), events (demonstrations, festivals), leisure (summer camps), and solidarity (strike funds, legal support, help for comrades in difficulty). Apart from a few marginal circles that have continued and sometimes intensified such communities of life and solidarity – *zones à défendre* (political occupation of land to prevent ecological destructions), squats, activist associations, artistic collectives – it is mostly religious communities that have invested this sphere of believing-together by chatting-, playing- and doing-together. In France, the current successes of the far-right National Rally may owe more to its (anti-Muslim) sociality of red wine and pork sausage than to the xenophobic arguments of its programme.

4. *Complexity trumps unanimity*. Our needs for sociality and proximity are all the more vivid as they are threatened by the development of our productive systems. These have become mind-bogglingly complex over the past two centuries, with the intensification of the division of labour and the extension of supply chains. More and more humans must coordinate increasingly differentiated and distant activities to collaborate in the production of goods that are ever more 'complicated' to

understand and unfold – the etymology of 'complexity' [*com-plicare*] pointing to a process of layer upon layer 'folding us with' each other. The smartphone is often waved as an emblem of this complication, with its seventy types of materials mobilised (including thirty different metallic elements) from four continents. As these superimposed layers of complexity multiply, our social organisations differentiate themselves into a growing number of tangled causalities and intersecting perspectives, of which it becomes increasingly difficult to construct a shareable understanding. Smartphone users generally only have eyes to cry when an investigative report gives them a glimpse of the production conditions that prevail in Congolese mines or in Chinese workshops. Depending on the perspective from which it is approached, the same object shines like a high-tech miracle, a neocolonial shame, a prosthetic brain, a vector of brutalization, a catalyst for profit, or a medium of emancipation. It is tangentially impossible to agree on its 'real' status: complexity trumps unanimity.

5. *Intelligibility trumps complexity*. As we have seen in the previous chapters of this book, reference to complexity has nonetheless become a cover for a falsely progressive discourse. Everything is so tangled that it becomes unimaginable to do anything concrete to redress the injustices structuring the world. Too complicated . . . Conspiracy thinking rides on the feeling of impotence self-inflicted on the left by complexity thinkers. The appeal of 'populist' rhetoric rests on the simple – mythical, mystifying – solutions it offers to complicated problems: stop immigration; lock up offenders; cut bureaucratic jobs; lower taxes; privatise public media; increase tuition fees; ban the construction of mosques; dollarise the economy. Although they are not unanimously endorsed, such solutions are attractive insofar as their causal effectiveness can be readily hallucinated: we can easily breathe their stories in and out together.

Denouncing 'populism' for its overly simplistic solutions, however, is no more effective than fact-checking Donald Trump's nonsense. Any human understanding of causal links consists of a simplification of the entanglement of infinite causal chains from which any event results. Anti-capitalism can be equally described as an ideology and as a conspiracist myth: it invites activists to breathe together in a common fight against the machinations of capitalists elevated to the rank of root causes of contemporary problems. This is partly true – insofar as any truth can only be a *partial* truth, *the* (all-encompassing) *truth* not belonging to the human realm. Conspiracism is clearly dangerous when it identifies the conspirators with an essentialised social group to be repressed (typically: Jews, Muslims, foreigners), and when it establishes its monocausal principle of partial intelligibility as the sole and exclusive source of explanation. But ideological myths make (partially) intelligible a tangle of causalities whose hypercomplexity always risks inhibiting any intervention. In doing so, they operate as a catalyst for political mobilisations: we act because we believe (in part wrongly) to have identified the decisive cause of a situation.

6. *Antagonism consolidates communities.* Another factor in adhering to certain opinions, closely linked to the previous one, is that we believe all the more strongly with our fellow human beings as we band together to *believe against* those we identify as adversaries. Conspiracy hypotheses help unite communities by attributing the frustration of certain needs to malevolent intentions. It is well known that antagonism consolidates communities. The uncanny recurrence of the accusation of cannibalistic paedophilia is likely explained by the fact that gratuitous horrendous violence imposed on children can only unite against it all people who consider themselves 'normal' and with good intentions. Here, too, however, the power of myth must be carefully dissected from the dangers of mystification, in order not to throw out the baby of necessary opposition and pugnacity with the conspiratorial bathwater.

There are very real conspiracies whose effects can be terribly destructive. Let us think of the meeting in Berlin of European powers (including Russia, the Ottoman Empire, and the US) between November 1884 and February 1885 to share the colonial exploitation of the African continent. Or the creation of the Global Climate Coalition in Washington, DC, in 1989, by an alliance of oil, mining, energy, forestry, and manufacturing industries, in tune with George H. W. Bush's White House, to protect these companies against limits on greenhouse gas emissions. Even if these conspiracies took the official form of conferences and well-established organisations, led by public figures (although keeping a good part of their transactions secret), it is difficult not to consider them, in retrospect, as anticipating quite precisely the current phantasmagoria of the deep state: a few (rich, white, male) decision-makers gather around a table to divide the exploitation of the world, for their buddies' benefit and at the cost of immeasurable suffering, unspeakable violence, and unprecedented destruction. Stories denouncing such collusions of interests are not conspiratorial per se. Neither is identifying adversaries and mobilising communities of action around the need to combat them. It is the daily routine of political mythocracy.

7. *Omni-mediatisation fosters multi-perspectivism.* The factors mentioned in the previous sections have conditioned political life for centuries. One of the main novelties of the current period is the unprecedented technical possibility, made affordable to a majority of the world's population, of becoming the source of media flows capable of spreading almost instantly across the planet. The miniaturisation and multiplication of audiovisual broadcasting/reception devices (smartphones, screen cameras) tends to multiply the contradictory perspectives, documenting our complex realities in their various aspects. As illustrated by street videos showing racist police violence, this multiplication puts into circulation representations (images, sounds, speeches, stories) that manifest very diverse – and potentially antagonistic – points of view and hypotheses about our tangled causalities. As demonstrated by high school student Darnella Frazier recording and broadcasting the murder of George Floyd on 25 May 2020 in the streets of Minneapolis, or by two young women posting on Twitter a video recording of Nahel Merzouk's murder in the streets of Nanterre on 27 June 2023, this type of 'sousveillance' has now become widespread, while it was exceptional in March 1991 when George Holliday filmed the beating of Rodney King, before transmitting it to a local Los Angeles TV channel.[11] Dominant myths about police behaviour – duly authorized and scripted from 'up there' – can be much more easily debunked by sousveillance practices.

11 See Steve Mann, Jason Nolan, and Barry Wellman, 'Sousveillance: Inventing and Using Wearable Computing Devices for Data Collection in Surveillance Environments', *Surveillance and Society* 1, no. 3 (2003).

This technical capacity to diversify points of view considerably alters the dynamics of mythocracy: while mass media throughout the twentieth century mostly relayed the perspectives (sometimes conflicting among themselves) of the privileged classes, nowadays cameras, smartphones, and social networks allow underrepresented points of view to gain visibility. Omni-mediatisation fosters multi-perspectivism.

8. *Affective attractivism trumps multi-perspectivism.* Multi-perspectivism, however, encounters an adversary within the very heart of the technology that favours it. The decentralised internet of the 1990s was based almost exclusively on *pull* gestures: I look for the information by getting out there to pull it from where it is (first by trial and error, later with the help of search engines). This allowed everyone to communicate with each other in peer-to-peer mode, without anyone knowing if you were an expert or a dog. In recentralising communications on a few hegemonic platforms, the internet of the 2010s based its expansion on *push* dynamics: I receive notifications, incentives, recommendations, and suggestions that bring content to my screen without me having to seek them. By accelerating the massification of followers and by basing their economic model on the commodification of attention, platforms tend to favour certain (more profitable) content: those that will exert the most irresistible attraction, and those that will capture our attentions more predictably.[12]

According to the magnetic analogy mobilised in Chapter 2, within the magnetic fields generated by the circulation of messages on platforms, content is structurally privileged by the currently dominant captological dynamics insofar as they (1) mobilise affects most intensely, (2) fit into previously marked positions, (3) polarise the most divisive oppositions, (4) deviate the most from the median positions perceived as expected, (5) manage to encapsulate the state of a field through a striking synthesis, and (6) bring out a singularity that shakes the field without making it explode.

All these (often mutually contradictory) traits clearly point towards an exacerbation of conspiratorial phantasmagories. Even if the overall

12 These issues have been developed in Yves Citton, *An Ecology of Attention*, Cambridge: Polity, 2016; and *Mediarchy*, Cambridge: Polity, 2019.

tendency seems to add fuel to the fire of already burning conflicts, these chaotic dynamics can play to or against any type of myth. Centripetal and centrifugal forces are in constant tension, to the rhythm of an unstable swing between acceptance by homophily and singularisation by deviation.[13] What remains fairly clear, however, is that such a magnetic field seems perfectly suited to welcome what the previous chapters have analysed as 'myths' – while it seems perfectly unsuitable to what general wisdom considers as rational, reflective, and sustained 'argumentations'.

Beyond the unpredictability of platform mythocracy, *attentional extractivism* – which bases the profits of platforms on the quantity of attention that they manage to harvest in order to resell it to advertisers – results in an *affective attractivism* – which tends to group perceptions around a restricted number of lines of cleavages, both pre-facilitated and unstable. This affective attractivism can be praised for its capacity to mobilise a massive number of agents around tags like #BlackLivesMatter and #MeToo, placing on the political agenda, with unprecedented speed and vigour, issues that the authorities systematically tended to repress in the past. At the same time, it can just as easily be criticised for the emotional ruts in which it generates and imprisons our indignations.[14]

Just when omni-mediatisation allows us to dream of a pluralistic media universe, where multiple perceptions of the world can coexist by correcting and complementing each other, the affective attractivism inherent to platform capitalism obliterates the development of multi-perspectivism. It exacerbates the polarisation of attention and affects around binary clashes, driven by the need for recognition rather than by attention to complexity. It reduces the multiplicity of points of view by trapping them in conflictual polarisations that favour the recognisable at the expense of the alien.

13 Wendy Hui Kyong Chun, *Discriminating Data: Correlation, Neighborhoods and the New Politics of Recognition*, Cambridge, MA: MIT Press, 2021.

14 Laurent de Sutter, *Indignation totale. Ce que notre addiction aux scandales dit de nous*, Paris: L'Observatoire, 2019.

9. *Vertigos of viral playfulness trump calculations of interests.* If there is one aspect of conspiracist mythocracy that most rationalist debunkers-from-above recurrently miss, it is its sarcastic, gaming, gambling, playful, and even joyful dimension. In this respect only, the designation of a 'post-truth' era is perhaps more accurate than it seems – as long as we understand it from the point of view of the role-playing game in which all players know full well that they are maintaining a fiction. Most actors understand that the point of the game is not so much the victory of truth as the rivalry between myths. The naivety of many debunkers lies in not seeing that, within this mythocratic playfield, truths and fictions are supposed to intertwine, support, and weave into each other, rather than repel each other.

Such a mythocratic playfield must be recontextualised in the framework sketched by the (in)famous statement attributed to Karl Rove, advisor to President George W. Bush, collected by Ron Suskind in the *New York Times Magazine* of 17 October 2004:

> The aide said that guys like me were 'in what we call the reality-based community', which he defined as people who 'believe that solutions emerge from your judicious study of discernible reality' . . . 'That's not the way the world really works anymore,' he continued. 'We're an empire now, and when we act, we create our own reality. And while you're studying that reality – judiciously, as you will – we'll act again, creating other new realities, which you can study too, and that's how things will sort out. We're history's actors . . . and you, all of you, will be left to just study what we do.[15]

Like it or not, over the past decades at least, the 'right' has operated from a much more insightful (if reckless) understanding of mythocracy than has the 'left'. Berlusconi, Bush, Orbán, Trump, Bolsonaro, Milei have managed to play rebels and gamble with history, while all of us have

15 Ron Suskind, 'Faith, Certainty and the Presidency of George W. Bush', *New York Times Magazine*, 17 October 2004.

been 'left' to just study what they did.[16] At the heart of this worryingly *wirklich* delirium (true insofar as effective) parades the figure of the *actor*, in the double but converging sense of the one who acts and the one who plays a role. Rove only takes note of the obvious: actor and agent become one on a political scene. As protagonists of a running myth (which could sound as a running joke, if the stakes were not so high), these sinister characters 'perform' better than their 'left' counterparts. While comparisons between the political scene and a theatrical stage have haunted many periods of past history, the rise of platform capitalism in the 2010s – simultaneous with the rise of video games in the cultural practices of intensely connected populations – marked the entry of political life into a much more *playful* universe, of which we are just beginning to glimpse some rules. The affective attractivism of social media irresistibly tickle the gaming instincts of the *Homo ludens* lying dormant in most of us.

The conspiratorial gamification hosted by the various platforms strikingly stimulates the four dimensions of play highlighted by Roger Caillois in his classic 1958 work *Man, Play and Games*.[17] Online, too, (1) we frequently play roles under borrowed identities (*mimicry*); (2) we expose ourselves to the chance of more or less fortunate serendipity (*alea*); (3) we are often led to compete for consideration and influence, under a constant barrage of critical appraisals, vengeful denunciations, and hostile rivalry (*agôn*); finally and more importantly still, (4) when a post or a tweet goes viral, when likes or retweets soar in an exponential curve, the buzzing hype generates a psychic experience of bungee-jumping vertigo (*ilinx*). The most implausible conspiracy theories as well as the most sinister forms of online harassment are driven by this vertiginously playful (and narcissistic) thrill, whose force of attraction is largely overlooked by debunkers obsessed with the sole compass of truth-value. From this point of view, the most enlightening model for understanding

16 Pablo Stefanoni, *La rébellion est-elle passé à droite?*, Paris: La Découverte, 2021; Aris Komporozos-Athanasiou, *Speculative Communities: Living with Uncertainty in a Financialized World*, Chicago: University of Chicago Press, 2022.

17 Roger Caillois, *Man, Play and Games*, Chicago: University of Illinois Press, 2001 [1958].

the conspiracist battleground of platform mythocracies should be found in Natasha Dow Schüll's brilliant and disquieting analysis of Las Vegas's slot machines.[18]

'We are the actors of history': from White House aides to young influencers, political antagonisms (*agôn*) are restructured and decided through mythocratic simulations (*mimicry*), to the point where the vertigo of viral playfulness (*ilinx*) takes precedence over calculations of interests and strategic rationalities, with unpredictable consequences (*alea*). How many film stars, rap idols, or political figures did we see carried away by the competitive spirit of the attraction game, making scandalous statements or taking perfectly indefensible positions – against their best interests and basic rationality – like moths to a flame, fascinated by the parallel rise of outrageousness and retweet count? Some of them apologise retrospectively at their expense, while others choose to always rush forward, overcoming vertigo by an ever steeper escalation, accumulating excess upon excess in the hope of reaching that highest level of the game where all will be forgiven – which apparently works for certain figures like Trump, who seem totally armoured against any return to reality.

This joyful dizziness fuels the myth of the winner: it is inherently cheerful and it smiles at the cheerful. This myth is genuinely lived by the business manager who sees his goods snapped up by distributors, or his shares rising on the stock market, as well as by the influencer who sees clicks, likes, and followers increase exponentially. Before being translated into hard cash or elected power, this myth is measured and experienced in speed of propagation, in positive feedback, and in a feeling of traction inherent to the dynamics of attractivism. It is the form of enjoyment and power specific to platform mythocracy: its vertigo (*ilinx*) is that of the surfer at the top of the wave, carried by the joint breathing of a conspiratorial communion.

10. *Generative neural networks undermine indexicality*. Such self-inflicted dizziness, resulting in self-destructive swerves of our obligation to self-design, is all the more threatening now that we are entering a

18 Natasha Dow Schüll, *Addiction by Design: Machine Gambling in Las Vegas*, Princeton, NJ: Princeton University Press, 2014.

media world bound to be permeated with deep fakes. Fact-finding and fact-checking will be made all the more difficult (skilled, costly) as generative pretrained transformers (GPTs) will soon allow anyone to flood the media sphere with perfectly realist contrafactual simulations. If the relentless (and environmentally unsustainable) development of generative AI follows its current course, it will put within the reach of any teenager the 'psychological operations' arsenal heretofore confined to heavily financed secret services.[19] This will further undermine whatever indexicality was left in the images and sounds flowing through our screens, as the distance between 'I've seen/heard it' and 'Therefore it happened' is bound to expand, growing less and less easily manageable. Even as we are still struggling to understand the stakes of the Web 2.0 revolution whereby 'everyone-becomes-media', we are already confronted with its next step, wherein 'everyone-becomes-PsyOperator' – a democratisation that is in no way incompatible with the strong presence of the more traditional agents of PsyOp (CIA, Kremlin, Chinese Communist Party, etc.), with armies of trolls on their payroll. The various analyses presented in this book will hopefully help brace ourselves for this further erosion of our capacity to establish a water-tight, stable, and obvious separation between reality and myth.

11. *Iconomorphosis supersumes reality.* Under the neologism of 'iconomorphosis', French philosopher Frédéric Bisson has recently developed a powerful theorisation of the ways in which the signs circulating through our various forms of audiovisual media overdetermine, reorient, reconfigure, and restructure our material realities. In phase 1 of iconomorphosis, 'the mediatic icon substitutes itself to the index upon which it is superimpressed, so that the possible object signified by the image substitutes itself to the real object it denotes'. In phase 2, through 'the materialisation of the icon, the possible crosses the threshold that separates the real and its representation; it materialises in our lives, through gestures, behaviors, affects'.[20]

19 See Konrad Becker, *Dictionary of Operations: Deep Politics and Cultural Intelligence*, New York: Autonomedia, 2013.

20 Frédéric Bisson, *Logique du Joker*, Paris: MF, 2023, p. 230.

An emblematic example of such an iconomorphic materialisation is the dramatic case of James Holmes, who shot twelve people in a movie theatre in Aurora, Colorado, during a preview of Christopher Nolan's *The Dark Knight Rises*, on 20 July 2012 – claiming 'I am the Joker', while wearing the make-up and costume of the fictional character. The 'sophism of Edenic ontology' (held by most debunkers) assumes that reality would virginally precede its representations. To the contrary, Bisson extends Baudrillard's intuition about (what I would call) *the iconomorphic supersumption* of our reality by the dynamics of simulation: in the same way that Antonio Negri extended Marx's intuition about the 'real subsumption' leading all forms and moments of our life to be infiltrated (from below, *sub*-sumption) by the financial logic of capital, similarly Bisson suggests that all spheres of our material life become permeated (from above, *super*-sumption) by iconomorphosis.

The story goes like this: our (spontaneous) hallucinations result from the dissemination of (socio-economic) 'semiotic inseminations'. In other words, as suggested by radical theorists from the 1970s, our reality itself functions as a conspiracy, insofar as we breathe together (in and out) the icons artfully designed by a huge economic sector of 'semiurgy'. To say that iconomorphosis supersumes reality is to account for the fact that fictional films generate actual killers, in the same manner that our myths about terrorism and conspiracies contribute to the scripting of actual terrorist violence and conspiracy thinking.

This is mythocracy to the power of four, since not only our stories (as concatenations of actions), not only our words (as references to states of things), not only our perceptions (as index of a certain reality), but *reality itself* appears as being deeply mythified (and therefore dangerously mystifying). This supersumption explains why, on both sides of what Naomi Klein described as a 'Mirror World' – populated by 'individuals not guided by legible principles or beliefs, but acting as members of groups playing yin to the other's yang' – 'we are having disagreements about who is in reality and who is in a simulation'.[21] Such dizzying

21 Naomi Klein, *Doppelganger: A Trip into the Mirror World*, New York: Farrar, Straus & Giroux, 2022, pp. 15 and 106.

disagreements should be heard as the contemporary translation of Sun Ra's (anti-)foundational questions: 'If you're not a reality, whose myth are you? If you're not a myth, whose reality are you?'

Literature and/as multi-perspectivism

Ending this book with an afterword on the current debates about conspiracism establishes the latter both as an illustration and as an application of the theses of *Mythocracy*. To sum it up in a formula: *(anti-)conspiracy thinking is a myth about a myth*. In the 'Mirror World' constructed along the whirlwind dynamics of platform capitalism, the conspiracism of QAnon followers and the anti-conspiracism of academic debunkers symmetrically respond to and mutually feed each other. They share a similar gesture of denouncing a myth from a point of view assumed to be exterior and superior to mythification/mystification. From the conspiracist perspective, those of us who continue to gobble our daily blue pills fall victim of the myth of the Matrix: the deep state controls every part of our life for its leaders' profit, while we continue naively to believe in institutions plotted to take advantage of us. From the debunkers' perspective, those of us who denounce reality as a scam fall prey to the myths of conspiracy thinking: evil manipulators and/or ignorant agitators spread unfounded fake news that erodes the impermeable separation a free and rational society should maintain between lies and truth.

By doing so, both sides produce or maintain a common myth: the myth of an intellectual superiority enjoyed by some humans above others, indissociable from the myth implying that those who do not think like ourselves can't think on their own. I will call it *the myth of uni-perspectivism*. The main lesson repeated in this book is that there is no such position above or outside the realm of the myth. (The same could be said about ideologies.) We can only choose our (better: more egalitarian, more solidary, more sustainable) myths to fight against other (worse: more exclusory, more oppressive, more ecocidal) myths. This overall lesson comes with at least five corollaries, which I will briefly address to conclude this afterword.

First, within the situation described by the eleven principles outlined above, our main practical task should be to further develop the tools, methods, teachings, practices, and supporting institutions admirably framed by Matthew Fuller and Eyal Weizman under the heading of *Investigative Aesthetics*.[22] Any serious 'politics of truth' needs to invest in the means necessary to conduct investigations, whether in the natural or social sciences, in political and environmental activism, in social justice, in international relations, in technology, or in the arts. We will always need reductive stories and partly mystifying myths in order to streamline the unbearable complexity of being. But these stories and these myths will be all the more helpful, and all the less dangerous, if they are fed (and permanently corrected) by a tireless fieldwork of fact-finding investigations.

Second, these investigations will need to associate the highest efforts of objectivation and distant analysis with the humble and *narrative* recognition of their situatedness. It is no coincidence that the two most insightful books recently published on conspiracy thinking should come from writers who place their own story at the core of their investigation. Naomi Klein's *Doppelganger* starts from, and constantly goes back to, what attracted her to the other side of the Mirror World: the frequent mistakes made between her and feminist writer Naomi Wolf, who had become a public ally of Steve Bannon's conspiracy-mongering. Wu Ming 1's *La Q di qomplotto* is more emblematic still: as a member of the far-left Italian collective Luther Blissett, he had participated in the writing of a novel that became an international best-seller in the early 2000s under the title *Q*; his investigation documents his surprise to see, fifteen years later, his fictional character (named Q) become the mythical protagonist (QAnon) of a planetary-wide far-right phantasmagoria of complot, which had metaleptically transgressed the boundary between fictional and actual worlds to play a decisive role in real-life elections.[23]

22 Matthew Fuller and Eyal Weizman, *Investigative Aesthetics: Conflicts and Commons in the Politics of Truth*, London: Verso, 2021.

23 See edizionialegre.it for an English summary of the as-yet untranslated book.

Both of these books provide a remarkably lucid, rational, enlightening analysis of conspiracism, no less knowledgeable, trustworthy, and rigorous than the best academic publications. Yet they investigate, and live, the worlds of conspiracism from-the-inside: as an entanglement of myths within which they too are dizzyingly trapped. Explicitly or implicitly, the voice which analyses the situation, and possibly sketches a solution, acknowledges to be also a part of the problem. Nowhere do they deny the fact that they navigate the troubled waters of mythocracy with mythical sails and a mythical compass. Far from diminishing the explanatory power of their investigation, this narrative and enunciative situatedness inhabits (and haunts) it with a more discriminating tone and a livelier intensity.

Third corollary: the point of view from-the-inside of the conspiratory turmoil adopted by these two books can be more generally indexed upon the *specific virtues of literature and literary studies.* In an age and in an academic division of labour wherein studying literary texts seems about as relevant, to face today's urgencies, as specialising in theology or Egyptology, the previous chapters of this book have attempted to reclaim a practical and political usefulness of approaching narratives as narratives, mobilising some of the analytical tools generated by literary theories during the second half of the twentieth century. On the specific issue addressed in this afterword, literary studies seem well ahead of cognitivism when it comes to shedding light on the conspiracist imaginary. Their quasi-absolute exclusion from the current debates on this issue perpetuates a pseudo-rational naivety, which their remobilisation would help to dispel. This would involve a triple backstepping from the ratio-supremacist common sense: *hermeneutical* (all knowledge results from an interpretative construction), *fictional* (factuality and causality are to be understood within, rather than in opposition to, narrativity and fictionality), and *enunciative* (whenever we express ourselves in public, our voices never directly reflect our identities and beliefs, but constantly play with complex and subtle games of distancing and reframing).

More importantly still, literary attention and literary sensibility teach us a certain prudence, a sense of nuance and discrimination inherently linked to being an expression lived-from-the-inside. In the Western culture of the past four centuries, what we now identify as 'literature' emerged as a collective adventure fuelled by countless individual attempts to rewrite our constitutive myths, during countless cross-disciplinary investigations based on experience elevated to the status of experimentation, made all the more valuable because it was unbounded by the disciplinary walls now associated with the laboratory. For this collective adventure, Sun Ra found the best possible name in calling his ensemble the Myth-Science Arkestra.

The fourth corollary qualifies the dominant literary tradition – focused on the identification and fetishisation of the author – by staging the contemporary literary experience-experimentation as a radical questioning of authorship and authority. As we have seen in the previous pages, what the brave knights of debunking describe as a 'post-truth' era should rather be labelled '*post-authority*'. We have not fallen from the Paradise of Truth (heroically conquered by the predominance of critical thinking) to the Hell of Myth (abandoned to the most gullible). Rather, we are entering an era when the prevalence of comfortable lies and the omnipresence of half-truths may be more realistically recognised under the corroding assaults of a form of hyper-criticism. The rampant discrediting of all positions of authority experienced during the Covid episode can be credibly assessed as the result of seeing too many authoritative and authoritarian voices (people and institutions) caught with their pants down while passing myth for truth.

We will always need to distribute trust (another word for authority) in order to stabilise and validate reliable conducts of factual accuracy. What may (hopefully) be coming to an end is the myth of the uni-perspectivist truth, arrogantly monopolised by those who got hold of positions of authority. What follows it is not so much the empire of lies as the more difficult task of having to reposition oneself in a new regime of plural truths, and of systematically problematic access to facts. This calls for the learning of a new investigative prudence, rather than for lamentations in apocalyptic tones.

Under this light, it is a blessing for literary studies to have been debunked from the hegemonic status enjoyed by literary theory in the

1970s. Now that they find themselves uncomfortably cornered in a marginal zone of useless non-expertise, devoid of any pretence to authority, they are best positioned to address our most pressing issues from an unassuming, radically transversal, and properly 'curious' vantage point. Their relegation to a dusty *cabinet de curiosités* encourages them to fully endorse the truly revolutionary mission of curiosity: seeking and disturbing the inconvenient kernels of truth that lie beyond the boundaries of preestablished authorised knowledge.[24]

Fifth corollary, and final remark for this book: the most precious aspect of the literary *curiosité* may be its inherent propensity to foster *multi-perspectivism*. Long before Russian theorist Mikhail Bakhtin redefined the novelistic genre as a polyphonic dialogue between heterogeneous and contradictory points of view, epistolary novels had accustomed their readers to appreciate one set of events from the multiple perspectives of various value systems. Long before Brazilian anthropologist Eduardo Viveiros de Castro taught us the cognitive, ethical, political, and environmental merits of the 'perspectivist' world-views developed by Amazonian populations, literary fictions had experimented with discovering eighteenth-century France through the gaze of a Peruvian princess, or with seeing modern life from the point of view of a human cockroach.[25]

Sun Ra viewing the racist US from his Saturnian Astro-Black perspective proves as deeply literary as Voltaire's Micromegas visiting Earth from Sirius. It leads him to radically decenter his characterisation of truth:

> 'Truth' can also be bad, as when a man says 'I'll kill you' and he does. The moment of truth in a bullfight is the time of the bull's death . . .

24 Enrico Campo and Yves Citton, eds, *The Politics of Curiosity: Alternatives to the Attention Economy*, London: Routledge, 2024.

25 Mikhail Bakhtin, *The Dialogic Imagination*, Austin: University of Texas Press, 1982; Eduardo Viveiros de Castro, *Cannibal Metaphysics*, Minneapolis: University of Minnesota Press, 2017; Françoise de Graffigny, *Letters from a Peruvian Woman*, New York: MLA Editions, 1993 [1749]; Franz Kafka, *The Metamorphosis* [1915] in *The Complete Stories*, New York: Schocken Books, 1971.

> Those who live by reality are slaves to truth. It's a kind of narcotic, a dope. When the police finds out the truth about you, they say they get the 'dope' on you.[26]

The value and the effects of 'truth' can be quite different, whether you approach them from the perspective of a white university professor, a police officer, or an impoverished Black youth: it can simultaneously be a worthy goal for some, and a mortal danger for others.

The epistemological stakes and the political demands of multi-perspectivism within the conspiracist context of digital omni-mediatisation have already been clearly articulated by Vilém Flusser in his 1983 *Towards a Philosophy of Photography*. They can be succinctly summarised in six points: (1) any photograph taken by a camera is (objectively) 'true'; (2) the photographer's intervention rests on the (subjective) perspective adopted to frame a given situation; (3) different perspectives can reveal contradictory aspects of this situation (all equally 'true'); (4) it is impossible to consider a given situation from all of its possible points of view; (5) each photograph changes reality by putting in circulation a certain view on it; (6) a democratic society ought to find institutional mechanisms to allow for contradictory perspectives to complement, rather than suppress, each other.[27]

After having been rather uncomfortable throughout this book about the current definitions of the 'left' and the 'right' in today's politics, this afterword could suggest a reconfigured contrast, which would drastically redistribute the traditional assignations. It would identify the left with the (admittedly difficult) acceptance and taking into account of the multi-perspectivism afforded by our new communication regimes, while the right would be identifiable by their authoritarian imposition of a uni-perspectivist construction of reality.

26 Quoted in John F. Szwed, *Space Is the Place: The Lives and Times of Sun Ra*, New York: Da Capo Press, 1998, p. 317.

27 Vilém Flusser, *Towards a Philosophy of Photography*, Göttingen: European Photography, 1984; Emmanuel Alloa, *Partages de la perspective*, Paris: Fayard, 2020.

Multi-perspectivism is no less 'mythical' than uni-perspectivism. It is just another way to tell a possible story for democratic regimes. It is a dream, it is a hope for 'what we never came to be that we should be', it is a script for altering our common destiny according to the powers of letters, words, narratives, research, and study – a literary conspiracy, for which Sun Ra provided an inspiring blueprint:

> Now, just like everybody else, when I first came on this planet, I didn't know anything, completely ignorant. As I look back on my childhood, I am amazed at how ignorant I was. But it's a good thing I was, because then I did not accept anything as being the truth. And that made me research, you see. And researching, I found out all these things.
>
> . . .
>
> Two women stayed after a meeting and they asked me: 'What must we do?' I said: It is written *Take words, my people, and return to me!* You got to put these words together properly. Like if you put some chemicals together, they become deadly. That's the way it is for words. You can put certain words together and they become deadly for you, and deadly for our nation, and deadly for everybody. Words produced the atomic bomb: symbols, words, that's the way they got it first. First, they put on these symbols, letters and words, and then they were able to produce it . . . Now whatever you're living here – our supposed 'living' – there's a blueprint, and it's equational, and these equations are about to kill you. Unless you get some more equations. Now sometimes I've been talking about 'altered destiny', that's the substitution of a destiny for the one you got. Because the one you got is spelled D.O.O.M. And it's knocking at your door. Therefore, it's impossible you get out, because there's such a thing as karma.
>
> So then, what must you do? You must appeal to God's Impossible Department. Because the possible can never save you, and the truth cannot save you, because the truth is what you do every day. It's what you have done in the past, what you think every day, and it's what you read in the newspapers. Everything out there that's happening is the

truth. And everything that happens in history is the truth. But that's not any good.

. . .

They say that history repeats itself, but history is only his-story. You haven't heard *my* story yet . . . My story is close to mystery. My story is better than history. Mystery is better than history. What's *your* story?[28]

28 Sun Ra, 'The Possibility of Altered Destiny', conference, 10 November 1979; last paragraph from Szwed, *Space Is the Place*, p. 317.

Acknowledgements

The title, form, and content of this book have been transformed by the suggestions, criticisms, requests for clarification, and original ideas which Jérôme Vidal contributed through several months of discussions at the Éditions Amsterdam. I owe enormous thanks to him, as well as to Charlotte Nordmann and to Aurélien Blanchard, for the rich dialogue which continued throughout the work on this project.

This book was made possible thanks to the institutional support (and support between friends) provided by Jean-François Perrin and Sarga Moussa in the UMR LIRE. The research on which the afterword is based was supported by the Université Paris 8, by the *Fabrique du littéraire* unit, and by the EUR ArTeC financed by the French National Agency for Research (ANR) through the PIA ANR-17-EURE-0008.

My deepest gratitude goes to David Broder for his outstanding job in translation, as well as to Sebastian Budgen, Jeanne Tao, and Michelle Betters, who have welcomed, curated, and promoted this English translation at Verso Books.

Heartfelt thanks also to Wu Ming (1, 2, 3 …), Enrico Manera, Giulia Boggio Marzet Tremoloso, and the good folks at the Edizione Alegre for their 2013 Italian Edition.

The writing of this book also benefited from the advice, suggestions, reactions, encouragement, support, meetings, and friendship I had from comrades and colleagues both near and far. There are too many to include all of them, but I shall at least mention Kamel Abdou, Saddek Aouadi, Maryvonne Arnaud, Jacques Berchtold, Laurent Bigorgne, Frédéric Bisson, Aurélien Blanchard, Daniel Bougnoux, Sylvain Bourmeau, Laurent Bove, Frédéric Brun, Enrico Campo, Pierre Chartier, Grégory Chatonsky, Chloé Chaudet, Yvette Chiffre, Rosemary and Gilbert Citton, Claude Coste, François Cusset, Rachel Danon, Christophe Degoutin, Marianne Dubacq, Éditions Amsterdam, Marc Escola, Don Foresta, Florence and Francis Goyet, Victor Grauer, Francesco Gregorio, Alain Grosrichard, Adrien Guignard, Timothy Hampton, Christophe Hanna, Stefano Harney, Jan Herman, Denis Hollier, Brian Holmes, Michel Jeanneret, Laurent Jenny, Ariel Kyrou, Catherine Langle, Yann Laporte, Bruno Latour, Sandra Laugier, Thierry Laus, Maurizio Lazzarato, Anna Longo, Dennis Looney, Frédéric Lordon, Laurent Loty, Christie McDonald, Erin Manning, Brian Massumi, Isabella Mattazzi, Giuseppina Mecchia, Abdelfateh Mertali, Pierre-François Moreau, Fred Moten, Philippe Mouillon, Yann Moulier Boutang, Sarga Moussa, friends both old and new at *Multitudes* journal, Nancy Murzilli, Toni Negri, Christopher Newfield, Frédéric Neyrat, Ben Opie, Jérôme Pelletier, Jean-François Perrin, Alexandre Pierrepont, Martial Poirson, Anne Querrien, Dominique Quessada, Jacopo Rasmi, Judith Revel, everyone at *La Revue internationale des livres et des idées*, Martin Rueff, Lionel Ruffel, Dominique Sainte-Rose, Lucia Sagradini, Dina Sahyouni, Marc Saint Upéry, Anne Sauvagnargues, Yannick Séité, Jean-Paul Sermain, Pascal Sévérac, Ariel Suhamy, Olivier Surel, Astrid Ténière, Michel Vanni, Marco Venturini, Francis Vérillaud, Anne and Bertrand Vibert, Maurizio Vito, Phil Watts, Damien Zanone, and – above all else – Marina Kundu.

Index